JOHN CLARE'S
AUTOBIOGRAPHICAL WRITINGS

JOHN CLARE'S AUTOBIOGRAPHICAL WRITINGS

EDITED BY ERIC ROBINSON

With wood engravings by John Lawrence

Oxford New York

OXFORD UNIVERSITY PRESS

1983

Oxford University Press, Walton Street, Oxford OX2 6DP

London Glasgow New York Toronto
Delhi Bombay Calcutta Madras Karachi
Kuala Lumpur Singapore Hong Kong Tokyo
Nairobi Dar es Salaam Cape Town
Melbourne Auckland
and associates in
Beirut Berlin Ibadan Mexico City Nicosia

Oxford is a trade mark of Oxford University Press

British Library Cataloguing in Publication Data
Clare, John, 1793–1864
John Clare's autobiographical writings.
1. Clare, John. 1793–1864—Biography
I. Title II. Robinson, Eric, 1924–
821'.7 PR4453.C6
ISBN 0-19-211774-2

Library of Congress Cataloging in Publication Data
Clare, John, 1793–1864.
John Clare's autobiographical writings.
1. Clare, John, 1793–1864—Biography. 2. Poets.
English–19th century–Biography. I. Robinson, Eric,
1924– II. Lawrence, John, 1933–
III. Title.
PR4453.C6Z467 1983 821'.7[B] 82-22497
ISBN 0-19-211774-2

Set by Rowland Phototypesetting Ltd
Printed in Great Britain by
Thomson Litho Ltd,
East Kilbride, Scotland

CONTENTS

MAPS

Maps drawn by Reginald Piggott; research by Bruce Bailey.

INTRODUCTION

The story of John Clare's life, which spanned the years 1793 to 1864, has sometimes seemed to eclipse the interest in his poetry. That the son of an illegitimate Northamptonshire thresher and amateur wrestler, Parker Clare, and his illiterate wife, Ann, should become a literary celebrity, hobnobbing at his publisher's house with Lamb, Hazlitt, Coleridge, and Keats's friends, Woodhouse and Reynolds, is unlikely enough. That he should publish four volumes of poetry (*Poems Descriptive of Rural Life and Scenery*, three editions in 1820 and the fourth in 1821, *The Village Minstrel and other Poems*, 1821, *The Shepherds Calendar, with Village Stories and Other Poems*, 1827, and *The Rural Muse*, 1835) is a testimony to his productivity if not to his popularity. That at the end of all this he should enter Dr Matthew Allen's asylum at High Beach, Epping, in 1837, and that, after escaping from there, he should be confined to the Northampton Asylum from 1841 till his death in 1864, forgotten by all but a few but still composing many poems, is a turn of the wheel of fortune befitting medieval tragedy. In the year after his death, Clare's story was told for the first time by Frederick Martin in his stimulating, if overcoloured and inaccurate *Life of John Clare*[1] and since then has been retold several times, often with more gush than gusto. More than a hundred years after his death Clare's poetry is being more widely read than ever before and Clare is beginning to take his rightful place among the great English poets of the Romantic Period, not inferior to Keats, Shelley, Coleridge, Wordsworth, or to the one whom Clare himself most revered, Byron. It is therefore appropriate that we should study closely what Clare had to say about himself, both in the *Sketches in the Life of John Clare* (first edited for the public by Edmund Blunden in 1931) and in the fragments of autobiography (brought to the attention of the public by J. W. and A. Tibble in *John Clare, A Life*, 1931, and *The Prose of John Clare*, 1951). Clare first started writing his life in early 1821 in order to assist John Taylor, his publisher, and those efforts resulted in the

---

[1] Published 1865: 2nd edition, ed. Eric Robinson and Geoffrey Summerfield, 1964

Sketches, but he continued to write passages down until 1828, when his fourth visit to London took place. I have assembled here all the fragments that I could find that seemed to be intended for an autobiography. I have also included Clare's *Journey out of Essex* dealing with his escape from Dr Matthew Allen's asylum in July 1841. For the remainder of his life we have to turn to his poems and to his letters. There is much that we still do not know.

Clare's autobiographical writings have perhaps been taken too much at face value as though the writer, being a countryman, could not have shaped his story to suit a particular reader or to create an image satisfying to Clare himself. There has also been a disposition among Clare's biographers and critics to make light of the fact that Clare had literary models, at least in part, for the kind of life that he wanted to write. The autobiographical writings make it clear that from his earliest days Clare was not a stranger to books and that some of those books were the same that had great influence upon James Boswell or John Aubrey or other great biographers. Unless we take into account Clare's self-consciousness and his literary background we shall fail to evaluate his autobiography properly. It is a tragedy that we do not have the fair copy of the autobiography for which the fragments were written. Since some of the fragments were written after 1821 it is clear that the *Sketches* cannot be the culmination of all the passages, and, as many of them are crossed through and marked 'done with', it is also evident that a fair copy of some sort must have existed. We know that it was Clare's practice so to mark his writings when a fair copy had been made either by him or by an amanuensis. The absence of the fair copy means that we are left with passages that duplicate each other entirely or in part and that we cannot be confident of the order in which Clare intended them to be presented. There are a few notes giving projected chapter-titles or suggesting 'for the next chapter' but they do not suffice to establish an unmistakable order. Perhaps one day the fair copy will turn up and we shall be able to see how right or how wrong I have been in the order adopted in this book. I have resisted the temptation, however, to create a continuous narrative as J. W. and Anne Tibble did in *The Prose of John Clare*, except for an occasional paragraph where I have indicated clearly what I have done. There is a little repetition but that is inevitable in the presentation of raw material such as these fragments are.

None of this is meant to be taken, however, as an apology for

Clare's writings. The *Sketches* and the fragments form together one of the raciest autobiographies in the English language. This autobiography has Nashe's gusto without his bibulous overflow, Cobbett's robustness without his didacticism and Traherne's sensitivity sharpened by a countryman's astringency. It needs ideally, like all Clare's work, to be read aloud, for the sound of his Northamptonshire, nay Helpston, voice vibrates throughout it. Clare grew to be critical of punctuation,[1] so that he increasingly dispensed with it. This means that the reader has to allow the meanings of the prose to dictate the rhythm and movement: one has to feel one's way carefully as if looking for a nest in a thicket. I have tried to help by leaving spaces between sentences, for sentences and natural breaks there are, if seldom pointed. But in the *Sketches* Clare sprinkled commas and semicolons all over the place and I have chosen to remove much of that punctuation to bring the work into closer alignment with his maturer method of composition. As he himself wrote: 'do I write intelligable   I am genneraly understood tho I do not use that awkward squad of pointings called commas colons semicolons etc . . .' I have also linked parts of a word together where Clare sometimes leaves them in separate parts, such as 'him self', because I am not sure how far the separation was Clare's deliberate intention. I have not changed spellings or standardized grammar because Clare's practice in such matters was highly personal and he came to object ever more strongly to such interference with his work. Emendation has led some previous editors to substitute a standardized word such as 'shrill' for the dialect word 'shill' or 'porch' for 'poach' and thus to cramp Clare's writings into a comformity entirely foreign to them. This I have avoided. But all editors of Clare tread a fine line and we must be influenced in part by the audience to which a particular book is directed. I do not believe, however, that we are justified in making verbs and subjects agree in number or in removing double negatives when it is certain that such practices were part of Clare's own speech and his own grammatical habits.

Although the peculiarities of Clare's use of language may not be attributed entirely to the Soke of Peterborough or Clare's village, yet there can be no question that he belonged to a specific place and time. From his birth in Helpston in 1793 to his death in Northampton in 1864, except for four visits to London and some months in Epping

---

[1] See Barbara Strang, 'John Clare's Language' in R. K. R. Thornton, *The Rural Muse: Poems by John Clare* (Carcanet New Press, 1982), pp. 159–73

Forest, he passed his days in the county of his birth. He lived at first under the same roof as his parents at Helpston, moved to another cottage in Northborough only a few miles away in 1832, and then from 1841 until 1864 spent the remainder of his life at St Andrew's, Northampton. His life-story is told against the background of a particular landscape with its fens, its heaths, its sheep-pastures and its market-towns and villages. (It is significant that Clare uses the word 'town' to denote any settlement however small.) He talks of Will-o'-the-wisps (or Jenny burnt-arses), of ghosts and poachers, of spires peeping over stiles, of bird-haunted thickets, of lonely farms and the threshers, gleaners, and weeders in his native fields. The skies of the fens always overshadowed him, and there is no writer from whom one gets a better sense of an unbroken horizon or of the scarlet flames of sunrise and sunset. In this landscape he breathed freely: once he left it he felt suffocated and began to lose touch with reality. He speaks constantly of the 'lordship', the area under the control of the lord of the manor, or of his 'world', the locality with which he was familiar. It is not uncommon to this day to find on the edge of English towns a pub called The World's End as though when one reached the boundary of a familiar settlement one dropped over the edge of the horizon. Clare's sense of self-identity is intimately involved with his awareness of his birthplace and of all the living things that he remarked within his locality:

I lovd the meadow lake with its fl[a]gs and long purples crowding the waters edge   I listend with delights to hear the wind whisper among the feather topt reeds and to see the taper bulrush nodding in gentle curves to the rippling water and I watchd with delight on haymaking evenings the setting sun drop behind the brigs and peep again thro the half circle of the arches as if he longs to stay

[A34, 15]

It is not of the landscape alone, however, that Clare writes. He tells us much about the people. His voice tells of the hardships suffered by poor men, their humiliations and their sense of oppression, but also of their joys, their festivities and their songs.[1] Sometimes, as in his 'Apology for the Poor' one hears his honest anger:

now if the poor mans chance at these meetings is anything better than being a sort of foot cushion for the benefit of others I shall be exceedingly happy but as it is I much fear it as the poor mans lot seems to have been so long remembered as to be entirely forgotten . . .

[1] See George Deacon, *John Clare and the Folk Tradition*, 1983

or when he speaks of one rude visitor:

he then asked me some insulting libertys respecting my first acquaintance
with Patty and said he understood that in this country the lower orders made
their courtship in barns and pig styes and asked wether I did   I felt very vext
and said that it might be the custom of high orders for aught I knew as
experience made fools wise in most matters but I assured him he was wrong
respecting that custom among the lower orders here

[A33, 1]

His story of the magistrate, Hopkinson, and his wife is a brilliant
satire upon condescension gone wrong. Such recitals are of a piece
with his poem, 'The Parish', which never got a hearing in Clare's own
day. Since *Piers Plowman* there has hardly been an authoritative
voice in English literature to speak for the ploughmen, the threshers,
the hedgers, shepherds, woodmen and horse-keepers until Clare
began to write. The farmer-journalist, William Cobbett, is heard
loud and clear and so, at a later date, is the gamekeeper, Richard
Jefferies. Joseph Ashby of Tysoe has been evocatively presented by
his daughter and is closer to the agricultural labourer. But none of
these is the equal of Clare. As Edmund Blunden said, Clare's
autobiographical writings contain

Fresh information and thoughts of a poet of the purest kind; originality of
judgment, bold honesty; illuminating and otherwise unobtainable observations on intricate village life in England between 1793 and 1821; a good
narrative – nearly as good as Bunyan – and plenty of picturesque expression.
It will be a long time before a voice again speaks from a cottage window with
this power over ideas and over language.[1]

The people of John Clare's autobiography – Will Farrow, the
cobbler, Morton, the magistrate, Henson, the bookseller and Ran-
ter-preacher, the servants at Milton Hall, the boy John Turnill, the
master of the kitchen-garden at Burghley – are as lively and as
individualized as characters from *The Canterbury Tales*. No play
ever had a richer cast. And when we move from individual persons to
meetings and occasions, such as singing and dancing with the
gypsies, visiting the fair as children, the drills of the militia at Oundle
or the night-life of London, there too all is light and colour, and well
might one say, 'the year was crowned with holidays' [B5, 46].
    As a story of Clare's life, however, we ought to recognize that
Clare's *Sketches* and the autobiographical fragments belong to the

[1] E. Blunden (ed.), *Sketches in the Life of John Clare*, 1931

tradition of those sixpenny chapbooks hawked by pedlars from door to door which shaped Clare's childhood imagination. Clare is the hero of his own chapbook: he is his own Tom Hickathrift, Dick Whittington, Jack and the Beanstalk or what-have-you. He was quite aware of the strangeness of his own rise to fame. Other tales of men and women rising from obscurity were part of folk-tradition. Even when totally fictional they were presented as true-life stories. Swift adopted the idiom in *Gulliver's Travels* and Defoe did the same in *Robinson Crusoe*. Gay's *Beggar's Opera* too belongs to the tradition of marvellous lives and adventures. Clare was even more deeply entrenched in the tradition than Defoe, Gay, and Swift because for many years the chapbooks were almost his sole literary diet. His imagination was nourished by the popular songs and stories that have always fed the minds of the poor and compensated them for their deprivations by a rich world of fantasy. Clare's dreams were made of tales of knight-errantry, the adventures of Robin Hood, the history of Joseph, and even the true stories of Chatterton, Kirke White, and Bloomfield. At all times of his life, sane or insane, Clare identified himself with some hero. In his insane years he seems to have been unable to keep fact and fiction apart: was he Clare or was he Byron, Burns, or Shakespeare? Was he Nelson or Ben Caunt, the prize-fighter? The fantasies of his insanity continue the fantasies of his earlier years as revealed in his autobiographical fragments. Did he really drub a bullying corporal in the army or was it merely that he would have liked to do so? Were the amorous advances made by the governess at General Birch Reynardson's house any more real than the games he played with Mrs Emmerson or Mary Howitt? Similarly, what visions of fame and popularity Clare cherished within himself and what desolation befell him at Northborough when he recognized that he was destined always to be the outsider, the vagrant, and the alien!

He wanted to believe in his own special destiny, to feel that he was marked out by fate. Was that not the meaning of his providential birth and survival contrasted with the early death of his twin sister? Was it not for this reason that he was twice saved from drowning and preserved from a dangerous fall when he was birds-nesting? Why was it that he was not buried in the debris of the barn where he and his companions had been drinking? The resemblances to Bunyan in *Grace Abounding* or to James Lackington, the Methodist bookseller, are all too clear. Was Clare not the Joseph about whom he read in the chapbook published by Henson? And when he tells us of his visits to London and his jaunts with the painter, E. V. Rippingille, the experiences are very similar to those he read about in Richard King's *The Tricks of London Laid Open*. He is fascinated by kidnappers, cheats, and ladies of the town. Even the description of the frauds in Waithman's shop cast Clare in the role of the gullible countryman, as portrayed in Richard King's chapbook. Later, in the *Journey out of Essex*, as Clare sets out on his epic walk, he presents himself as a general marshalling his forces and we attribute this fantasy to his madness, but it continues a side of his character that had long been established.

In the *Sketches in the Life of John Clare*, the poet wishes to present himself to his evangelical publisher and to his patrons, Lord Radstock and Mrs Emmerson, as a very proper object for their support. He therefore puts himself forward as Hogarth's Industrious Apprentice, which Clare had undoubtedly seen: 'I resigned myself willingly to the hardest toils and tho one of the weakest was stubbor[n] and stomachful and never flinched from the roughest labour   by that means I always secured the favour of my masters and escaped the ignominy that brands the name of idleness . . .' Is this the same boy about whom we are told in the autobiographical fragments that he avoided apprenticeship by 'shamming Abraham', i.e. by pretending to be sick? Or who was always flopping down in the hedgerow to write his poems when the farmer was not looking? Or who ran away from the nurseryman because the work was too hard? It may not have been that Clare intended to mislead but that he was too easily influenced in his youth by what his London friends thought that he ought to be. What we see sometimes therefore, is what Clare *wanted* to be true of himself. A weakling among his schoolmates, a 'silly shanny boy', abandoned by his childhood sweetheart, a half-witted rhymer – no wonder that he aspired to be cleverer at mathematics than the schoolmaster, stronger than the bullying corporal, and a gay Lothario among the girls!

In other respects besides this love of chapbooks Clare mirrors the culture of fellow countrymen of his time. Consider the numbers of books on mathematics and land-surveying that he mentions. In a period of General Acts of Enclosure, of drainage-schemes and new methods of farming, one way to self-betterment was through the study of geometry and surveying or through book-keeping and accounts. The books he mentions – Bonnycastle, Ward, Vyse and others – all went into many editions and must have been purchased by the rural poor all over the country. Even in the days of his insanity Clare held on to the same ambitions for his son, Charles: 'you must not forget Learning – Ainslies Landsurveying and Cobbins Arithmetic are your School books – you should read them still.'[1] When the children were very young he bought them fairy-stories: as they grew older he was concerned about schoolbooks. Similarly his early attempts to acquire grammar and spelling, though he abandoned them, were shared by thousands of other aspiring autodidacts of the early nineteenth century.

Clare was much more widely read, however, than other labouring men. Like them he read the Bible (cf. Elizabeth Newbon's father), *Old Moore's Almanack*, *Pilgrim's Progress*, Thomas Tusser's *Five Hundred Points of Good Husbandry*, *Old Nixon's Prophecies*, and *Mother Shipton*, but he also came to share in the reading of many of the educated people of his day. He read Pope, Thomson and Cowper, Swift, Goldsmith, Defoe and Paine, and the natural history of Nicholas Culpeper, John Ray, and Erasmus Darwin. He also read Bloomfield, Chatterton, Kirke White, as well as Milton, Byron, Chaucer, Keats and many other poets.[2] It is true that he said that he would rather have written *Babes in the Wood* than *Paradise Lost* but he had read both. To track Clare in his snow is a much more difficult task than those who regard him as a simple rustic realize. His personal library was larger and probably more closely read than those of many present-day academics.

Besides his reading we must take into account Clare's knowledge of ballads and their music, of dances and dance-tunes, some of which he collected from gypsies, his extensive acquaintance with festivals, Morris dances, bull-runnings, statute fairs, Maydays, Valentine's Eves, Plough Mondays, and a host of other occasions. He submitted an extensive essay on such matters to William Hone, editor of the *Every Day Book*. His knowledge of the local flora and fauna was unparalleled,[3] he claimed to be able to speak gypsy-slang and his 'Don Juan' shows how familiar he was with London slang, and he was assistant to his friend, Artis, in some of the archaeological digs in

---

[1] Northampton MS 30: John Clare to Charles Clare, 15 October 1849

[2] See D. Powell's list of Clare's library in D. Powell, *Catalogue of the John Clare Collection* in the Northampton Public Library (Northampton, 1964)

[3] See M. Grainger, *The Natural History Prose Writings of John Clare* (Oxford, 1983) and E. Robinson and R. Fitter, *John Clare's Birds* (Oxford, 1982)

the neighbourhood of Castor. The autobiographical writings reflect all this rich variety of curiosity. Clare's breadth of culture has been underestimated because few literary critics of today could claim a range of interest in any way approaching his. The modern scholar, moreover, tends to acquire his knowledge not from conversation but through the written word. Clare not only read, he listened and he observed.

The autobiographical fragments are, as we have said, different in emphasis from the *Sketches*. They are much more openly critical of the middle classes, revealing Clare's aversion for simpering misses and pompous magistrates, for pretentious militia officers and grasping farmers, and, what could not have been acceptable to Clare's publisher, John Taylor, his increasing distrust of booksellers. On 30 December 1824, Clare wrote to the Revd H. F. Cary, translator of Dante: 'I have not yet finished my life . . . I feel anxious to finish it and I feel also anxious that you should see it and I shall be greatly obliged for your opinion of it as I mean if I live to publish it   I have gotten 8 chapters done and have carried it up to the "Poems on Rural Life" etc . . .' According to Clare's *Journal* for 19 January 1825 he had then completed a ninth chapter. I have not been able to reconstruct all these chapters with accuracy. Where a chapter title of Clare's own invention is used, it is printed without comment: where I have made up my own title, it is enclosed within square brackets. There is no *conclusive* proof that the autobiography was ever completed. Frederick Martin's reference to Clare's 'very curious autobiographical memoirs' may refer to nothing more than the cancelled fragments that we still have. Since there is no established order for the fragments I have done the best I can and I have given all the MS references so that the interested scholar may read them for himself in the context in which they occur. A glossary is provided at the end of the volume and there are additional notes on matters which the reader may find difficult to follow or which require further information. We have also provided two maps.

It is now possible to begin to understand Clare in his own context – geographical, social, and cultural. What kind of writer did he aspire to be? He wanted to write songs that people like himself would enjoy. He did not wish to separate himself from ordinary men and women. He wanted to explore the vices of the age. A chapbook in the Harding Collection at the Bodleian Library (A127, 36), Oxford, has a title which would have appealed to Clare:

An Explanation of the Vices of the Age: Shewing the Knavery of Land lords, the Imposition of Quack Doctors, the Roguery of Petty Lawyers, the Cheats of Bum-Bailiffs, and the Intrigues of Lewd Women . . .

He was a countryman and an English countryman. Though he detested corruption he did not wish to destroy monarchy or aristocracy; though he despised hunting parsons, he respected clergymen who had a sympathy for the poor; though he rejected mock-modesty and puritanism, no man had a greater regard for women than he, nor a greater sensitivity to their feelings and their suffering. He was a poet but he was no namby-pamby. His names for himself – Honest Jack and Random Jack – reveal what he thought of himself. It is a tribute to our own age that John Clare is coming into his own.

SELECTED READING

E. Blunden (ed.), *Sketches in the Life of John Clare* (London, 1931)

F. W. Martin, *The Life of John Clare*, 2nd edition, with an Introduction and Notes by E. Robinson and G. Summerfield (London, 1964).

E. Blunden, *Keats's Publisher, A Memoir of John Taylor* (London, 1936)

J. W. and A. Tibble, *John Clare, A Life* (London, 1932)

J. W. and A. Tibble, *John Clare, His Life and Poetry* (London, 1956)

M. Grainger, *The Natural History Prose Writings of John Clare* (Oxford, 1983)

G. Deacon, *John Clare and the Folk Tradition* (London, 1983)

E. Robinson and R. Fitter, *John Clare's Birds* (Oxford, 1982)

J. Barrell, *The Idea of Landscape and the Sense of Place, 1730–1840: An Approach to the Poetry of John Clare* (Cambridge, 1972)

E. Storey, *A Right to Song: The Life of John Clare* (London, 1982)

NOTE ON THE TEXT

In *Sketches in the Life of John Clare* and *More Hints in the Life* I have removed much of Clare's punctuation in order to bring it more into line with his later practice, as demonstrated in the *Autobiographical Fragments* and *Journey out of Essex*. Thus in *Sketches* I have generally omitted full stops and a large number of unnecessary commas and semicolons. In order to help the reader, however, I have left spaces between sentences in all the different autobiographical writings printed here. I have chosen to print words like 'him self' as one word, since it is not always clear that Clare was doing more than lifting his pen from the page, though in some instances the habit was probably deliberate. Odd spellings have been retained and where they might create special difficulty have been included in the Glossary alongside other unfamiliar words. The best test for the reader to adopt, however, is to read the word aloud.

I have printed the *Autobiographical Fragments* in the most rational order I could devise, since to print the fragments in the order in which they appear in the manuscripts, as catalogued by David Powell and Margaret Grainger, would simply produce confusion. I always indicate in square brackets at the side, thus [A25, 32], the location of the passage in the manuscripts. If the MS is from the Peterborough Museum collection, it is preceded by a capital letter, according to the numbering given in Miss Grainger's catalogue. The number following the comma within the square brackets is then the page number. [A32, 12R] for example, means that the material appears upside down on page 12 of Peterborough MS A32.

A space between square brackets in the text means that Clare has left a space in which he intended later to fill in a word or words but has failed to do so. Textual notes, or footnotes made by Clare himself, are printed at the bottom of the page. Informational notes are printed at the back of the book and are keyed by superior figures in the text.

In this text, intended for the general reader, I have not shown minor deletions and alterations but have concentrated on mentioning those which seem to me to be of importance to the meaning or to illustrate Clare's intentions in some significant way.

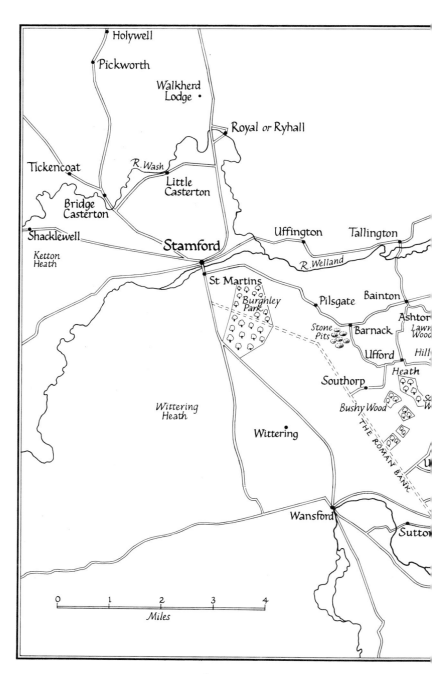

Holywell

Pickworth

Walkherd
Lodge •

Royal or Ryhall

Tickencoat

R. Wash

Little
Casterton

Bridge
Casterton

Shacklewell

Ketton
Heath

Stamford

Uffington

Tallington

R. Welland

St Martins

Burghley
Park

Pilsgate

Bainton

Ashtor

Stone
Pits

Barnack

Lawr
Woo

Ulford

Hill

Heath

Southorp

Bushy Wood

Wittering
Heath

Wittering

THE ROMAN BANK

Wansford

Sutto

0   1   2   3   4

Miles

CLARE'S COUNTRYSIDE

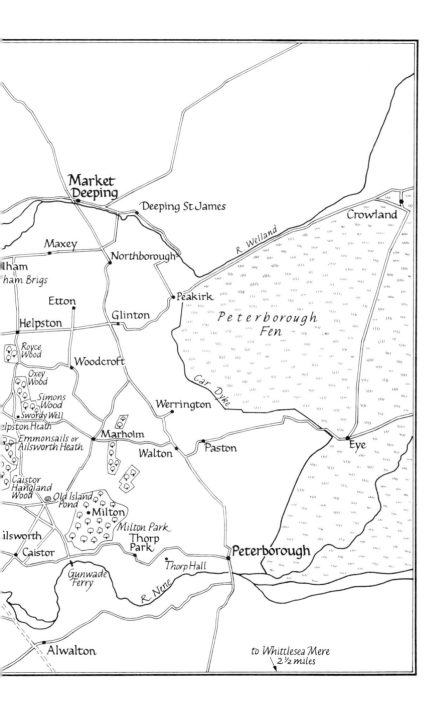

SKETCHES IN THE LIFE OF JOHN CLARE

WRITTEN BY HIMSELF
& ADDRESSED TO HIS FRIEND
JOHN TAYLOR ESQR
MARCH 1821

There is a pleasure in recalling ones past years to reccolection: in this I believe every bosom agrees and returns a ready echo of approbation and I think a double gratifycation is witness'd as we turn to a repetition of our early days by writing them down on paper

on this head my own approbation must shelter its vanity while thus employ'd, by consieting self-satisfaction a sufficient appology. But I am carless of fame and fearless of censure in the business, my only wish being to give a friend pleasure in its perusal for whom and by whose request it is written and as I have little doubt of being able to accomplish that matter those who (strangers to the writer) that it displeases need not be startled at the disappointment

I was born July 13, 1793 at Helpstone, a gloomy village in Northamptonshire, on the brink of the Lincolnshire fens; my mothers maiden name was Stimson, a native of Caistor, a neighboring village, whose father was a town shepherd as they are calld, who has the care of all the flocks of the village   my father was one of fates chance-lings who drop into the world without the honour of matrimony   he took the surname of his mother, who to commemorate the memory of a worthless father with more tenderness of love lorn feeling than he doubtless deservd, gave him his sirname at his christening, who was a Scotchman by birth and a schoolmaster by profession and in his stay at this and the neighboring villages went by the Name of John Donald Parker   this I had from John Cue of Ufford,[1] an old man who in his young days was a companion and confidential to my run-a-gate of a grandfather, for he left the village and my grandmother soon after the deplorable accident of misplaced love was revealed to him, but her love was not that frenzy which shortens the days of the victim of seduction, for she liv'd to the age of 86 and left this world of troubles Jan 1. 1820. Both my parents was illiterate to the last degree   my mother knew not a single letter and superstition went so far with her that she beleved the higher parts of learing was the blackest arts of witchcraft and that no other means coud attain them   my father could read a little in a bible or testament and was very fond of the supersti[ti]ous tales that are hawked about a sheet for a penny, such as old Nixons Prophesies, Mother Bunches Fairey Tales, and Mother Shiptons Legacy[2] etc he was likewise fond of Ballads and I have heard him make a boast of it over his horn of ale with his merry companions at the Blue bell public house which was next door that he coud sing or recite above a hundred   he had a tollerable good voice and was often calld upon to sing at those convivials of bacchanalian merry makings

in my early years I was of a waukly constitution, so much so that my mother often told me she never coud have dreamd I shoud live to make a man, while the sister that was born with me[3] being a twin was as much to the contrary a fine livley bonny wench whose turn it was to die first for she livd but a few weeks, proving the old saying for once mistaken 'that the weakest always goeth to the wall.' As my parents had the good fate to have but a small family, I being the eldest of 4, two of whom dyed in their Infancy my mothers hopfull ambition ran high of being able to make me a good scholar, as she said she expirenced enough in her own case to avoid bringing up her childern in ignorance, but god help her, her hopful and tender kindness was often crossd with difficultys, for there was often enough to do to keep cart upon wheels, as the saying is, without incuring an extra expence of putting me to school, though she never lost the oppertunity when she was able to send me nor woud my father interfere with her kind intentions till downright nessesity from poverty forced him to check her kind intentions, for he was a tender father to his childern and I have every reason to turn to their memorys with the warmest feelings of gratitude and satisfaction, and if doing well to their childern be an addition to rightousness I am certain god cannot forget to bless them with a portion of felicity in the other world, when souls are calld to judgment and recieve the reward due to their actions commited below. In cases of extreeme poverty my father took me to labour with him and made me a light flail for threshing, learing me betimes the hardship which adam and

Eve[4] inflicted on their childern by their inexperienced misdeeds, incuring the perpetual curse from god of labouring for a livlihood, which the teeming earth is said to have produced of itself before, but use is second nature, at least it learns us patience   I resignd myself willingly to the hardest toils and tho one of the weakest was stubbor[n] and stomachful and never flinched from the roughest labour   by that means I always secured the favour of my masters and escaped the ignominy that brands the name of idleness   my character was always 'weak but willing'. I believe I was not older then 10 when my father took me to seek the scanty rewards of industry   Winter was generally my season of imprisonment in the dusty barn   Spring and Summer my assistance was wanted elswere in tending sheep or horses in the fields or scaring birds from the grain or weeding it, which was a delightfull employment, as the old womens memorys never faild of tales to smoothen our labour, for as every day came new Jiants, Hobgobblins, and faireys was ready to pass it away. as to my schooling, I think never a year passd me till I was 11 or 12 but 3 months or more at the worst of times was luckily spared for my improvment, first with an old woman in the village and latterly with a master at a distance[5] from it   here soon as I began to learn to write, the readiness of the Boys always practising urgd and prompted my ambition to make the best use of my abscence from school, as well as at it, and my master was always supprisd to find me improved every fresh visit, instead of having lost what I had learned before for which to my benefit he never faild to give me tokens of encouragment   never leisure hour pass'd me with out making use of it   every winter night our once unletterd hut was wonderfully changd in its appearence to a school room   the old table, which old as it was doubtless never was honourd with higher employment all its days then the convenience of bearing at meal times the luxury of a barley loaf or dish of potatoes, was now coverd with the rude begg[in]ings of scientifical requ[i]sitions, pens, ink, and paper one hour, jobbling the pen at sheep hooks and tarbottles, and another trying on a slate a knotty question in Numeration, or Pounds, Shillings, and Pence, at which times my parents triumphant anxiety was pleasingly experiencd, for my mother woud often stop her wheel or look off from her work to urge with a smile of the warmest rapture in my fathers face her prophesy of my success, saying 'shed be bound, I shoud one day be able to reward them with my pen, for the trouble they had taken in giveing me schooling', and I have to return hearty thanks to a kind providence in bringing her prophesy to pass and giving me the pleasure of being able to stay the storm of poverty and smoothen their latter days; and as a recompense for the rough beginnings of life bid their tottering steps decline in peacful tranquility to their long home, the grave. here my highest ambition was gratifyd for my greatest wish was to let my parents see a printed copy of my poems   that pleasure I have witness'd and they have moreover livd to see with astonishment and joy their humble offspring noticed by thousands of friends and among them names of the greatest distinction, the flower of honour[6] of his native country   surely it is a thrilling pleasure to hear a crippled father seated in his easy chair comparing the past with the present, saying 'Boy who coud have thought, when we was threshing together some years back, thou woudst be thus noticed and be enabled to make us all thus happy.' About this time, which my fathers bursts of feeling aludes too, I began to wean off from my companions and sholl about the woods and fields on Sundays alone   conjectures filld the village about my future destinations on the stage of life, some fanc[y]ing it symtoms of lunacy and that my mothers prophecys would be verified to her sorrow and that my reading of books (they woud jeeringly say) was for no other improvment then quallyfiing an idiot for a workhouse, for at this time my taste and passion for reading began to be furious and I never sholld out on a Sabbath day but some scrap or other, was pocketed for my amusment   I deeply regret usefull books was out of my reach, for as I was always shy and reserved I never woud own to my more learned neighbours that I was fond of books, otherwise then the bible[7] and Prayer Book, the prophetical parts of the former, with the fine hebrew Poem of Job, and the prayers and simple translation of the Psalms in the latter was such favourite readings with me that I could recite abundance of passages by heart   I am sorry to find the knowledge of other books shoud diminish the delight ones childhood experiences in our first perusal of those divine writings. I must digress to say that I think the manner of learing children in village schools very erronious, that is soon as they learn their letters to task them with lessons from the bible and testament and keeping them dinging at them, without any change, till they leave it   A dull boy, never turns with pleasures to his school days when he has often been beat 4 times for bad readings in 5 verses of Scripture, no more then a Man in renewd prosperity to the time when he was a debtor in a Jail   Other books as they grow up become a novelty and their task book at school, the Bible, looses its relish   the painful task of learning wearied the memory   irksome inconvenience never prompts reccolection   the bible is laid by on its peacful shelf and by 9 Cottages out of 10 never disturb'd or turnd too further then the minutes reference for reciting the text on a Sunday, a task which most chr[i]stians nowadays think a sufficient duty at least in the lower orders   I cannot speak with assurance only where experience informs me   so much for village schools   About now all my stock of learning was gleaned from the Sixpenny Romances of 'Cinderella', 'Little Red Riding Hood', 'Jack and the bean Stalk', 'Zig Zag', 'Prince Cherry',[8] etc and great was the pleasure, pain, or surprise increased by allowing them authenticity, for I firmly believed every page I read and considerd I possesd in these the chief learning and literature of the country   But as it is common in villages to pass judgment on a lover of books as a sure indication of laziness, I was drove to the narrow nessesity of stinted oppertunitys to hide in woods and dingles of thorns in the fields on Sundays to read these things, which every sixpence thro the indefatigable savings of a penny and halfpenny when collected was willingly thrown away for them, as oppertunity offered when hawkers offerd them for sale at the door   to read such things on Sundays was not right   while nessesity is a good apology for iniquity and ignorance is more so I knew no better and it may be said that ignorance is one of the sweetest hopes that a poor man carries to the grave, when his manhood muses oer the exclamation of his dying Saviour, asking and offering the same plea for the worst of Sinners 'Father forgive them: they know not what they do'   [digressions may become tiresome and ill grounded opinions may be reckoned consciets but while it is pleasant to turn out of the road for a beautiful blossom tis no less human but nothing short of humanity to release the plundering fox from the snare   hopes unrealized are hopes in reality   blessings long hoped for when real are hopes no longer]*   Clergymen may say tis an enlightened age when a man can have oppertunitys to hear good from bad every Sunday, he has no longer the cloak of ignorance to skulk from iniquity as the west indian and the cherokee digressions may become tiresome and ill grounded opinions may be reckoned consciets but, while it is pleasant to turn out of the way for a b[e]autiful blossom, tis nothing short of humanity to release the plund[er]ing fox from the snare – hopes unrealized are hopes in reality   blessings possesd are hopes no longer   tis the weakness and not the fault of nature to throw a cloak over its imperfections when it seeks for heaven as a better place then it posseses   A staff to the maimed and a couch to the weary traveller are desirable blessings and usful to wish for as blessings thats wanted.

I have often absentet my self the whole Sunday at this time nor coud the chiming bells draw me from my hiding place to go to church, tho at night I was sure to pay for my abscence from it by a strong snubbing   I at length got an higher notion of learning by going to school and every leisure minute was employd in drawing squares and triangles upon the dusty walls of the barn   this was also my practice in learning to write   I also devourd for these purposes every morsel of brown or blue paper (it matterd not which) that my mother had her tea and sugar lapt in from the shop   but this was in cases of poverty when I coud not muster three farthings for a sheet of writing paper   the saying of 'a little learning is a dangerous thing' is not far from fact   after I left school for good (nearly as wise as I went save reading and writing) I felt an itching after every thing   I now began to provide my self with books of many puzzling systems

---

* This passage heavily deleted by Clare.

Bonnycastles Mensuration, Fennings Arithmetic, and Algebra[9] was now my constant teachers and as I read the rules of each Problem with great care I preseverd so far as to solve many of the questions in those books   my pride fancyd it self climbing the ladder of learning very rapidly, on the top of which harvests of unbounded wonders was concieved to be bursting upon me and was sufficient fire to promt my ambition, but in becoming acquainted with a neighbour, one John Turnill,[10] who was a good mathematical scholar, I found I was not sufficient to become master of these things without better assistance as a superficial knowledge of them was next to nothing and I had no more   he kindly enough put me in a plan but cirscumstances soon calld him from me and I luckily abandond the project, not without great reluctance – I was not thought fit for some other employment then th[r]eshing with my father which the neigh-bours said was far to hard for my weak constitution and the first step taken for my releasment from it was an application to put me apprentice to a shoemaker[11] to a neighbour in the town, but this, on my being apprisd of it, I disliked, for at that time I hardly knew what I liked   I was such a silly, shanny boy that I dreaded leaving home were I had been coddled up so tenderly and so long and my mother was determined if I was a trade that I shoud have my choice, far as cirscumstances woud let me, for they coud give not a sixpence with me – however my lot was not for shoe making nor did I ever repent missing it – a next door neighbour, who kept the Blue Bell public house, got me a week or two to drive plough for him, having a small cottage of 6 or 8 acres, and knowing me and my parents he usd me uncommon well   his name was Francis Gregory[12]   he was a single man and lived with his Mother   they both used me as well as if I was their own and after I had been there awhile I got used to them   they hired me for a year, the only year I livd in hired service in my life   my master was of very bad health and dyd a year or two after I left   I have reason to drop a good word to his memory   my friend John Turnill wrote his epitaph on his grave stone, such as it is; for he used to dabble in poetry tho I saw very little of it – Here I got into a habit of musing and muttering to ones self as pastime to divert melancholly, singing over things which I calld songs and attempting to describe scenes that struck me   tis irksome to a boy to be alone and he is ready in such situations to snatch hold of any trifle to divert his loss of company and make up for pleasenter amusments, for as my master was weak and unwell he seldom went to work with me unless necessary as ploughing etc   I always went by my self to weeding the grain, tending horses and such like. Once every week I had to go for a bag of flower to Maxey, a village distant about 2 Miles, as it was sold cheaper then at home and as my mistress was an economist she never lost sight of cheap pennyworths   in the short days of winter its often been dark ere I got home and even by times dusk before I started

I was of a very timid disposition   the traditional Registers of the Village was uncommonly superstitious (Gossips and Granneys) and I had two or three haunted Spots to pass for it was impossible to go half a mile any were about the Lordship were there had nothing been said to be seen by these old women or some one else in their younger days. therefore I must in such extremitys seize the best

remedy to keep such things out of my head as well as I coud, so on these journeys I mutterd over tales of my own fancy and contriving into ryhmes as well as my abilities was able; they was always romantic wanderings of Sailors, Sol[d]iers etc following them step by step from their starting out to their return, for I always lovd to see a tale end happy and as I had only my self to please I always contrivd that my taste shoud be suited in such matters   Sometimes I was tracking my own adventures as I wishd they might be going on from the plough and flail to the easy arm chair of old age reciting armours intrigues of meeting always good fortune and marrying Ladies etc

Hope was now budding and its summer skye warmd me with thrilling extacy and tho however romantic my story might be I had always cautions, fearful enough no doubt, to keep ghosts and hobgoblins out of the question   what I did was to erase them and not bring them to remembrance, tho twas impossible, for as I passd those awful places, tho I dare not look boldly up, my eye was warily on the watch, glegging under my hat at every stir of a leaf or murmur of the wind and a quaking thistle was able to make me swoon with terror

I generaly kept looking on the ground and I have been so taken with my story that I have gone muttering it over into the town before I knew I got there   this has often embarrasd me by being overheard by some one who has asked me who I was talking too   I think I was 13 years of age now but trifling things are never pun[c]tually rememberd as their occurence is never strikingly impressd on the memory, so I cannot say with assurance   none of these things was committed to paper   this summer I met with a fragment of Thompsons Seasons[13]   a young man, by trade a weaver, much older then myself, then in the village, show'd it me   I knew nothing of blank verse nor ryhme either otherwise than by the trash of Ballad Singers, but I still remember my sensations in reading the opening of Spring   I cant say the reason, but the following lines made my heart twitter with joy:

> Come gentle Spring ethereal mildness come
> And from the bosom of yon dropping cloud
> While music wakes around, veild in a shower
> Of shadowing roses, on our plains desend.

I greedily read over all I coud before I returnd it and resolvd to posses one my self, the price of it being only 1^s/6^d I expressd my supprise at seeing such a fine poam so carlessly handld, most part of Winter being gone, but the owner only laughd at me and said 'twas reckoned nothing of by himself or friends'   he and his friends were methodists and he presented Wesleys hymns as a rival of exellence   I said nothing but thought (whatever his religion might be) the taste of him and his friends was worth little notice   I have seen plenty of these fanatics to strengthen my first opinion, as some of them will not read a book that has not the words Lord and God[14] in it   this I assert as a fact to my knowledge and I have always lookd on their concieted affectations with disgust   their founder was rather credolous but I believe him a good man and reverance his Memory   his followers, both in preaching and practice, have brought his principles into disgrace   I have seen plenty to justify the remark. On the next Sunday I started to stamford to buy Thompson, for I teazd my father out of the 1^s/6^d and woud not let him have any peace till he consented to give it me, but when I got there I was told by a young shop boy in the street who had a book in his hand which I found to be 'Collins Odes and poems' that the booksellers woud not open the shop on a Sunday   this was a dissapointment most strongly felt and I returnd home in very low spirits, but haveing to tend horses the next week in company with other boys I plannd a scheme in secret to obtain my wishes by stelth, giving one of the boys a penny to keep my horses in my absence, with an additional penny to keep the Secret   I started off and as we was generally soon with getteing out our horses that they might fill themselves before the flyes was out I got to Stamford I dare say before a door had been opend   I loiterd about the town for hours ere I coud obtain my wishes   I at length got it with an agreeable dissapointment in return for my first, buying it for 6^d less then I had propos'd and never was I more pleasd with a bargain then I was with this shilling purchase   On my return the Sun got up and it was a beautiful morning and as I did not like to let any body see me reading on the road of a working day I clumb over the wall into Burghly Park[15] and nestled in a lawn at the wall side   the Scenery around me was uncommonly beautiful at that time of the year and what with reading the book and beholding the beautys of artful nature in the park I got into a strain of descriptive ryhming on my journey home   this was 'the morning walk'[16] the first thing I commited to paper   I afterwards wrote the evening walk[17] and several descriptions of Local Spots in the fields which I had frequented for Pootys, flowers, or Nests in my early child hood   I burned most of these after I got to consiet I knew better how to make poetry   others I corrected perhaps 20 times over till their origional form was entirley lost such as the Morning walk now extant   I always turn to this years service with F. Gregory as one of the pleasentest occurrences in my existence   I was never hurried in my toils for he was no task master or swore at for commiting a fault   a gentle chiding he always deemd sufficient for any thing that I might do wrong   I believe this usuage and this place to have been the Nursery for fostering my rustic Song   after leaving here awhile somthing came into my head that I woud be a gardiner and for this purpose I went with my father to Burg[h]ley, the Seat of one of my kindest benefactors and Patrons, the Marquis of Exeter, to whom at that time and till the publication of my first Vol of poems I was a stranger. we went to the Master of the Kitchen Garden[18] as most suitable for my destination of working in future in the village were flower gardens are but little store set bye, as the taste of Farmers turns entirely on profit   it may suffice to say we succeeded in getting the wishd for situation. our circumstance in appearing before the Master of the garden will show the mistaken notions of grandeur and

distinction in a clown that has not seen the world   my father as well
as my self thought that as he appeard with white stockings and neck
cloth and as he was under such a great man as a Marquis he must
certainly be homaged as a gentleman of great consequence himself so
with all humilitation to his greatness we met him with our hats in our
hands and made a profound Bow even to our knees ere we proceeded
in the enquirey   I accordingly went the next week as a temporary
apprentice for 3 years for I was not bound   I did not like his looks
from the first and to my inconveneonce provd a good phisigionomist
in the end, so after I had been here nearly a twelve month I fled him,
for I coud stand him no longer   I was very timid and fearful and he
was always fer sending me to Stamford in the night and swearing at
me in his passions for things which were two trifling to be called
faults, tho to give him his due he usd me better then he had done
others before and even after I left him gave me a good word as a still
and willing boy   on this ramble[19] I visited Grantham, Newark etc,
and then returnd to my parents, were I commenced Gardiner, but my
employment in that character was short, for I liked to work in the
fields best   the continued sameness of a garden cloyed me and I
resumed my old employments with pleasure were I coud look on the
wild heath, the wide spreading variety of cultured and fallow fields,
green meadows, and crooking brooks, and the dark woods, waving
to the murmering winds   these were my delights and here I coud
mutter to myself as usual, unheard and unnoticd by the sneering
clown and conscieted cox comb, and here my old habits and feelings
returnd with redoubled ardour, for they left me while I was a
gardiner   I now venturd to commit my musings readily to paper but
with all secresy possible, hiding them when written in an old unused
cubbard in the chamber, which when taken for other purposes drove
me to the nessesity of seeking another safety in a hole under it in the
wall   here my mother when clearing the chamber found me out and
secretly took my papers for her own use as occasion calld for them
and as I had no other desire in me but to keep them from being read
when laid in this fancied safe repository, that desire seemd compleated and I rarely turnd to a reperusal of them   consequently my
stolen fugitives went a long time ere they was miss'd   my mother
thought they was nothing more then Copies as attempts of improving my self in writing   she knew nothing of poetry, at least little
dreamed her son was employd in that business, and as I was ashamed
of being found out as an attempter in that way, when I discoverd her

thefts I humourd her mistake a long time and said they was nothing more then what she supposed them to be so she might take them. but when I did things that I liked better then others I provided safer lodgings for them – at length I begun to shake off this reserve with my parents and half confess what I was doing   my father woud sometimes be huming over a song, a wretched composition of those halfpenny ballads, and my boast was that I thought I coud beat it   in a few days afterwards I used to read my composition for his judgment to decide, but their frequent critisisms and laughable remarks drove me to use a process of cunning in the business some time after, for they damp'd me a long time from proceeding. My method on resuming the matter again was to say I had written it out of a borrowd book and that it was not my own   the love of ryhming which I was loath to quit, growing fonder of it every day, drove me to the nessesity of a lie to try the value of their critisisms and by this way I got their remarks unadulterated with prejudice – in this case their expressions woud be, 'Aye, boy, if you coud write so, you woud do.' this got me into the secret at once and without divulging mine   I scribbld on unceasing for 2 or 3 years, reciting them every night as I wrote them when my father returnd home from labour and we was all seated by the fire side   their remarks was very useful to me   at somethings they woud laugh   here I distinguishd Affectation and consiet from nature   some verses they woud desire me to repeat again as they said they coud not understand them   here I discoverd obscurity from common sense and always benefited by making it as much like the latter as I coud, for I thought if they coud not understand me my taste shoud be wrong founded and not agreeable to nature, so I always strove to shun it for the future and wrote my pieces according to their critisisms, little thinking when they heard me read them that I was the author   My own Judgment began to expand and improve, at least I consieted so and thinking my critisisms better then theirs I selected my pieces approvd of by them and even found most of em fit for nothing but my mothers old purposes, for as I kept sorting them over and over there was few that escaped that destiny in the end. what first induced me to ryhme I cannot hardly say   the first thing that I heard of poetry that may be called poetry was a romantic story, which I have since found to be Pomfrets 'Love triumphant over reason'[20] by reading of it over since to my father who rememberd the Story, but I coud benefit little by this as I used to hear it before I coud read and my father was but a sorry reader of poetry to improve his hearers by reciting it   the relating any thing under the character of a dream is a captivating way of drawing the attention of the vulgar and to my knowledge this tale or vision as it is calld of Pomfrets is more known among the lower orders then any thing else of poetry at least with us   the Romance of 'Robinson Crusoe' was the first book of any merit I got hold of after I coud read   twas in the winter and I borrowd it of a boy at s[c]hool who said it was his uncles and seemed very loath to lend it me, but pressing him with anxious persuasions and assuring him of its safety while in my hands he lent it me that day to be returnd in the morning when I came to school, but in the night a great snow fell which made it impossible to keep my promise as I coud not get, Glinton being 2 miles from our village were I went to school, so I had the pleasure of this delightful companion for a week   new ideas from the perusal of this book was now up in arms   new Crusoes and new Islands of Solitude was continually mutterd over in my Journeys to and from school but as I had not the chance of reading it well I coud not come at the spirit of the thing to graft a lasting impression on the memory, which if I had woud perhaps have been little benefit to my future attempts   I also got an early perusal of The Pilgrims Progress which pleased me mightily – All I can reccole[c]t of the old book of Pomfrets, which my father used to read to me, was that it was full of wooden cuts and one at the beginning of every poem, the first of which was two childern holding up a great Letter   These pictures lured me to make an end of the book for one day I made use of an oppertunity to cut them out and burnt the rest to avoid detection – But to return to the narritive, having made use of my parents critisisms till (as I said before) my consiet fancyd I coud do without em, I ryhmd and read them in secret and my mother giving me a small box to put my books, clothes, etc in, with a lock and key, as she said I was now a big boy and to learn me how to be saving, she first learned me how to take care of my own things by resigning them to my care with this prudent admonition and advice, 'You must now, my boy, think of somthing to do you good   you must go to service after all if you wish to get on and as you dont like farmers service I will seek a friend that shall get you somthing better   so leave off writing and buy no more books, tho I own its better then spending your money in beer, but you want cloths and ought to save every farthing for that purpose   I give you this box and you will find it useful when you get from me to keep your few things together   when you once get from me you will think nothing of it and you'll find it far better then drudging at home year after year in the barn and the field for little or nothing.' this advice however good it might be was but little attended too   the box when in my possesion made me an exelent receptacle for my writings and books were they lay snug and safe from all dangers and I continued as hot as ever at reading and scribbling and, as I always looked sullen when my mother talkd of Service, she at length gave up teazing me, tho I have often heard her discourse with my father that her hopes were lost and that I shoud never be anything   this when heard dampd me a little but I preseverd with my avocations and as they both began to dislike my love of books and writing, thinking it of no longer use since I had determind to stick at hard labour, I pursued it with all secresey possible and every shilling I coud save unknown to them I bought books and paper with   my Library about now consisted of the following: 'Abercrombies Gardiners Journal,' 'Thompsons Seasons,' A Shatterd Copy of 'Miltons Paradise lost,' 'Wards Mathematics,' Fishers 'Young mans companion,' 'Robin Hoods Garland,' 'Bonnycastles Mensuration,' and 'Algebra,' 'Fennings Arithmetic,' 'Death of Abel,' 'Joe Millers Jests,' A 'Collection of Hymns,'[21] with some odd Pamphlets of Sermons by the Bishop of Peterborough — I now began to value my abilitys as superiour to my companions and exalted over it in secret, tho by learing them at school they had the boast of reading and writing better and coud use their compasses at ovals, triangles, Squares etc and talk about plotting grounds etc and many things which, tho I knew a superficial knowledge of, the groundworks was greek to me, but I cared little for these things for I considerd walking in the track of others and copying and dinging at things that had been found out some hundreds of years ago had as little merit in it as a child walking in leading strings ere it can walk by itself   when I happend with them in my sunday Walks I often try'd their taste by pointing out some striking beauty in a wild flower or object in the surrounding senery to which they woud seldom make an answer, and if they did twas such as 'they coud see nothing worth looking at' turning carless to reasume their old discourse and laughing at my 'droll fancies' as they woud call them   I often wondered that, while I was peeping about and finding such quantitys of pleasing things to stop and pause over, another shoud pass me as carless as if he was blind   I thought somtimes that I surely had a taste peculialy by myself and that nobody else thought or saw things as I did   still as my highest ambition at that time was nothing else but the trifle of pleasing ones self, these fancys coud dishearten me very little while that gratification was always at hand, but a cirscumstance occurd which nearly stopd me from writing even for my own amusment   borrowing a school book of a companion, having some entertaining things in it both in prose and Verse with an introduction by the compiler, who doubtless like myself knew little about either (for such like affect to give advice to others while they want it themselves), in this introduction was rules both for writing as well as reading Compositions in prose and verse, were, stumbling on a remark that a person who knew nothing of grammer[22] was not capable of writing a letter nor even a bill of parcels, I was quite in the suds, seeing that I had gone on thus far without learing the first rudiments of doing it properly for I had hardly hard the name of grammer while at school – but as I had an itch for trying at every thing I got hold of I determ[i]ned to try grammer, and for that purpose, by the advice of a friend, bought the 'Universal Spelling Book'[23] as the most easy assistant for my starting out, but finding a jumble of words classd under this name and that name and this such a figure of speech and that another hard worded figure I turned from further notice of it in instant disgust for as I knew I coud talk to be understood I thought by the same method my writing might be made out as easy and as proper, so in the teeth of grammer I pursued my literary journey as warm as usual, working hard all day and scribbling at night or any leisure hour in any convenient hole or corner I could shove in unseen, for I always carried a pencil in my pocket having once bought at Stamford fair a dozen of a Jew for a Shilling which lasted me for years   while nessesity as I got up towards manhood urged me to look for somthing more then pleasing ones self, my poems had been kept with the greatest industry under wishd concealment, having no choice to gratify by their disclosure but on the contrary chilling damp with fear whenever I thought of it, the laughs and jeers of those around me when they found out I was a poet was present death to my ambitious apprehensions for in our unletterd villages the best of the inhabitants have little more knowledge in reading then what can be gleaned from a weekly Newspaper, Old Moors Almanack, and a Prayer Book on Sundays at Church, while the labouring classes remain as blind in such matters as the Slaves in Africa – but in spite of what they might say and do, Nessesity as I said before urgd me to think of Somthing   my father, who had been often crippled for months together with the rumatics for 10 or 12 years past, was now tottaly drove from hard labour by them and forced to the last shifts of standing out against poverty – My fathers Spirit was strongly knitted with independence and the thoughts of being forced to bend before the frowns of a Parish to him was the greatest despair, so he stubbornly strove with his infirmitys and potterd about the roads putting stones in the ruts for his 5 shillings a week, fancying he was not so much beholden to their forced generosity as if he had taken it for nothing I myself was of a week constitution and a severe indisposition keeping me from work for a twelvemonthe ran us in debt   we had back rents to make up, shoe bills, and Bakers etc   my fathers assistance was now disabled and the whole weight fell upon myself, who at the best of times was little capable to bear it, with the hopes of clearing it off – my indisposition, (for I cannot call it illness) origionated in fainting fits, the cause of which I always imagined came from seeing when I was younger a man name Thomas Drake after he had fell off a load of hay and broke his neck   the gastly palness of death struck such a terror on me that I coud not forget it for years and my dreams was constantly wanderings in church yards, digging graves, seeing spirits in charnel houses etc   in my fits I swooned away without a struggle and felt nothing more then if I'd been in a dreamless sleep after I came to my self but I was always warnd of their coming by a chillness and dithering that seemd to creep from ones toe ends till it got up to ones head, when I turnd sensless and fell; sparks as if fire often flashd from my eyes or seemd to do so when I dropt, which I layd to the fall – these fits was stopt by a Mr Arnold M.D.[24] of Stamford, of some notoirety as a medical gentleman and one whom I respect with gratful remembrances for he certainly did me great benefit, tho every spring and autum since the accident happend my fears are agitated to an extreem degree and the dread of death involves me in a stupor of chilling indisposition as usual, tho I have had but one or two swoonings since they first left me

In this dilemma of Embaresment which my fathers misfortune with the addition of my own above mentioned involvd us I began to consider about the method of revealing the Secret of my poetry   I had a confidential friend, one Thomas Porter[25] of Ashton-Green, a lone cottage about a mile from helpstone, who being a lover of books was a pleasant companion and to whose house I went almost every sunday for several years   our tastes was parrarel excepting poetry he lovd to walk the wood for wild flowers and to pore over old book

stalls at a fair   such like pastimes to him as myself was the greatest
entertainments we coud meet with   to him I showd the first
Specimen of my talent at poetry but being a bad Judge of it and
considering the scirscumstance of its coming from me he said little of
it but kept the secret inviolate   I cared little about his reserve in
stating his opinion as I knew he understood little to give a just one   I
askd him if he understood it and he merely said 'yes', for he was a
strict observer of nature and acquainted with most of her various
pictures thro the changes of Seasons   this reccomendation was
plenty for me as I found his eyes viewd things as mine did and his
notice observed them as I expressd them and wether prose or poetry
he knew of its merits no further   from this time I began to select my
pieces and copy them off, for the inspection of sombody that might
be a judge but who I knew not or where to apply   I a year or two
after went to Deeping Fair and applyd to a Bookseller[26] there for a
book of blank Paper but having none that I wanted he promised to
bind me one up and send it, in the mean time seeming half inclined to
enquire what use I was going to put it to and I on my part as willing to
inform him and being at that time releasd from my timid embaras-
ment of reserve from a free application of Ale in the fair, I bluntly told
him my intentions as he was a printer of that extent of business in
having types sufficient to enable him to print a pamphlet or small
book now and then when he coud happen of employment   he
doubtless fancyd I was a bargain, so he wishd to see some of my
poems and while after I took him 'The setting Sun' 'To a primrose'
etc which with doubtless little credit to his taste he seemed to highly
approve and we enterd into proposals about the manner most
beneficial to get them out and as a specimen of his abilities in printing
he shewed me the 'Life of Joseph', then in the press printing for if I
recolect right 'W. Baines Paternoster row London', which, tho I little
understood the elegance of printing, thought it deservd small praise
as to that matter but the manner of printing my poems was to me of
little consequence   to get them printed at all was sufficient so I
readily agreed that he was capable of publishing my trifles and the
best way for so doing he said was by subscription   force p[o]ints us
to no choice or else I detested the thoughts of Subscription as being
little better then begging money from people that knew nothing of
their purchase, who when they had got it woud laugh and jeer the
writer for jeerings sake, for theres nothing more common then
consiet attributing the word foolish to and laughing at what it dont

understand, reckoning all vanity thats above the comprehension of its own little knowledge and such was most of the individuals around me which made me decline coming to an imediate agreement, tho want of money was another obstacle that coud not be surmounted just then as he said people must be informed of it before they coud subscribe and that a prospectus of the plan with a Specimen of the poetry etc was quite nessesary, 300 of which he said when I had drawn one up he woud print on a double leaf of foolscap 8vo for £1 for he seemed timid to write one himself, as I proposed, which made me consider him incapable of publishing a selection with any credit to me as my judgment of what woud do etc was worth nothing, but this he woud do at any time wether I saw him again or not if I woud but inform him by letter and send an 'Address to the Public' which I knew little about addressing   soon after this I left Helpstone in company with an out o town labourer who followed the employment of burning lime, name Stephen Gordon, who came from Kingsthorp near Northampton, who got me from home with the promise of many advantages from working with him which he never intended or at least never was able to perform   we at first worked for Mᵣ Wilders at Bridge Casterton in Rutland   the whole addition to my fortunes accumulated here was the acquaintance with a young girl who was destined for my future companion thro this life and a poor mans meeting with a wife is reckoned but little improvment to his con- dition and particular with the embaresments labourd under at this time   we staid at this place till the latter end of the year and then went to Pickworth, a hamlet which seems by its large stretch of old foundations and ruins to have been of town of some magnitude in past times tho it is now nothing more then a half solitude of huts and odd farm houses scatterd about some furlongs asunder   the marks of the ruins may be traced 2 miles or further from beginning to end here by hard working nearly day and night I at last got my £1 saved for the printing the proposals, which I never lost sight of, and getting a many more poems written as ex[c]ited by change of Scenery, and from being over head and ears in love above all the most urgent propensity to scribbling I fancyd myself more qualified for the undertaking, considering the latter materials much better then what I had done, which no doubt was the case, so I wrote a letter from this place imediatly to Henson of M. Deeping, wishing him to begin the proposals and address the public himself, urging he coud do it far better then myself but his Answer was that I must do it, after which I made some attempts but having not a fit place for doing any thing of that kind, lodging at a public house and pested with many other inconviniences, I coud not suit myself with doing it in a hurry, so it kept passing from time to time till at last I determined good or bad to produce somthing and as we had another lime kiln at Ryhall[27] about 3 miles from Pickworth I often went there to work by myself were I had leisure to study over such things on my journeys of going and returning to and fro; and on these walks morning and night I have droped down 5 or 6 times, to plan this troublesome task of An address etc   in one of these musings my prosing thoughts lost them selves in rhyme, in taking a view as I sat neath the shelter of a woodland hedge of my parents distresses at home and of my laboring

so hard and so vainly to get out of debt and of my still added perplexitys of ill timed love – striving to remedy all and all to no purpose – I burst out in an exclamation of distress, 'What is Life', and instantly recolecting such a subject woud be a good one for a poem I hastily scratted down the 2 first Verses of it as it stands as the begining of the plan which I intended to adopt and continued my jorney to work, but when at the kiln I coud not work for thinking about what I had so long been trying at; so I set me down on a lime skuttle and out with my pencil for an address of some sort, which good or bad I determind to send off that day and for that purpose when finished I accordingly started to Stamford about 3 miles from me   still along the road I was in a hundred minds wether I shoud throw all thoughts up about the matter or stay while a fitter oppertunity to have the advice of some friend or other but on turning it over in ones mind agen a second thought soon informd me that I had none   I was turnd adrift on the broad ocean of life and must either sink or swim: so I weighd matters on both sides and fancied let what bad woud come they coud but ballance with the former   if my hopes of the Poems failed I shoud be not a pin worse then usual – I coud but work then as I did already – nay I considerd I shoud reap benefit from disapointment   their downfall woud free my mind from all foolish hopes and let me know that I had nothing to trust to but work, so with this favourable idea I pursued my intention, dropping down on a stone heap before I got in the town to give it a second reading and correct what I thought amiss, as I found my printer had little abilitys that way, I was feign to do my best at it to escape being laughed at   When I got to the Post Office they wanted a Penny as I past the hour, but as I had none and hating to look so little as to make the confession I said with a little petteshness that it was not mine and that I shoud not pay for other peoples letters   the man lookd a little supprisd at the unusual garb of the letter which I was half ashamd of – directed with a pencil, written on a sheet of paper that was crumpled and grizzld with lying in ones pocket so long and to add to its novelty seald with shoemakers wax. I saw his smile and retreated as fast as I coud from the town   in the course of another week 100 of printed proposals came, directed to pickworth, accompanyd with a letter wishing me to meet him at a public house in Stamford on a set day to discuss on further particulars, which turnd out to be nothing more particular then paying him for his printing and when he presented his bill I found he had added 5^s/- more to the £1 agreement   this led me into his principles of overreaching and encroaching and from that time I considerd him in his true light as being no friend of mine further then interest directed him, which turnd out exactly the case   I distributed my papers accordingly but as I coud get at no way of pushing them into higher circles then those with whom I was accquainted they consequently passd off as qu[i]etly as if they had still been in my possesion unprinted and unseen   as soon as he got 100 Subscribers he said he woud begin to print, which after awhile he pretended he had got, so I lost aweeks work to go home and arange matters but when I got there to him he said he coud not begin the book unless I advanced him £15,   this was plenty for me   I now found the man what I considerd him and determind in my mind he shoud not print it at all tho I said nothing then – I had not 15 pence nor 15 Farthings to call my own then – so I gave up all thoughts of his doing it   At this season of difficulty when I was embaras'd over head and ears in debt from down right nessesity I was still playing the fool with myself and coud not help running unnessary expences even then   I had been taking the 'Enquirer'[28] by Nos and had consequently ran in debt with a Bookseller to make up the matter this was a Mr Thompson, who kept the 'New public Library' in the high street, Stamford   how to get straight with him I did not know but to let him see I had some prospect in the wind and hoping he woud befriend me in the matter a little by thinking he woud get his money in so doing I sent him 3 or 4 prospectuses with a short note and the names of 3 or 4 Subscribers, but he treated my humble vanity with contempt and told the bearer (Thomas Porter of Ashton) that the money was what he wanted and the money he woud have   Mr Drury[29] had taken the Shop and seeing the prospectuses, thinking no doubt he might do it with benefit, paid the money immediatly without knowing further of me then what my friend related nor of my abilities then the prospectus specified, for his account of first meeting with the Sonnet to the Setting Sun[30] in MSS is all a hoax and of no other foundation then his own fancy: but wether a mistake or intended falsity I cant justly assert, but I am apt to imagine what I am loath to discover   we have all foibles, and be it as it may, I respect him. accordingly from the accidental cirscumstance of seeing the prospectus, he hunted me up on the following Sunday in company with a friend   I was not at home then, being at a neighbou[r]s house in the village known as a harmless resort of young men by the appelation of 'Bachellors Hall'[31] the possesors of which being two bachellors, John and James Billings,[32] whom I am still fond of visiting as companions tho much older then myself in spite of snarling mischief-makers who would feignly belye me into discredit for so doing, by pretending nightly depredations are misterously and frequently going forward, such as stealing Game etc   I never saw any such thing comited there, or any were else, and I woud give it on oath, not only for myself but on the credit of these men, that such calumnitors are liars of the vilest and most dangerous class and that I should always feel myself more safer in the company of my old neighbours then in those of that description   But again to our narrative   on being fetchd home with the news that gentlemen[33] was waiting to see me, I felt very awkard and had a good mind to keep away   I always felt and still feel very irksome among super-iours so that its nothing now but down right force that hauls me into it   however I made my appearance and they both said they had came to become subscribers   I thankd them   they moreover wishd to see some of my MSS   what I had I showd them and they was seemlingly pleasd with them   they also askd me on what terms I stood with Henson of Deeping   I told them and hinted my intention of leaving him   they said little either for it or against it, but to their credit perhaps it may be justice to remark that they observd if I had pledgd my word of honour to him not to break it by any means – I said nothing further about it but thought that as he had broke his word and seemd by his actions to set very little store by honour in the matter that I had little cause to be sticking at that point and shoud be guilty of very small faults if I set as little store by mine on the occasion, for an agreement once found unjustifiable or broken in any part is no longer honourable, while receeding from it is nothing more then Justifying ones self from an error – they said before they left me, at least Mʳ Drury did, that if I got the MSS from Henson he shoud like to see them and woud then arange matters with me if I pleased and print them without any advancment of money on my part   this was what I wanted and just suited me so I promised him he shoud   they made ready for starting and Mʳ Drurys friend invited me to come over and dine with him in the ensuing week but doubtless repenting of his free spoken kindness and thinking if he 'gave me an inch I shoud take an ell' by making unasked additional visits and by that means become troublesome, for theres nothing more common here now adays, so he opened the door agen and said 'If you get the MSS from deeping Mʳ Clare, we shall be glad to see you if not we can say nothing further about the matter.' thus ended the exibition of my two proffers of subscription like a showmans touchstone of 'presto, quick, change, and be gone, soon as the words spoke, the tricks done.' I was hipt most cursedly at what ended their visit and wishd I had not came home   what ever his reasons was for chewing his kindness over again I know not   if he by second thoughts fancyied I might be an intruder he afterwards found himself mistaken, for I never paid it even according to his alterd conditions. Drury may make what he pleases of his meeting with me at first if I shoud ever become of that consequence in his opinion to require that notice – he may contradict, add, alter, or shuffle it about in what shape he pleases – here is the plain truth without the least desire to offend or wish to please any of the parties conserned – I respect them on the list of my other friends as far as they are respectable and thats all I can say in this part of the Story or all I care about the consequence. I have one fault which had ought to be noticed, a heated spirit that instantly kindles in too hasty bursts of praise or censure   this will be found in my corespondence   when I fancy my self injured I cannot brook it, no more then stifle my gratitude when I am under obligations: one flowes as freely as the other   nor do I repent it   when I am under misconsceptions and accuse wrongfully I shall meet forgiveness; when I do not I neither need it nor require it   my spirit of independence I set store by myself and I rest alike careless of succeeding callumniatures who by adducing their consiets as examples may abuse me either for wanting or possesing it Just as they please to decide – so be it – tryed friendship shall never find me ungratfull in the end or shifting after benefits – I wish others to see me as freely as I will them, which no doubt plenty of them does, tho under the mistery of false colours – what I have and shall say in this sketch is matured by reflection, so I wish every thing at least the substance to remain as it is written. I shall recant nothing. The same week my mother went over to Deeping fetched the MSS home again and as soon as I got them in my possesion I started off to Drurys   To get the book printed for no expence on my part and a certain sum gaind by it in the bargain was a temptation I coud not let slip   when I appeared with them he gave me a Guinea as an ansel or ernest to the bargain and I readily left them and proceeded as he wishd in sending others as I copied them out, with no other agreement then word-of-mouth at that time he praised some gentlemen into whose hands he intended to entrust the MSS uncommonly and I felt very anxious of knowing who the gentlman shoud be but he kept it as a secret a long time and at length told me twas John Taylor[34] of London a cousin of his   moreover he read me extracts from some of the above gentlemans letters to convince me of his abilities and I deemd it very lucky that such a man shoud fall in the way to correct and supperintend the publication and I have still the happiness to remember that when the thing came to be realized I met with no dissapointment but found the good character of the gentlemen given by Drury was not exaggerated in the least, but on the contrary, many things before unknown to me served to heighten my expectations rather then diminish them – Drury by some jealous advisers, or one how or other, wanted an agreement after a time had expired and wishing to please everybody as far as I was able, I with some reluctance signed one with out considering in the least what it might contain for tho it was read over to me I took no heed of it as I knew nothing about such things – but reccolecting afterwards of hearing somthing about not only the present publication then in hand but what ever publications I might be encouraged to publish was all bound and apprenticed to this agreement – this I coud not stand, so I determined to break all such bondages and acted accordingly. and now leaving this long digression of trifleing I shall resume the story of my occupations and labours   I continued to work at Pickworth till the winter and then went to Casterton were I stopt a little while again with Mr Wilders till the frost set in that he coud not employ me longer   I then returnd home and had a good winters work of Scribbling etc for the forthcoming book   after the Spring came on I was sent for again to work for Mr Wilders were I continued all summer till the latter end of the year when a drop of wages against our first agreement made me leave the place   My amourous intrigues and connections with Patty,[35] the girl before mentioned, now began to disclose dangers which marriage alone coud remedy   I was little fit or inclined for marrying but my thoughtless and ram headed proceedings, as I was never all my life any thing else but a fool, commiting rashly and repenting too late having injured her character as well as my own as for mine, I cared not a farthing about it   twas bad enought I knew and made ten time worse by meddling lyars but the ruination of one whom I almost adored was a wickedness my heart, however callous it might be to its own deceptions, coud not act   the wide mouth of the world was open against her, swallowing everything that started to discredit her and sounding their ecchos in my ears to torment me and set me against her   hurt and vex me it did, but I felt more affection for her then ever and I determind to support her   I had that satisfaction on my consience that she was the only one I ever had injured and I had that oppertunity of easing my present trouble by making her amends   I therefore made use of it and married her March 16 1820 and my only repentance was that I had not became acquainted with her sooner then I did. I shoud have been as rich had I married 5 or 6 years sooner as I had been while single, for after I grew up I got into many scrapes I shoud other wise have shunned in the company of one I esteemed, for till my arival at Casterton my dealings with love was but temporary   when a face pleasd me I scribbled a Song or so in her praise, tryd to get in her company for the sake of pastime meerely as its calld on a Sunday eve a time or two and then left off for new alurements in fresh faces that took my fancy as supperiors – but these trifles, were as innosent and harmless as trifling had I kept free from all others. temptations were things that I rarely resisted when the partiallity of the moment gave no time for reflection I was sure to seize it what ever might be the consequence. still I have been no ones enemmy but my own   my easy nature, either in drinking or anything else, was always ready to submit to persuasions of profligate companions who often led me into snares and laughd at me in the bargain when they had done so. such times as at fairs, coaxed about to bad houses, those painted pills of poison, by whom many ungarded youths are hurried to destruction, like the ox to the slaughter house without knowing the danger that awaits them in the end – here not only my health but my life has often been on the eve of its sacrafice by an illness too well known, and to[o] disgusting to mention. but mercey spared me to be school'd by experience who learnd me better. perhaps its not improper or too insignificant to mention that my first feelings of love was created at school even while a boy   a young girl, I may say a child, won my affections not only by her face which I still think very handsome but by her meek modest and quiet disposition, the stillest and most good natured girl in the school   her name was Mary[36] and my regard for her lasted a long time after school days was over but it was platonic affection, nothing else but love in idea for she knew nothing of my fondness for her, no more then I did of her inclinations, to forbid or encourage me, had I disclosed after wards – but other Marys etc excited my admiration and the first creator of my warm passions was lost in a perplexd multitude of names that woud fill a vol to Callender them down ere a bearded chin coud make the lawfull appology for my entering the lists of Cupid. Thus began and ended my amourous career. My faults I believe to be faults of most people – nature like a bird in its shell came into the world with errors and propensitys to do wrong mantled round her as garments and tho not belonging to her substance are so fastned round her person by the intricate puzzles of temptation that wisdom has not the power or the skill to unloose her nott that fastens them – virtue, or innoscence, pretending perfection in this world is to common sense a painted Sepulchre. the mercey of perfection must look on all with many indulgences or the best will fall short of their wishd reward.

In matters of religion I never was and I doubt never shall be so good as I ought to be – tho I am at heart a protestant perhaps like many more I have been to church [more] often then I have been seriously inclined to recieve benefit or put its wholsome and reasonable admonitions to practice – still I reverence the church and do from my soul as much as anyone curse the hand thats lifted to undermine its constitution – I never did like the runnings and racings after novelty in any thing, keeping in mind the proverb 'When the old ones gone there seldom comes a better.' The 'free will' of ranters,[37] 'new light' of methodists, and 'Election Lottery' of Calvanism I always heard with disgust and considered their enthusiastic ravings little more intelligable or sensible then the belowings of Bedlam. In politics I never dabbled to understand them thoroughly   with the old dish that was served to my forefathers I am content. but I believe the reading a small pamphlet on the Murder of the french King many years ago with other inhuman butcheries cured me very early from thinking favourably of radicalism   the words 'revolution and reform' so much in fashion with sneering arch infidels thrills me with terror when ever I see them – there was a Robspiere, or somthing like that name, a most indefatigable butcher in the cause of the french levellers, and if the account of him be true, hell has never reeked juster revenge on a villian since it was first opened for their torture – may the foes of my country ever find their hopes blasted by diss- appointments and the silent prayers of the honest man to a power that governs with justice for their destruction meet always with success. thats the creed of my consience – and I care for nobody else's – all have liberty to think as they please and he is a knave that cheats his heart with false appearances, be his opinions as they may – here is as faithful account of myself as I can possibly give   I have been as free to disclose my own faults as a meddler is those of his neighbours – and by so doing have doubtless baffled the aims of skulking assasins from throwing weapons in the dark with the force they woud have done had I made myself better then I am. 'Tell truth and shame the devil'

I am
ever faithfully
yours etc
John Clare

To John Taylor Esqr
London.

[Northampton MS 14]

MORE HINTS IN THE LIFE ETC

I have dipt into several sorts of Studies at several times in my boyish days   my vanity was such that what ever Book in art or Science I could come at I fancied I could learn it and Instantly with as much ardour and Enthuiseism (perhaps) as the author that wrote it. I have sat down studying it page by page with an anxious delight not to be describd but where any thing happened to come above my Comprehension it was a Painfull task   I have had repeated t[o]uches at a Mathematics Question for a month together and while it remaind a Secret I have had with out knowing the cause such a longing Sickness on me that I could eat (in the time) little or nothing   In this manner I eagerly dipt into Most arts and Sciences that came in my way

These where Mathematics Particulary Navigation and Algebra Dialling Use of the Globes Botany Natural History Short Hand with History of all Kinds Drawing Music etc etc   I had once a very great desire to learn the Latin Language but the happy fate of not meeting with proper Books in that age of Vanity saved me the trouble of Expeirencing many an aching head (Study always left a sinking sickening pain in my head otherways unaccountable) and many an Envious Staring throbbing thro my bosom which always was the case when I found my attempts in vain − etc

On Sundays I Generally stole from my Companions whose Manners and Play was noways Agreable to me and sholld into the Woods Where I was most happy as I always lovd to be by myself   I have spent whole days (Sundays) in Searching Curious wild Flowers of which I was very fond and I often wondered when in Company with others that they never noticed them and that they never in the least noticed my remarks on such and such beauties when I have stooped down and cropped the flower to explain my Ideas in vain   I was very fond of 'birds Nesting' as we us'd to call it when I was a Child but this hard hearted practise of Robbing Poor birds was soon laid aside as I grew up   Searching of Snail shells we call 'Pooties' was a Favou[r]ite Amusement − I must remark too the Aspiring Pride of being first Scholar in the school (as I always was)   If I had the least fear of a Superior I labourd night and day at my Question till the

Masters praises put me out of doubt – This Vanity had its Origin at the first (or nearly so) school I went to   A Mr Seaton once Schoolmaster at Glinton us'd to give his best scholars premiums that is such as Got Tasks and spelling the best and the most of either   he always took a great delight (as I could percieve) in Questioning and rewarding me even som times when I did not deserve it but his reasons for so doing I cannot tell as I was quite a stranger to him   he once set me a task of getting a Chap[ter] of Job   I think the 3rd   this suprisd me   I accordingly compleated the task in the Christmas week   I was rewarded exellently for my abilities with 6^d and praises of the Master   ever after the boys where so dampt that they woud not try in things in which I was concernd so that I got the prizes without trouble and have come in for some time as much as threepence in a Week   this I savd unknown to my parents to buy books etc

I forgot to mention that I was while at school very much delighted with the perusal of 'Robinson Crusoe' as lent me by a school fellow   it is an entertaining book and the effect of its perusal was such that I still remember it with pleasure

Grammer I never read a page of in my Life nor do I believe my master knew any more then I did about the matter

I have a Superficial Knowledge of the Mathematics which I gaind partly by self Tuition (as I was very fond of them once) and partly by the assistance of a Friend whom I shall ever remember with Gratitude*

I never went to meals with out employing every leisure minute in the perusal of a book   practiseing thus I began to read and comprehend the meaneing of what I read well   [Northampton MS 22]

* Mr John Turnill Late of Helpstone now in the Excise [Clare's footnote].

AUTOBIOGRAPHICAL FRAGMENTS

I cannot trace my name to any remote period a century and a half is the utmost and in this I have found no great ancestors to boast in the breed – all I can make out is that they were Gardeners Parish Clerks and fiddlers and from these has sprung a large family still increasing were kindred has forgotten its claims and 2nd and 3rd cousins are worn out [A32, 7]

[*Holidays*]

What ups and downs have I met with since I was a boy   how barren the world looking about me   now years come and go like messengers without errands and are not noticd for the tales which they tell are not worth stopping them to hear   nothing but cares and dissa[point]ments   when I was a boy a week scarcly came without a promise of some fresh delight   Hopes were always awake with expectations   the year was crowned with holidays [B5, 46]

and then the year usd to be crownd with its holidays as thick as the boughs on a harvest home   there was the long wishd for Christmass day the celebrated week with two sundays when we usd to watch the

29

clerk return with his bundle of ever greens and run for our bunch to stick the windows and empty candlesticks hanging in the corner or hasten to the woods to gett ivy branches with its joccolate berrys which our parents usd to color with whitening and the blu[e]bag sticking the branches behind the pictures on the walls

then came Valentine   tho young we was not without loves   we had our favourites in the village and we listend the expected noises of creeping feet and the tinkling latch as eagerly as upgrown loves

wether they came or not it made no matter   dissapointments was nothing in those matters then   the pleasures of anticipation was all — then came the first of april   o how we talkd and harpd of it ere it came of how we woud make april fools of others and take care not to be catchd our selves when as soon as the day came we were the first to be taken in by running unconsiously on errands for Piegons milk glass eyd needles or some such april fool errands   when we were undecieved we blushd for shame and took care not to be taken in till the day returnd agen when the old deceptions were so far forgotten as to decieve us again

then there was the first of may   we were too young to be claimants in the upgrown sports but we joined our little interferances with them and run under the extended hankerchiefs at duck under water[1] with the rest unmolested   then came the feast when the cross was throngd round with stalls of toys and sweets horses on w[h]eels with their flowing manes and lambs with their red necklaces box cuckoos and we lookd on these finerys till the imaganation almost coaxed our itching fingers to steal and seemd to upbraid our fears for not daring to do it   then the sweet meats was unbounded   their was barly sugar candied lemon candied hore[h]ound and candied pepper-mint with swarms of colord sugar plumbs and tons of lollipop   our mouths waterd at such luxurys   we had our penny but we knew not how to lay it out   there was ginger bread coaches and ginger bread milk maids   to gratifye two propensitys the taste and the fancy together we bought one of these gilded toys and thought we had husbanded our pennys well till they was gone and then we went runing and coaxing our parents for more thinking of making better bargains when we got money agen   then there was eastwell spring[2] famous in those days for its spaws and its trough at the fountain were we usd to meet of a sunday and have sugard drink   then came the she[e]p [s]heerings were we was sure of frumity from the old shepherds if we sought the clipping pens and lastly came the harvest

home and its cross skittles   ah what a paradise begins with the
ignorance of life and what a wilderness the knowledge of the world
discloses   surely the garden of eden was nothing more then our first
parents entrance upon life and the loss of it their knowledge of the
world   [B8, 127R–126R]

surely our play prolonging moon on spring evenings shed a richer
lustre then the mid day sun that surrounds us now in manhood for its
poetical sunshine hath left us   it is the same identical sun and we
have learned to know that – for when boys every new day brought a
new sun   we knew no better and we was happy in our ignorance –
there is nothing of that new and refreshing sunshine upon the picture
now   it shines from the heavens upon real matter of fact existances
and weary occupations   [A46, 106]

[Leisure]

I loved to employ leisure in wandering about the fields watching the
habits of birds to see the wood pecker s[w]eeing away in its ups and
downs and the jay birds chattering by the wood side its restless
warnings of passing clowns the travels of insects were the black
beetle nimbld along and the opening of field flowers   such amuse-
ments gave me the greatest of pleasures but I coud not acco[u]nt for
the reason why they did so   a lonly nook a rude bridge or woodland
style with ivy growing around the posts delighted me and made
lasting impressions on my feelings but I knew nothing of poetry then
    yet I noticd every thing as anxious as I do now and every thing
pleasd me as much   I thought the gipseys camp by the green wood
side a picturesque and an adorning object to nature and I lovd the
gipseys for the beautys which they added to the landscape   I heard
the cuckoos 'wandering voise' and the restless song of the Nightin-
gale and was delighted while I pausd and mutterd its sweet jug jug as I
passd its black thorn bower   I often pulld my hat over my eyes to
watch the rising of the lark or to see the hawk hang in the summer sky
and the kite take its circles round the wood   I often lingered a
minute on the woodland stile to hear the wood pigions clapping their
wings among the dark oaks   I hunted curious flowers in rapturs and
muttered thoughts in their praise   I lovd the pasture with its rushes
and thistles and sheep tracks   I adored the wild marshy fen with its
solitary hernshaw sweeing along in its mellan[c]holy sky   I wan-

31

dered the heath in raptures among the rabbit burrows and golden blossomd furze   I dropt on a thymy mole hill or mossy eminence to survey the summer landscape as full of raptures as now   I marked the varied colors in flat spreading fields checkerd with closes of different tinted grain like the colors in a map the copper tinted colors of clover in blossom the sun tand green of the ripening hay the lighter hues of wheat and barley intermixd with the sunny glare of the yellow c[h]arlock and the sunset imitation of the scarlet head aches with the blue corn bottles crowding thier splendid colors in large sheets over the lands and 'troubling the corn fields' with destroying beauty the different greens of the woodland trees the dark oak the paler ash the mellow Lime the white poplar peeping above the rest like leafy steeples the grey willow shining chilly in the sun as if the morning mist still lingerd in its cool green   I felt the beauty of these with eager delight   the gad flyes noon day hum the fainter murmer of the bee flye 'spiring in the evening ray' the dragon flyes in their spangld coats darting like 'winged arrows down the stream' the swallow darting through its one arched brig the shepherd hiding from a thunder shower in an hollow dotterel the wild geese scudding along and making all the letters of the Alphabet as they flew the motley clouds the whispering wind that mutterd to the leaves and summer grass as it flutterd among them like things at play   I observd all this with the same raptures as I have done since but I knew nothing of poetry   it was felt and not utterd   most of my sundays was spent in this manner about the fields with such merry company   I heard the black and the brown beetle sing their evening songs with rapture and lovd to see the black snail steal out upon its dewy baulks   I saw the humble horse bee at noon 'spiring' on wanton wing   I lovd to meet the woodman whistling away to his toils and to see the shepherd bending oer his hook on the thistly green chatting love storys to the listening maiden while she milked her brindld cow   the first primrose in spring was as delightful as it is now   the copper colord clouds of the morning was watchd and the little ups and downs and roly poly child mountains of the broken heath with their brown mossy crowns and little green bottoms were the sheep feed and hide from the sun   the stone quarry with its magnified pre-cipic[e]s   the wind mills sweeing idly to the sum[m]er wind   the steeples peeping among the trees round the orisons circle

I noticd the cracking of the stubbs to the increasing sun while I gleand among them   I lovd to see the heavey grassopper in his coat

of delicate green bounce from stub to stub   I listend the hedge
cricket with raptures
    the evening call of the patridge   the misterious spring sound of
the land rail that cometh with the green corn
    I lovd the meadow lake with its fl[a]gs and long purples crowd-
ing the waters edge   I listend with delights to hear the wind whisper
among the feather topt reeds and to see the taper bulrush nodding in
gentle curves to the rippling water and I watchd with delight on
haymaking evenings the setting sun drop behind the brigs and peep
again thro the half circle of the arches as if he longs to stay

[A34, 16–15–14]

I had plenty of leisure but it was the leisure of solitude for my
Sundays was demanded to be spent in the fields at horse or cow
tending   my whole summer was one days employment as it were in
the fields   I grew so much into the qu[i]et love of nature[s] presence
that I was never easy but when I was in the fields passing my sabbaths
and leisures with the shepherds and herd boys as fancys prompted
somtimes playing at marbles on the smooth beaten sheep tracks or
leap frog among the thimey molehills somtimes ranging among the
corn to get the red and blue flowers for cockades to play at soldiers or
runing into the woods to hunt strawberrys or stealing peas in church
time when the owners was safe to boil at the gipseys fire who went
half shares at our stolen luxury   we heard the bells chime but the
fields was our church and we seemd to feel a religious poetry in our
haunts on the sabbath while some old shepherd sat on a mole hill
reading aloud some favorite chapter from an old fragment of a Bible
which he carried in his pocket for the day a family relic which possesd
on its covers and title pages in rude scrawls geneoligys of the third
and fourth Generations when aunts uncles and grandmothers dyd
and when cousins etc were marri[e]d and brothers and sisters born
occupying all the blank leaves in the book and the title pages
bhorders which leaves were prese[r]ved with a sacred veneration tho
half the contents had been sufferd to drop out and be lost
    I lovd this solitary disposition from a boy and felt a curosity to
wander about spots where I had never been before   I remember one
incident of this feeling when I was very young   it cost my parents
some anxiety   it was in summer and I started off in the morning to
get rotten sticks from the woods but I had a feeling to wander about
the fields and I indulged it. I had often seen the large heath calld

33

Emmonsales[3] stretching its yellow furze from my eye into unknown solitudes when I went with the mere openers and my curosity urgd me to steal an oppertunity to explore it that morning   I had imagind that the worlds end was at the edge of the orison and that a days journey was able to find it   so I went on with my heart full of hopes pleasures and discoverys expecting when I got to the brink of the world that I coud look down like looking into a large pit and see into its secrets the same as I believd I coud see heaven by looking into the water   so I eagerly wanderd on and rambled among the furze the whole day till I got out of my knowledge when the very wild flowers and birds seemd to forget me and I imagind they were the inhabitants of new countrys   the very sun seemd to be a new one and shining in a different quarter of the sky   still I felt no fear   my wonder seeking happiness had no room for it   I was finding new wonders every minute and was walking in a new world often wondering to my self that I had not found the end of the old one   the sky still touched the ground in the distance as usual and my childish wisdoms was puzzled in perplexitys   night crept on before I had time to fancy the morning was bye   the white moth had begun to flutter beneath the bushes the black snail was out upon the grass and the frog was leaping across the rabbit tracks on his evening journeys and the little mice was nimbling about and twittering their little earpiercing song with the hedge cricket whispering the hour of waking spirits was at hand when I knew not which way to turn but chance put me in the right track and when I got into my own fields I did not know them everything seemd so different   the church peeping over the woods coud hardly reconcile me   when I got home I found my parents in the greatest distress and half the vill[a]ge about hunting me   one of the wood men in the woods had been killed by the fall of a tree and it servd to strengthen their terrors that some similar accident had befallen myself as they often leave the oaks half cut down till the bark men can come up to pill them which if a wind happens to rise fall down unexpected   [A34, 8]

I usd to be fondly attachd to spots about the fields and there were 3 or 4 were I used to go to visit on sundays   one of these was under an old Ivied Oak in Oxey wood were I twisted a sallow stoven into an harbour which grew into the crampd way in which I had made it two others were under a broad oak in a field calld the Barrows and Langley Bush[4] and all my favourite places have met with misfortunes the old ivied tree was cut down   when the wood was cut down and my bower was destroyed the woodmen fancied it a resort for robbers and some thought the crampd way in which the things grew were witch knotts and that the spot was a haunt were witches met   I never unriddeld the mystery and it is believd so still for I got there often to hide myself and was ashamed to acknowledge it – Lee Close Oak was cut down in the inclosure and Langley bush was broken up by some wanton fellows while kidding furze on the heath – the Carpenter that bought Lee Close oak hearing it was a favorinte tree of mine made me two rules and sent me and I prese[r]ved a piece of the old Ivy the thickest I have ever seen   [A33, 7]

What a many such escapes from death doth a boys heedless life meet with   I met with many in mine   once when wading in the

meadow pits a lot of cow tending boys we tryd to to[p] each others tasks   we had gone several times and it was my turn to attempt again when I unconscously got beside a gravel ledge into deep water when my heels slipt up and I siled down to the bottom   I felt the water choke me and thunder in my ears and I thought all was past but some of the boys coud swim and so I escapd   another time we were swiming on bundles of bull rushes when mine getting to one end suddenly bouncd from under me like a cork and I made shift to struggle to a sallow bush and catching hold of the branches I got out but how I did it I know not for the water was very deep and yet we had dabbld there sunday after sunday without the least fear of danger
    once when birds nesting in the woods of which I was very fond we found a large tree on which was a buzzards nest   it was a very hard tree to climb   there were no twigs to take hold of and it was two thick to swarm so we consulted for awhile some proposing one thing and some another till it was decided that a hook tyd to the end

35

of a long pole that woud reach to the collar of the tree woud be the best to get up by   in taking hold of it and swarming several attempted to no purpose and at last I tryd tho I was rather loath to try the experiment   I succeeded at getting up to the collar which swelld in such a projection from the tree that I coud not make a landing without hazarding the dangerous attempt of clinging with my hands to the grain and flinging my feet over it. I attempted it and faild so there I hung with my hands and my feet dangling in the air   I expected every moment to drop and be pashd to pieces for I was a great height but some of my companions below while some ran away had the shrewdness to put the pole under me and by that means I got on the grain just in time before I was quite exausted and savd my life

another time when I was grown up I went to the woods to gather acorns and getting on a tree which was very full I sat on a large grain dashing them which broke and I fell to the ground about 14 or 15 foot were I lay for a long time and knew nothing   on coming to my self I crawld up and saw that the large grain just lodgd above me   I was agonized   I coud not catch my breath unless by deep groans and I got over that   [B7, 92–1]

In spring the leafing hedges brings to my memory the times when I anxiously rambld about them at leisure hours hunting the birds nest[s] and pootys and I cannot help peeping among them still tho I feel almost ashamed of my childish propensitys and cannot help blushing if I am observed by a passing neighbour

Thus the same thing of every thing   flowers have happy assosiations of youth   they are its sweetest chronicles   the herdsmen cannot neglect the wild thyme on the hill that made him seats when a boy or the blue caps in the wheat [with] which he trim[m]ed his cockade to play at soldiers   to the old woman the little blue flower aside the brook called in botany water mouse ear brings the lovers reccolections when she was young   she still stoops down and fancys that it smile[s] upward in her eye forget me not   [B3, 60]

At the end of a little common when I was a boy called Tankers Moor there was a little spring of beautiful soft water which was never dry   it used to flow from under an edding at the end of the land out of a little hole about as deep and round as a cuttin[g] – it used then to dribble its way thro the grass in a little ripple of its own making no bigger than a grip or cart rut – and in this little spring head there used to be hundreds of the little fish called a minnow not so big as the struttle and these used to be found in that hole every year but how they came there I could not tell   some years a quantity of struttle was found and often a few gudgeons – when a boy we used to go on a sunday in harvest and leck it out with a dish and string the fish on rushes – and therebye thinking ourselves great fishers from the number we had caught not heeding the size   [A49, 73]

the Marquis was then a boy   I have him in my minds eye in his clean jerkin and trowsers shooting in the park or fishing on the river
[A34, 13]

tho I always felt in company a disbelief of ghost witches etc yet when I was a lone in the night my fancys created thousands and my fears was always on the look out every now and then turning around to see if aught was behind me   I was terribly frighted on seeing a will o wisp for the first time and tho my fears grew less by custom for there are crowds about our fenny flats yet I never coud take them on the credit of philos[oph]y as natural phenomenons at night time but always had a suspicion of somthing supernatural belonging to them – I have had a many 'night fears' and usd to be terribly anoyd when a boy in takeing the horses away at the evening to heath in spring time when the badgers made a horrible squeeling noise in the woods resembling the screams of a woman and the crooning of the [wood pigeons] but the worst fright I ever met with was on a harvest night when I workd at Bassets of Ashton   we was always late ere we gave over work as harvesters generally are and ere we finishd our suppers it was nigh midnight by the time I started home which was but the distance of a short mile but I had a terror haunting spot to cross calld Baron parks in which was several ruins of roman camps and saxon castles and of course was people[d] with many mysterys of spirits
    the tales were numberless of ghosts and goblings that were seen

there and I never passd it without my memory keeping a strict eye to look for them and one night rather late I fan[c]yd I saw somthing stand wavering in the path way but my hopes put it off as a shadow till on coming nearer I found that it was somthing but wether of flesh and blood was a question   my astonishd terrors magnified it into a horrible figure   it appeard to have ears of a vas[t] length and the hair seemd to hang about it like [   ]   I trembld and almost wishd the earth woud open to hide me   I woud have spoke but I coud not and on stopping at the stile to look were it was my increasd terror found it close at my heels   I thought it was nothing but infernal now and scarce [know]ing what I did I took to my heels and when I got home I felt nearly fit to dye   I felt assurd that ghosts did exist and I dare not pass the close the next day till quite late in the day when every body was abroad when to my supprise I found it was nothing but a poor cade foal[5] that had lost its mother and had been raisd with milk till it was grown up and had been turnd ther[e] to wean it the day before it followd me again and my disbelief in ghosts was more hardend then ever   [D2, 10]

'Will with a whisp' 'Jimmy Whisk' Jack with a lanthorn   in this november month they are often out in the dark misty nights – on 'Rotten Moor' 'Dead Moor' Eastwell moor – Banton green end Lolham Briggs Rine dyke furlong and many other places in the lordship[6]   I have my self seen them on most of these spots – one dark night I was coming accross the new parks when a sudden light wild and pale appeared all round me on my left hand for a hundred yards or more accompan[i]ed by a crackling noise like that of peas straw burning   I stood looking for a minute or so and felt rather alarmed when darkness came round me again and one of the dancing jack a la[n]thens was whisking away in the distance which caused the odd luminous light around me – crossing the meadow one dark sunday night I saw when coming over the Nunton bridge a light like a lanthorn standing on the wall of the other bridge   I kept my eyes on it for awhile and hastened to come up to it – but ere I got on the bridge I looked down it and saw the will of whi[s]p vapour like a light in a bladder whisking along close to the water as if swimming along its surface but what supprised me was that it was going contrary to the stream   [A49, 49]

38

[*Northborough*]

There is a saying or rather an old superstition connected with this place as well known round the neighbourhood as some of the sayings of Gotham are – when any one who was awkard at his work and would not be shown his companions would say – 'Send him to Norborrey (Northborough) hedge corner to hear the wooden cuckoo sing'[7] and this spot was one of the curiositys that my imagination when a boy yearnd to see – from the frequency of the above saying it grew a natural curiosity and a sort of classic spot for the travels of my fancys – but I never learnt from where it sprung – I apprehend it was some foolish charter of some feudal occupier of the old castle in the days of chivalry – for in a neighbourhood a little distant an old man told me there was a little spot about as large as a pinfold enclosed with quick which fence the parish was obliged to mend and repair every year on a particular day under the foolish appelation of 'hedging the cuckoo in' – in our fields there was a similar enclosure called the 'Cow pen' but the custome if customes there were of repairing etc were all lost and forgotten long before I was born – yet the ghost stories conected with its lonely situation was as fresh as a dew fall   they are forgetting the old memories now and the young ones are too caring to heed them – but I do assure you I would not pass such spots now at nightfal if I could help and to pass them at midnight   [A46, 154]

Chusing Friends

Among all the friendships I have made in life those of school friendship and childish acquaintance are the sweetest to remember
    there is no deseption among them   their is nothing of regret in them but the loss   they are the fairest and sunniest pages memory ever doubles down in the checkerd volume of life to refer to   there is no blotches upon them – they are not found like bargains or matters of interest nor broken for selfish ends – I made but few close friendships for I found few with the like tastes inclinations and feelings
    One of my first friendships was with Richard the brother of John Turnill   it began with infancy from playing at feasts by the cottage wall with broken pots and gathering the crumpled seeds of the mallow for cheeses making houses and fires of sticks stones and clay

39

to the second stage of hunting birds nests and painted pooty shells
among the dewy boughs and busy growing grass in the spring and the
partnerships of labours toils and sunday leisures but death came
while we were growing up into each others pleasures like twin
flowers and took him away before our budding friendships could
blossom – yet it was [an] image of happiness – what numberless
hopes of successes did we chatter over as we hunted among the short
snubby bushes of the heath or on hedge rows and crept among the
black thorn spreys after the nest of the nightingales and what happy
discourses of planning pleasures did we talk over as we lay on the soft
summer grass gazing on the blue sky shaping the passing clouds to
things familiar with our memorys and dreaming of the days to come
when we shoud mix with the world and be men little thinking that we
shoud chew the cud of sweet and bitter fancys when we met it   but
he never did   I have mentiond were he dyd and was buried a while
back   his brother Johns acquaintance began with learning me on
winter nights to write and sum   he was of a studious musing turn of
mind and fond of books always carr[y]ing one of some sort or other
in his pocket to read between toils at leisure hours   they were
somtimes sixpenny books of storys and at other times the books
which he usd at school for he had been [at] boarding school and read
in books there that are unknown in a village school   I remember
being often delighted with one which he repeated by heart in ryhme a
story of a young lady being killd in battle by a shield ball[8] while
seeking her lover and another tale in prose of the old man and his ass[9]
which was a favour[i]te and he always contrivd to bring the News
paper in his pocket in weeding time which I was always very anxious
to read   his father was a fa[r]mer and I usd to work for them in the
weeding and haymaking seasons   his mind was always anxious
after knowledge and too restless to stick to any thing long so he had a
superficial knowledge of many things and a solid information with
none   one season he woud be learned and occupied with Mathematics working problems of algebra or Geometry   he was also
ambitious of shining in the almanack diarys and attempted to
unriddle the puzzles for the prizes and to ryhme new charad[e]s
reddles rebuses on a slate which he fitted to his pocket and making
dials on a board and fixing them on the top of his weed hook shaft to
enquire the hour of the day   then before he had formd half an
acquaintance with them he woud be making his telescopes of paste
board and studying the stars with the assistance of a book which he

had purchasd a cheap penny worth at some second hand book stall
somtimes he woud be after drawing by perspective and he made an
instrument from a shilling art of painting which he had purchasd that
was to take landscapes almost by itself   it was of a long square shape
with a hole at one end to look thro and a number of diferent colord
threads crossd into little squares at the other   from each of these
squares different portions of the Landscape was to be taken one after
the other and put down in a facsimile of these squares done with a
pencil on the paper   but his attempts made but poor reflelctions of
the objects and when they were finishd in his best colors they were far
from being even poor shadows of the origional and the sun with its
instantaneous sketches made better figures of the objects in their
shadows   once he happend in with Lilys astrology at Deeping fair
and then his head was forever after Nativitys and fortune telling by
the stars   his mother was skilld in huswife phisic and Culpeppers
Herbal[10] and he usd to be up after gathering herbs at the proper time
of the planets that was said to rule them expecting they woud
perform Miracles – I remember the last thing which he was busy after
were studying a book on bees and a restless desire after glass hives
once he got a book on the mysterys of nature which told him how to
turn metals into gold to find jewels in a toads head and gather brake
seed on midsummer eve for my[s]tical purposes which I have now
forgotten   but in the midst of all his inventions and thirst for
knowledge a couzin came down from London who had a power of
getting him a place in the excise his present occupation so his parents
hopes were ripend and he was sent to school and then to the excise
and all his hopes anxietys crowds of schemes and happy memorys
were left unfinishd behind him to make room for new ones

[A25, 34–32]

I usd to spend many of my winter nights and sabbath leisures when I
grew up in the world at a neighbours house of the name of Billings
it was a sort of meeting house for the young fellows of the town were
the[y] usd to join for ale and tobacco and sing and drink the night
away   the occupiers were two Bachelors and their cottage was calld
bachelors hall   it is an old ruinous hut and hath needed repairs ever
since I knew it for they neither mend up the walls nor thatch the roof
being negligent men but quiet and innofensive neighbours   I still
frequent their house   it has more the appearence of a deserted
hermitage then an inhabited dwelling   I have sat ta[l]king of witch

and ghost storys over our cups on winter nights till I felt fearful of
going home   John Billings the elder had a very haunted mind for
such things and had scarce been out on a journey with the night
without seeing a gost a will o whisp or some such shadowy mysterys
and such reccolections of midnight wanderings furnishd him with
storys for a whole winters fire side   I usd to go often to the wood to
pill oaks in the winters evening or in fact any thing chance started and
once we went on a sabbath day   there was three of us and James
Billings was the gunner for I had no eye to kill any thing even if I was
close to it tho my will perhaps was as good as the rest and on rustling
about among the bushes we started a hare which hopd on a little way
and stood to listen when my companion lifted his old gun to take a
aim and a sudden shock tingld in my ears like the momentary sound
of broken glasses   we was astounded and look on each others faces
with vacancy – the gun had bursted and all the barrel was carr[i]ed
aw[a]y to the lock and part of the lock likwise   we saw danger in
each others faces and dare not make enquirey what was the matter as
all of us expected we were wounded but as soon as the fright was over
we found none of us was hurt   what became of the gun we coud not
tell for we coud not find a fragment but that which he held in his hand
– was not this an alarm to tell our conscence that we were doing
wrong and wether it was chance or providence that interferd it was a
narrow escape   I felt the warning for once and never was caught on
the same errand again   [A25, 31]

John Billings was an inofensive man   he believes every thing that he
sees in print as true and has a cupboard full of penny books   the king
and the cobler Seven Sleepers[11] accounts of People being buried so
many days and then dug up alive Of bells in churches ringing in the
middle of the night Of spirits warning men when they was to dye etc
each of the relations attested to by the overseers churchwardens etc
of the parish were the strange relations happend always a century
back were none lives to contradict it   such things as these have had
personal existances with his memory on as firm footings as the bible
history it self   he is fond of getting cuckcoos blue bells Primroses
and any favou[ri]te flowers from the fields and woods to set in his
garden and his sundays best leisures is when the weather and seasons
permits him to ramble by the river sides a fishing and we have spent
many sundays together in that diversion   [A25, 30]

these are universal feelings and the stuff which true poesy is made of
is little else   it is the eccho [of] what has been or may be   when the
reader peruses real poesy he often whispers to [himself] 'bless me I've
felt this myself and often had such thoughts in my memory' tho he
was ignorant of poetry   nature is the same everywere   the little
daisey wears the self same golden eye and silver rim with its delicate
blushing stains underneath in our fenny flats as it does on the
mountains of switzerland if it grows there – my companion had no
knowledge of poesy by books   he had never read Thompson or
Cowper or Wordsworth or perhaps heard of their names yet nature
gives every one a natural simplicity of heart to read her language tho
the grosser interferences of the world adulterate them like the bee by
the flower and deaden the heart with ignorance – he usd often to
carry a curious old book in his pocket very often a sort of jest book
calld the Pleasant art of money catching[12] and another of Tales
whose title was 'Laugh and be fat' and he felt as happy over these
while we wild away the impatience of a bad fishing day under a green
willow or an odd thorn as I did over Thompson Cowper and Walton
which I often took in my pocket to read   my companions books
were very old and curious   the one on 'Money catching' there was a
tale in it of Jougler Percy and the Butchers dog and several rules and
receipts for savings and cheap living and a colection of proverbs and
a long poem of 40 or 50 verses the middle of which was gone   I
fancyd some of the verses good and I think they are written by a poet
perhaps Randolph for there was some of his poems in the Vol
particulary a satirical one on 'Importunate duns'   the verses I
aluded to above are entitled lessons of Thrift some jests by Tarlton
I copyd some of them out some years back and I will insert them
here*   [A25, 9]

Lord Radstock[13] was my best friend   it was owing to him that the
first Poems succeeded   he introduced them into all places were he
had connections got them noticed in newspapers and other [places]
and if it did nothing more it made them known – he kindly undertook
to settle my affairs with my Publishers which they kindly enough on
their parts deferred and its not settled yet – he wrote Taylor a letter
wishing him to draw up an agreement in 'black and white' as his
Lordship expressd it as faiths in men was not to be trusted   Taylor

---

* Not yet identified in the Peterborough MSS. Richard Tarlton (d. 1588), comic
actor, wit, and hero of the anecdote collection *Tarlton's Jests*.

pretended to be insulted at this and wrote his Lordship a genteel saucey one that setteld the affair in the present confusion of no settlings at all   nay they will neither publish my poems or give them up

Lord Radstock at first sight appears to be of a stern and haughty character but the moment he speaks his countenance kindles up into a free blunt good hearted man one whom you expect to hear speak exactly as he thinks   he has no notion of either offending or pleasing by his talk and care[s] as little for the consequences of either   there is a good deal of the bluntness and openheartedness about him and there is nothing of pride or fashion   he is as plain in manner and dress as an old country squire   a stranger woud never guess that he was speaking to a Lord and tho he is one of the noblest familys in England he seems to think nothing [of his position]   I have often observed this in real Titles   while a consieted bastard squire expects Sir at the end of every word a Lord seems to take no notice how he is talkd too – the first is jealous of his gentility and knows that his title is nothing but the breath of words the latter knows that his was born with him and it is a familiar that sits easy on his name – his Lordship is a large man of a commanding figure   the bust by Behnes[14] is very like but wants expression as does the engraving   his Lordship has only one fault and that is a faith that takes every man [at his face value]   he and Lord Fitzwilliam[15] are the two best patrons I have had   [B6, 84R]

[The Revd Isaiah Holland[16] was another friend] and [one] who had given his undisguised opinion of them [i.e. Clare's poems] when praise was of most value and when nobody else had even ventured an opinion except a doubt of their merits and whom I ought to have mentiond first on my list of friends   he came over as soon as the book was publis[h]ed and before I was aware of its fate but I instantly read my success in his countenance for he opend the door eagerly and laughd as he shook me by the hand saying 'Well am not I a good prophet'   I told him that I had not heard the fate of the book as yet and he said then I am more happy in being the herald of good News for I can assure you that your utmost hopes have succeeded as I recieved a letter this morning from a literary friend who spoke it as a certainty that your poems woud take and he has given them hearty praise   this enlivend me and we chatterd over the results of the future all the afternoon – when he first came to see me I was copying

44

out the 'Village funeral' to send to Drury and as he leand overy my shoulder to read it he said 'these are the things that will do and if they do not succeed the world deserves a worse opinion then I am inclind to give it but go on and be not cast down by the doubts or surmises of anyone' this was the prophecy to which he aluded when he came to tell me of my success – I dedicated the poem of the Woodman to him as a trifling return for his kindness the chance that led me to his acquantance was his meeting with one of the papers printed by Henson of Deeping and he made further enquireys at a farmers house were he used to visit who was well acquanted with me and my family and as they gave a favourable account of my character as a quiet inoffensive fellow he expressed a desire to see me and sent for me but I did not like to show my head any were at that time so my mother went over in my stead when as he asked her several enquireys and desired her to caution me against Hensons printing the poems as he thought it woud go a great way to ruin the success they might meet with else were and said he woud come over to see me as he accordingly did he was excessively fond of Kirk White[17] such a friendship as this is worth the remembrance he had no other interest then that of wishing me well and did it heartily he now lives at St Ives and if the Newspapers tell the truth he is married

[A25, 21–2]

[Books]

My acquantance of books is not so good as late oppertunitys might have made it for I cannot and never coud plod thro every a book in a regular mecanical way as I meet with [it] I dip into it here and there and if it does not suit I lay it down and seldom take it up again but in the same manner I read Thompsons Seasons and Miltons Paradise Lost thro when I was a boy and they are the only books of Poetry that I have regularly read thro yet as to history I never met with the chance of getting at [it] yet and in novels my taste is very limited Tom Jones Robinson Crusoe and the Vicar of Wakefield are all that I am acquainted with they are old acquantan[ces] and I care not to make new ones tho I have often been offerd the perusal of the Waverly Novels I declind it and [though] the readily remaining in ignorance of them is no trouble yet my taste may be doubted for I hear much in their praise and believe them good – I read the vicar of

Wakefield over every Winter and am delighted tho I always feel diss-appointed at the end[ing] of it happily with the partings   my mind cannot feel that it ends happily with [the] reader   I usd to be uncommonly fond of looking over catalogues of books and am so still   they [are] some of the earliest readings that oppertunitys alowd me to come at   if ever I bought a penny worth of slate pencils of Wafers or a few sheets of Paper at Drakards they were to be lapt in a catalogue and I considerd them as the most va[l]uable parts of my purchase and greedily lookd over their contents and now in cutting open a new book or Magazine I always naturaly turn to the end first to read the book list and take the rest as a secondary pleasure

Anticipation is the sweetest of earthly pleasures   it is smiling hope standing on tiptoes to look for pleasure – the cutting open a new book the watching the opening of a new planted flower at spring etc   [A34, 1]

The first books I got hold of beside the bible and prayer book was an old book of Essays with no title and then a large one on Farming Robin hoods Garland and the Scotch Rogue[18] – The old book of Farming and Essays belongd to an old Mr Gee who had been a farmer and who lived in part of our house which once was his own – he had had a good bringing up and was a desent scholar and he was always pleasd to lend me them even before I coud read them without so much spelling and guesses at words so as to be able to make much of them or understand them   [A31, 216]

I became acquainted with Robinson Crusoe very early in life having borrowd it of a boy at Glinton school of the name of Stimson who only dare lend it me for a few days for fear of his uncles knowing of it to whom it belongd yet I had it a sufficient time to fill my fancys with new Crusoes and adventures

From these friendships I gathered more acquaintance with books which like chances oppertunitys were but sparing   [A25, 32]

[Learning]

As to my learning I am not wonderfully deep in s[c]i[e]nce nor so wonderfully ignorant as many may have fancied from reading the accounts which my friends gave of me   if I was to brag of it I might

46

like the village schoolmaster boast of knowing a little of every thing a jack of all trades and master of none   I puzzled over every thing in my hours of leisure that came in my way Mathematics Astronomy Botany and other things with a restless curiosity that was ever on the enquiry and never satisfied and when I got set fast with one thing I did not tire but tryed at another tho with the same success in the end   yet it never sickened me   I still pursued Knowledge in a new path and tho I never came off with victor[ie]s I was never conqured*

[B3, 81]

The neighbours believing my learning to be great thought it a folly in me to continue at hard work when they fancyd I might easily better my self by my learning and as Lord Milton[19] was a great friend to my father they persuaded me to go to Milton[20] to see what he woud do for me and the parish clerk a man of busy merits who taught the sundy school offerd to go with me as he knew his Lordship better then I did by seeing him at the Sundy school often   I accepted the proposal and started once more upon ambitious and hitherto fruitless errands   I remember the morning   we saw two crows as soon as we got into the fields and harpd on good luck and success and my companion gave me advice with the authority of a patron as well as a frend   as soon as we got there on making the nessesary enquiries we was told that his Lordship woud see us bye and bye and hour passd after hour till night came and told us we was dissapointed and the porter conforted us by saying we shoud call again tomorning but my friend the Clerk had more wits in the way and we met his Lordship the next day at the heath farm near home which he was in the habit of visiting often   as soon as we came up to his Lordship my companion began to descant on my merrits in a way that made me hang my head but I found he had a double errand for before he finishd his tale of my [talents] he pulld an antique box out of his pocket which he had found in leveling some headlands near eastwell spring a spot famous

---

* Another version of this first paragraph appears at B4, 99:

As to my learning if I was to brag over it I might make shift to say a little about mathematics Astronomy Botany Geography and others of the Abst[r]use Arts and sciences for I puzzld over such matters at every hour of leisure for years as my curosity was constantly on the enquiry and never satisfied and when I got set first with one thing I did not despair but tryd at another tho with the same success in the end   yet it never sickend me   I still pursued knowledge in a new path and tho I never came off victor I was never conquored

for summer sunday revels   it was in the for[m] of an apple pye and
containd several farthings of king charles the firsts or second[s] reign
and begd his lordship to do somthing for me and upon hearing to
whom I belongd he promisd he woud   his Lordship smild and took
it and gave him a good exchange for his curosity which raisd the
clerks voice in the conclusion of his story of me and when his
Lordship heard to whom I belongd he promisd to do somthing for me
but such trifling things are soon shovd out of the memorys of such
people who have plenty of other things to think of   I heard no more
of it and workd on at my old employments as usual   I had now
many schemes and plans in my mind of what I coud or might do   I
had improvd by frequent trials in ryhming and often felt that I might
gain some notice in times to come   I fancyd too that I was book
learnd for I had gotten together by savings a quantity of old books of
motly merits all of which Drury got for a little or nothing   I will
reccolect some of them   there was the yong mans best companion
Dilworths Wingates Hodders Vyses and Cockers Arithmetic   the
last was a favourite with me and I kept it   Bonnycastles and Horners
Mensuration and Wards Mathematics Leybourns and Morgans
Dialling Female Shipwright Robinson Crusoe Pilgrims Progress
Martindales Land surveying and Cockers Land surveying Hills
Herbal Balls Astrology Culpeppers Herbal Rays History of the
Rebellion Hudibras some Numbers of Josephus Parnels Poems
Miltons Paradise Lost Thompsons Seasons Sam Westleys Poems
Hemmings Algebra Sturms Reflections Harveys Meditations Wal-
lers Poems Westleys Philosophy Thompsons Travels Lestranges
Fables of Esop A book on Commets Life of Barnfield more Carew
The Art of Gauging Duty of Man Watts Hymns Lees Botany Waltons
Angler Kings Tricks of London laid open The Fathers Legacy or
seven stages of Life[21] Bloomfields Poems   some of these were great
favourites particularly Waltons Angler tho I never caught any more
fish then usual by its instructions   I bought it at a book stall kept by a
shoe maker of the name of J Adams at Stamford for 2 shillings and I
gave it to my friend O. Gilchrist[22]   the Female Shipwright was a
winter evening favourite in my first book days   it b[e]longd to my
uncle and was a true story printed by subscription for the woman
whose history it related   Bloomfields Poems was great favourites
and Hills Herbal gave me a taste for wild flowers which I lovd to hunt
after and collect to plant in my garden which my father let me have in
one corner of the garden and on happening to meet with Lees

Botany* second hand I fell to collecting them into familys and tribes but it was a dark system and I abandond it with a dissatisfaction

I also was fond of gather[ing] fossil stones   tho I never knew these was the subject of books yet I was pleasd to find and collect them which I did many years tho my mother threw them out of doors when they was in her way   a Dr Dupere of Crowland collected such things and my friend John Turnell got some for him   this gave me the taste for fossil hunting   my friend Artis[24] had what was left when I became acquainted with him   my habits of Study grew anxious and restless and increasd into a multiplicity of things poetry natural history Mathematics etc but I had little ambition to write down any thing but my ryhmes   these were on local circumstances mostly and on spots and things which I felt a fondness for   two or three of a Satirical nature I will insert here   the 'Elegy on the Death of a quack' was written on a quack Docter who came to Deeping and whom the dupd people calld Docter Touch as it was rumourd about on his first appear[en]ce there that he curd all diseases by touching the patient with his hand which made the Villages round all anxious to know the truth of it   lame and blind and such felt a vain hope that he might be inspird and sent on purpose for their relief and Deeping was threatend to be as crowded with cripples as the Pool of Beth-sheba   my Father and Will Farrow the shoemaker mentiond awhile back† went over to Deeping directly on his arrival there to assertain the truth and leave their infirmitys behind them if possible but experience put a new face on the story   the fellow did not cure them by touch but by blisters which he laid on in unmercifull sizes at half a guinea a blister and the money was to be paid down before he did his work   this last demand compleatly shook my fathers faith as to his mission for he understood that [the] prophets of old curd for nothing and he expected to see modern miracles performd in the same

* At B3, 73 Clare has written:

   I have puzzled wasted hours over Lees Botany to understand a shadow of the system so as to be able to class the wild flowers peculiar to my own neighbourhood for I find it woud require a second Adam to find names for them in my way and a second Solomon to understand them in Lennsis system – moder[n] works are so mystified by systematic symbols that one cannot understand them till the wrong end of ones lifetime and when one turns to the works of Ray Parkinson and Gerrard[23] were there is more of nature and less of Art it is like meeting the fresh air and balmy summer of a dewey morning after the troubled dreams of a nightmare

   † Clare either had another order in mind for his observations on Farrow or a passage about him is missing from the MSS.

manner but when he found it was no such thing he and his companion refusd to have any thing to do with the medical prophet who was very importunate and even abusive at their credulity   when they returned home and told their tale I sat down and wrote the following Epitaph . . .

[A25, 4]

On the Death of a Quack

Here lyes Lifes Cobler who untimly fell
By name of Doctor Drug 'em known to all
His frequent visits mad[e] him known full well
For where he'd business he ne'er faild to call
Fools praisd his power as great in saving Life
And for that purpose many a journey made
To Village Lout and Tradesmans Wimsy Wife
But some there must be to incourage trade
For want of them full many a trade wou'd stop
and what wou'd docters do if 't wa'n't for fools?
They then might keep at home and shut up shop
Their pills and and mixtures would be usless tools
– The Doctors Drugs one certain Virtue claims
Which in his Wondorous Bills he never puts
E' faith why dont they? – 't' woud increase their fame
To empty Pockets well as scour the Guts
At this our Drug 'em was Expert enough
The Art he practis'd knew it wondorous well
While money lasted he ne'er faild of Stuff
And Fools would buy 'em – he knew how to sell
And faith of Custom from his noted skill
He never faild – his fame the Village spred
Tho ignorant of the cause – too strong a Pill
Has worked a Patient now and then to dead
Yet still his fame and customers increas'd
Who he by Practise prov'd not over nice
And playd as good a part wi' them at least
For as they E'k'd his fame – he Ek'd his Price
His Drugs went off – (and Doctors will be paid)
So money tumbld in most wondorous free
But Fortunes Sun shine often finds a shade
The happest crosses meet – and so did he
Death – who'd ta'en many a Patient off his hands

And wether want of Work – Or wether whim
What caus'd his coming – no one understands
But he was hunting and he hunted him
No Lingering – Illness'd Journyman he sent
Himself at once – nor made one doubtful stop
Spite of his being a Doctor – Boldly went
And Seizd him in his Garrison – his Shop
Where all his Weapons dreadfully displayd
Bid bold Defiance on each hand Bill Read
And Pills and Powders desperate sallies made
Pelting like hail Round the Besiegers head
But Death feard nought – yet when the Phisic flew
The stink so nausious – made him turn about
And forcd him to Retreat awhile to spew
But frequent Sallies wore the Doctor out
A Time to prove his Art was fairly bid
Patients Expected – (Fools have little wit)
That he would play his part (– well so he did)
But then it faild and then the fools were bit
They provd too well his Art of Getting Pelf
But tother Art was either Lost or past
If he sav'd them he cou'd not save him self
So here Poor Drug 'em lies a Quack at Last [1, 235]

the fellow stopt at Deeping a good while for he found plenty of
believers to mentain his hoaxing pretentions   in his bills he made a
great parade against all knowledge and the faculty and made a boast
of his ignorance by stating what he thought a better plea in making
his patients believe he was born a docter by being the seventh son of a
parent who was himself a seventh son and the seventh son of a
seventh son is reckond among the lower orders of people as [a]
prodigy in medicine who is born to perform miracles so he readily got
into fame amongst them till 2 or 3 patients dyd under his hands and
then on the turning of the tide he decayd in the night   I wrote
another long tale on the Docter and the shoemaker but it is not worth
inserting*   the following was written on an old woman with a
terrible share of tongue who was actually married to a sixth husband
and survivd them ...   [A25, 4–6]

* 'The Quack and the Cobler'. This poem appears in Pforzheimer Misc. MS 197,
where Clare refers to it as 'a true tale'.

On the Death of a Scold

A scolding woman's worse then hell
Her tongue can never cease
She loves in quarrels to oppose
And hates the thoughts of peace
So hags delight to see the storm
Deform the smiling skye
And joys to hear the thunder roll
And see the light'ning flie
They know their tools is ready then
To prosper every spell
Which the black arts of malice plans
In journey work for hell

But that which seems as choise in those
Which bear the hellish mark*
May be the effect of fear and dread
Hells mysterys are dark
Tis said their bodys when spells fail
Is like their souls condemn'd
And when they fail of Nickeys prey
He foxlike seizes them
So of old scolding nelly trix
The same thing may be said
Who after marrying husbands six
And scolding all to dead
She looking out for further work
A seventh still desir'd
But as Experience makes fools wise
Her customers grew tir'd
So when her tongue could find no more
To load with its abuse
It silencd not from being old
But only want of use
So Nicky seeing trade had faild
And no one car'd to come
He thought it time to shut up shop
And took his darling home   [A4, 8]

* For an account of these marks and mysterys see Mr Sinclairs 'Satans Invisible World discovered' [Clare's note].

I only regret the loss of one of my early poems a sort of Pastoral   the title was 'labour and luxury'   the plan was a labourers going to his work one morning overheard a lean figure [accosted] in a taunting manner by a bloated stranger the phantom of luxury whence the dialogue ensues   labour makes its complaints and the other taunts and jeers him till the lean figure turns away in dispair   [A25, 6]

Beginnings with the World

I never had much relish for the pastimes of youth   instead of going out on the green at the town end on Winter sundays to play foot ball I stuck to my corner stood poreing over a book   in fact I grew so fond of being alone at last that my mother was feign to force me into company for the neighbours had assured her mind into the fact that I was no better then crazy   [B8, 1128R]

My scholarship was to extend no farther than to qualify me for the business of a shoemaker or Stone Mason so I learnd cross multipli-cation for the one and bills of accounts for the other but I was not to be either   at last a man of the Name of Mowbray of Glinton woud have taken me for a trifle and another at home namd Farrow a little deformd fellow was desirious of taking me merely out of kindness to my father but the trifle they wanted coud not be found and I did not much relish the confinment of apprentiship   this Will Farrow was a village wit a very droll fellow a sort of Easop   his shop usd to be a place of amusment for the young ploughmen and labour[er]s on winter evenings   he was famous for a joke and a droll story and had a peculiar knack at making up laughable anecdotes on any circum-stance which happend in the village – and a satirical turn for applying nicknames to people who was almost sure to be call[d] by the one given till the day they dyd and remem[b]erd by it afterwards when their own was forgotten   many of his names are now afloat in the village – he has a brother living now who was a sailor 21 years and who kept a Journal of his life which he got me to copy out in part there was nothing particular in it but a mention of Lord Byron who saild in the same ship and was known among the sailors as a Traveller and not as a poet and I myself was ignorant of him alltogether when I copied out his account of him
    I cannot ascertain what time it was when he saild with him but doubtless child Harrold had no existance with the world then

53

I have since reflected on this interesting circumstance and often tryd to remember it   he describd him as a odd young man lame of one foot on which he wore a cloth shoe who was of a resolute temper fond of bathing in the sea and going ashore to see ruins in a rough sea when it required 6 hands to manage the boat   such additional trouble teazd the sailors and teazd them so much that his name became a bye word for unessesary trouble   Tom Farrow I believe was then an able seaman in the Fox Cutter   he now lives at Deeping St James and follows his trade of a Mason and bricklayer

[B8, 103–4]

After I had done with going to school it was proposd that I shoud be bound apprentice to a shoe maker but I rather dislikd this bondage I whimperd and turned a sullen eye upon every persuasion till they gave me my will   A neighbour then offerd to learn me his trade to be a stone mason but I dislikd this too and shoyd off with the excuse of not liking to climb tho I had clumb trees in raptures after the nests of Kites and magpies   my parents not liking to force me to any thing against my inclination their hopes was once more at a stand   I was then sent for to drive plough at woodcroft castle* of Oliver Crom-well memory   tho Mrs Bellairs[25] the mistress was a kind good woman and tho the place was a very good one for living my mind was set against it from the first and I was uneasily at rest   one of the disagreeable things was getting up so soon in the morning as they are much earlier in some places then in others and another was getting wetshod in my feet every morning and night for in wet weather the moat usd to over flow the causway that led to the porch and as there was but one way to the house we was obligd to wade up to the knees to go in and out excepting when the head man carried the boys over on his back as he somtimes woud   I staid here one month and then on coming home to see my parents they coud not persuade me to return   they now gave up all hopes of doing any good with me and fancied that I shoud make nothing but a soldier but luckily in this dilemma a next door neighbour at the Blue Bell Francis Gregory wanted me to drive plough and as I suited him he made proposals to hire me for a year which as it had my consent my parents readily agreed to   it was a good place   they treated me more like a son then

---

* At A46, 153 Clare writes: 'Here is one of the old Castles here that was in such requisition in the days of Cromwell and the holes in the wall then used for the cannon have never been filled up – it is a dreary looking building close to the turnpike'.

a servant   I believe I may say that this place was the nursery for my
ryhmes   [B8, 101]

F. Gregory

He was fond of amusement and a singer tho his notes was not more
varied then those of the cuckoo as he had but 2 Songs one calld 'the
milking pail' and the other 'Jack with his broom'[26]   his jokes too
were like a pack of cards   they were always the same but told in a
different turn   [O2, 2]

I livd at this place a year and left with the restless hope of being
somthing better then a plough man   my little ambitions kept
burning about me every now and then to make a better figure in the
world and I knew not what to be at – A bragging fellow name
Manton from Market Deeping usd to frequent the public house
when I livd there   he was a stone cutter and sign painter   he usd to
pretend to discover somthing in me as deserving encouragment and
wanted to take me apprentice to learn the misterys of his art but then
he wanted the trifle with me that had dissapointed my former
prosperitys   he usd to talk of his abilitys in sculpture and painting
over his beer till I was almost mad with anxiety to be a sign painter
and stone cutter but it was usless   such things made my mind
restless and on hearing from a friend Tom Porter of Ashton Green
that the Kitchen Gardiner at Burghley wanted an apprent[ice] I*
                                                                    [B3, 83]

I was with them without a salary   I thought it was a chance of being
somthing so I got my father to go with me to see if I might be excepted
                                                                    [A34, 7]

[*Clare considered various opportunities of employment before he
entered the kitchen-garden at Burghley: as a shoemaker's apprentice
with Will Farrow, as a stonemason's apprentice with George Shelton, as a sign-painter (this possibly with Mowbray of Glinton), and
as a clerk to his uncle's employer at Wisbeach. Before the last of these
opportunities arose he also worked as a ploughboy for Mrs Bellairs
at Woodcroft Castle. Upon his rejection at Wisbeach he entered the*

---

* Page torn off here but it is clearly continued at A34, 7.

55

service of Francis Gregory at the Blue Bell. It was from Gregory's service that he moved to Burghley. It is impossible to preserve the order of these events in Clare's autobiographical fragments and so we must now retrace our steps a little and hear what Clare has to say about George Shelton, Woodcroft Castle, and Wisbeach before once again taking up the narrative at the point where he left Gregory's and started work at Burghley. Ed.]

George Shelton too a Stone Mason woud have taken me but I got off by urging a dislike to climbing tho my fondness for climbing trees after birds nests went against me and my parents hopes were almost gone as they thought I sham[me]d abraham with a dislike to work and a view to have my liberty and to remain idle but the fact was I felt timid and fearful of undertaking the first trial in every thing   they woud not urge me to any thing against my will so I livd on at home taking Work as it fell   I went weeding wheat in the Spring with old women listening to their songs and storys which shortend the day and in summer I joind the haymakers in the meadow or helpd upon the stacks   when I was out of work I went to the woods gathering rotten sticks or picking up the dryd cow dung on the pasture which we call cazons for fireing   thus I livd a season spending the intervals at play along with she[e]ptenders or herd boys in lone spots out of sight for I had grown big enough to feel ashamd of it and I felt a sort of hop[e]less prospect around me of not being able to meet manhood as I coud wish for I had always that feeling of ambition about me that wishes to do somthing to gain notice or to rise above its fellows   my ambition then was to be a good writer and I took great pains in winter nights to learn my Friend John Turnill setting me copies who by the bye was far from a good writer himself   I was fond of books before I began to write poetry   these were such that chance came at – 6py Pamphlets that are in the possesion of every door calling hawker and found on every book stall at fairs and markets whose titles are as familiar with every one as his own name   shall I repreat some of them   'Little red riding hood' 'Valentine and Orson' 'Jack and the Jiant' 'Tom Long the carrier' 'The king and the cobler' 'Sawney Bean' 'The seven Sleepers' 'Tom Hickathrift' 'Johnny Armstrong' 'Idle Laurence' who carried that power spell about him that laid every body to sleep – 'old mother Bunch' 'Robin Hoods garland' 'old mother Shipton and old Nixons Prophecys' 'History of Gotham' and many others[27]   shall I go on   no these have memorys as common as Prayer books and Psalters with the peasantry   such were the books that delighted me and I savd all the pence I got to buy them for they were the whole world of literature to me and I knew of no other   I carried them in my pocket and read them at my leisure and they was the never weary food of winter evenings ere Milton Shakspear and Thompson had an existe[nce] in my memory and I even feel a love for them still   nay I cannot help fancying now that cock robin babes in the wood mother hubbard and her cat etc are real poetry in all its native simplicity and as it shoud be   I know I am foolish enough to have fancys different from others and childhood is a strong spell over my feelings but I think so on and cannot help it after I had been left to my idle leisures while doing jobs as I coud catch them I was sent for to drive plough at Woodcroft Castle of Oliver Cromwell memory* . . . it is a curious old place and was made rather famous in the rebellion of Oliver Cromwell – some years back there was a curious old bow found in one of the chimneys and the vulgar notion was that it was the identical bow that belongd to robin hood so readily does that name assosiate itself in the imagination with such things and places   I had a coin of Cromwells brought me last year by a neighbour pickd up in the neighboring field as large as a crown piece which I gave to my friend Artis   I stopt at this first place about a month and then on coming home to see my parents they coud not persuade me to return   they now gave up all hopes of doing any thing with me and fancyd that I shoud make nothing but a soldier   it was but a bad start to be sure and I felt ashamd of myself almost but my mind woud be master and I coud not act other wise   in this dilemma my Uncle who livd as footman with a counselor at Wisbeach came over to see us and said there was a vacancy in his masters office and he woud try to get me the place as he was certain I was scholar good enough for it and tho my father and mother was full as certain of it I doubted my abilitys very strongly but was glad to accept the proposal of going over to try   [B8, 104–5]

Wisbeach

My uncle morris came over to see us and said he woud ask his master to take me as a writer

My hopes of bettering my station with the world was agen

---

* This passage continues with a description very similar to that given above, from B8, 101, and here omitted.

revised and I started for Wisbeach with a timid sort of pleasure and when I got to Glinton turnpike I turnd back to look on the old church as if I was going in to another co[u]ntry   Wisbeach was a foreign land to me for I had never been above 8 miles from home in my life and I coud not fancy england much larger then the part I knew   at Peterboro Brig I got into the boat that carrys passengers to wisbeach once a week and returns the third day a distance of 21 miles for eighteenpence   I kept thinking all the way in the boat what answers I shoud make to the questions askd and then I put questions to myself and shapd proper replies as I thought woud succeed and then my heart burnt within me at the hopes of success and thoughts of the figure I shoud make afterwards when I went home to see my friends dressd up as a writer in a law[y]ers office   I coud scarcely contain my self at times and even broke out into a tittering laugh but I was dampd quickly when I thought of the impossibilitys of success for I had no prepossesing appearance to win favours for such a place   my mother had turnd me up as smart as she coud   she had pressd me a white neckcloth and got me a pair of gloves to hide my coarse hands but I had out grown my coat and almost left the sleeves at the elbows and all my other garments betrayd too old an acquantance with me to make me as genteel as coud have been wishd but I had got my fathers and mothers blessings and encouragments and my own hopes in the bargain made me altogether stout in the dreams of success   at length the end of my journey approachd when the passengers lookd out to see wisbeach brig that stretches over the river in one arch   my heart swoond within me at the near approach of my destiny 'to be or not to be'   I kept working my wits up how to make the best use of my tongue while the boatmen was steering for the shore and when I was landed my thoughts was so busy that I had almost forgot the method of finding out the house by enquiring for Counseler Bellamys

people star[e]d at me and pausd before they pointed down the street as if they thought me mistaken in the name   'And are you sure it is Counseller Bellamys you want' said another   'I am sure of it' I said and they showed me the house in a reluctanty way   when I got up to the house I was puzzld as I often have been in finding but one entrance were a fine garden gate with a 'ring the bell' seemd to frown upon me as upon one too mean to be admitted   I pausd and felt fearful to ring

[B3, 78]

58

I was puzzld what to do and wish[d] myself a thousand times over in my old corner at home   at length my hand trembld and pulld the bell it wrang and to my great satisfaction my uncle came being the only man servant and bade me welcome – I have told master about your coming said he   you must not hang your head but look up boldly and tell him what you can do – so I went into the kitchen as bold as I coud and sat down to tea but I ate nothing   I had filld my stomach with thoughts by the way   at length the counsellor appeard and I held up my head as well as I coud but it was like my hat almost under my arm   'Aye aye so this is your Nephew Morris is he' said the couns[e]llor   'yes Sir' said my uncle   'Aye aye so this is your Nephew' repeated the counsellor rubbing his hands as he left the room   'well I shall see him agen' – but he never saw me agen to this day – I felt happily mortified for the trial was over   I was not much dissapointed for I thought all the way that I cut but a poor figure for a law[y]ers clerk   so far it seems I was right   the next morning my uncle said that his mistress had bade him to make me welcome and to keep me till sunday morning when the boat returnd to Peterbro so I spent Saturday a looking about the town after amusement   I was fond of peeping into booksellers windows and found one full of paintings as specimens of a painter who was taking portraits and teaching drawing in the town after fame   the[se] was the early travels of a name well known with the World now – Rippingille[28] – I remember one of them was the 'Village ale house' another was a pencil sketch of the Letter carrier in the town whose face seemd to be familiar with every one that passd by   the rest I have forgotten – I little thought when I was looking at these things that I shoud be a poet and become a familiar accquantance with that painter who had blinded the windows with his attempts for fame – Poets and painters grow ashamd of their early productions and perhaps my friend Rippengill will not thank me for bringing up this assosiation of his early days yet I dont see what occasion they have to feel so for all things have a begining and surely it is a pleasure in happiness to review the rough road of anxietys and trouble in gaining it – on Sunday morning my uncle saw me to the boat and I left Wisbeach and my disapointment behind me with an ernest tho melancholy feeling of satisfaction and I made up for my lost ambition by the thoughts of once more seeing home and its snug fireside   my parents welcomd me with a mellancholy smile that bespoke their feelings of diss-apointment   as I sat upon my corner stool and related my adventures but good luck was at my elbow with a more humble and suitable occupation   Francis Gregory our neighbour at the blue bell wanted a servant and hir[e]d me for a year   I was glad and readily agreed   it was a good place and they treated me more like a son then a servant and I believe this place was the nursery for that lonly and solitary musing which ended in rhyme   I usd to be generaly left alone to my toils for the master was a very weak man and always ailing and my labours were not very burthensome being horse or cow tending weeding etc when I made up for the loss of company by talking to myself and enga[gi]ng my thoughts with any subject that came uppermost in my mind   one of my worst labours was a journey to a distant village name Maxey in winter afternoons to fetch flour once and somtimes twice every week   in these journeys I had hanted spots to pass   as the often heard tales of ghosts and hobgobblings had made me very fearful to pass such places at night it being often nearly dark ere I got there I usd to employ my mind as well as I was able to put them out of my head so I usd to imagine tales and mutter them over as I went on making my self the hero somtimes making my self a soldier and tracing the valours of history onwards thro varius successes till I became a great man   somtimes it was a love story not fraught with many incidents of knight errant[r]y but full of successes as uncommon and out of the way as a romance travelling about in foreign lands and induring a variety of adventures till at length a fine lady was found with a great fortune that made me a gentleman and my mind woud be so bent on the reveries somtimes that I have often got to the town unawares and felt a sort of dissapointment in not being able to finish my story tho I was glad of the escape from the haunted places   I know not what made me write poetry but these journeys and my toiling in the fields by myself gave me such a habit for thinking that I never forgot it and I always mutterd and talk[d] to myself afterwards and have often felt ashamd at being overheard by people that overtook me   it made my thoughts so active that they became troublesome to me in company and I felt the most happy to be alone   On sundays I usd to feel a pleasure to hide in the woods instead of going to church to nestle among the leaves and lye upon a mossy bank w[h]ere the fir like fern its under forest keeps

'In a strange stillness'*

* This line inserted from A34, 16.

watching for hours the little insects climb up and uown the tall stems
of the woodgrass and broad leaves

'Oer the smooth plantain leaf a spacious plain'*

or reading the often thumbd books which I possesd till fancy 'made
them living things'   I lovd the lonly nooks in the fields and woods
and many favourite spots had lasting places in my Memory   'the
boughs that when a school boy screend my head' before inclosure
destroyd them   [A34, 18–17]

Gardener Boy at Burghley

It was thought that I shoud never be able for hard work and I chusd
the trade of a Gardener when A companion of mine Thomas Porter
of Ashton told me that the master of the kitchen gardens at burghley
wanted an apprentice so off my father took me   it was a fine sabbath
morning and when we arrivd he mistaking every body for a gentleman that wore white stockings pulld off his hat to the gardiner as if it
had been the Marquis himself   I often thought after wards how the
fellow felt his consequence at the sight for he was an ignorant proud
fellow   he took me and I was to stop three years   my work for the
time I staid was taking vegetables and fruit down to the hall once or
twice a day and go on errand to Stamford as requird . . .†
                                                      [A34, 12–11]

and I was often sent to Stamford at all hours in the night for one thing
or other somtimes for liquors and somtimes to seek him by the
mistresses orders and as I was of a timid disposition I [was] very often
fearful of going and instead of seeking him I usd to lye down under a
tree in the Park and fall a sleep and in the Autum nights the ryhme usd
to fall and cover me on one side like a sheet which affected my side
with a numbness and I have felt it ever since at spring and fall and I
often times think that the illness which oppresses me now while I
write this narative proceeds from the like cause tho I have often made
the fields a bed since then when I have been at merry makings and

* This line, a quotation from 'Summer' in Robert Bloomfield's *The Farmer's Boy*,
is inserted from A34, 16.

† No words are omitted but I have interrupted this passage, which continues below
at '. . . the man was of so harsh a temper', in an attempt to preserve some continuity in
the narrative.

stopt out when all were abed and at other times when I had taken too much of Sir John Barleycorn and coud get no further   after I had been there a few weeks I savd my money to purchase Abercrombies Gardening which became my chief study   the gardens was very large but when I was there   and I remember finding some curious flowers which I had never seen before growing wild among the vegetables   one was a yellow head ache perrenial and another was a blue one anual   I never saw none like them before or since [A34, 4]

I learnt irregular habbits at this place which I had been a stranger too had I kept at home   tho we was far from a town yet confinement sweetens liberty and we stole every oppertunity to get over to Stamford on summer evenings   when I had no money to spend my elder companion woud offer to treat me for the sake of my company there and back agen and to keep me from divulging the secret to my master by making me a partner in their midnight revels   we usd to get out of the window and climb over the high wall of the extensive gardens for we slept in the garden house and was locked in every night to keep us from robbing the fruit I expect – Our place of rendevouse was a public house calld 'the Hole in the wall' famous for strong ale and midnight merriment kept by a hearty sort of fellow calld Tant Baker (I suppose the short name for Antony)[29]   he had formerly been a servant at Burghley and his house in consequence was a favourite place with the burghley servants always   he dyd last year 1822 very rich – I wrote a long poem in praise of his ale in the favourit scotch metre of Ramsay and Burns   it was not good but there are parts of it worthy as I think of a better fate then being utterly lost   it has long been out of my possesion   My friend Gilchrist told me after I had shown it to him that the house had been long celebrated by drunken Barnaby and that he himself had gained a nich[e] of [im]mortality for Tant Baker in a new Edition of that work
[A34, 13]

G. Cousins

I workd with a man here of a very singular character who knew more ghost storys and marvelous adventures then I had ever met with before and he was one of the most s[i]mple mind   he even believd any thing that was imposd on him for truth in a serious manner and nothing but a laugh at his credulity woud shake his faith   he was of a good memory and the only books he read was Abercrombies gardening and the Bible and he woud repeat a whole chapter by heart and remember the texts which he heard at church years bye   he believd in witches and often whisperd his suspicions of suspected neighbours in the Village   he had a great taste for looking about churches and church yards and woud go ten miles on a sunday to visit one which he had not seen before to read the epitaphs and get those he likd best by heart   he had an odd taste for gentlemans coats of arms and collected all the livery buttons he coud meet with   he had workd in the garden 33 years   his name was George Cousins   he was one of the most singular inofensive men I ever met with   [A34, 11]

. . . the [master of the kitchen gardens] was of so harsh a temper that none likd him and the foreman being weary of the place as well as myself he persuaded me to go with him so we got up early one morning in the autumn and started for Grantham* which we reachd the first night a distance of 21 miles and I thought to be sure I was out of the world   we slept at an alehouse calld the crown and anchor and I wishd my self at home often enough before morning but it was too late then   our enquireys not meeting work there we travelld on to Newark on trent† and there we got Work at a Nurserymans of the name of Withers and lodgd at a lame mans house of the Name of Brown whose son was a carpenter and celebrated for making fiddles

I felt quite lost while I was here tho it was a very livly town but I had never been from hom[e] before scarc[e]ly farther then out of the sight of the steeple   I became so ignorant in this far land that I coud not tell what quarter the wind blew from and I even was foolish enough to think the suns course was alterd and that it rose in the west and sat in the east   I often puzzld at it to set my self right but I still thought so   I remember the fine old castle that stands bye the river and I stood upon the bridge one night to look at it by moonlight and if I remember rightly there is a brick mansion raisd up in its ruins

* Clare has a very damaged passage which appears to refer to their arrival in Grantham: '[by the time we go]t there it was night   when we [woke at last on] the next day it appeard to me [the air was full o]f rattling repetition noise as if all [the people in the] streets was turning skreekers and knocking at shutters [   ] we learnd since that they were stocking weavers' [A34, 9].

† The following passage seems to refer to Newark. It will be noticed that the account of the enlisting in the militia does not seem to square with that at A34, 11–10 which follows: 'While here we went to a little village feast calld Baldwick and the Nottingham shire Militia was then very brief in getting substitutes or recruits   we got fresh' [A34, 15].

which are inhabited and the light from their windows gleaming thro
the ruins gave it an awful appearance at night somthing akin to the
old ruined castles inhabited by banditti in roman[c]es   we did not
stay here long for the master did not give us wages sufficient paying
us one part and promising us the rest if we suited him by a further
trial so we got up earlier then usual one morning to start and as we
was not much burthend with luggage we easily stole away unde-
tected and left our credit with our host ninepence half penny in debt
    we got to Stamford the same night but dare not show ourselves in a
public house so we went thro and lay under a tree in the park   the
ryhme fell thick in the night and we was coverd as white as a sheet
when we got up   [A34, 12–11]

We workd a while in the nursery at hoeing the weeds up between the
young trees and as the ground was baked very hard in the sun it was
much too heavy for my strength for I was but a boy   the wages we
got was small tho the master promisd us more if we suited him by a
further trial but neither the wages or work suited me for my mind was
ill at rest   the strength of my companion was stubborn enough for
any toil but mine was young and feeble and like my mind strange and
unfit with the world   the Nottinghamshire Milit[i]a was then recruiting at Newark* and I fled my toils and listed tho I was of a timid
disposition but Militia had not that terror hanting name of a regular
soldier   I went to Nottingham to be sworn in but was found too
short and felt very glad of the escape afterwards – (the road parts at
the foot of Newark bridge into a Y and that towards the left was the
road for Not[tingham]   I had often heard of Nott[ing]ham in Robin
Hoods Songs and thought it was some [*incomplete*]   [A34, 11–10]

I now followd gardening for a while in the Farmers Gardens about
the village and workd in the fields when I had no other employment
to go too   poetry was a troublsomely pleasant companion anoying
and cheering me at my toils   I coud not stop my thoughts and often
faild to keep them till night so when I fancyd I had hit upon a good
image or natural description I usd to steal into a corner of the garden
and clap it down but the appearance of my employers often put my

---

* The confusion over this militia episode is increased by a deletion at this point
which reads: 'the Nottinghamshire Militia was then recruiting in the town and I woud
have listed but . . .', and by the single name, Moulton, which appears after the phrase
'I fled my toils and listed . . .'

fancys to flight and made me loose the thought and the muse together for I always felt anx[i]ous to consceal my scribbling and woud as leave have confessd to be a robber as a ryhmer   when I workd in the fields I had more oppertunitys to set down my thoughts and for this reason I liked to work in the fields and bye and bye forsook gardening all together till I resumd it at Casterton   I usd to drop down behind a hedge bush or dyke and write down my things upon the crown of my hat and when I was more in a hip for thinking then usual I usd to stop later at nights to make up my lost time in the day   thus I went on writing my thoughts down and correcting them at leisure spending my sundays in the woods or heaths to be alone for the purpose and I got a bad name among the weekly church goers forsaking the 'church going bell' and seeking the religion of the fields tho I did it for no dislike to church for I felt uncomfortable very often but my heart burnt over the pleasures of solitude and the restless revels of ryhme that was eternaly sapping my memorys like the summer sun over the tinkling brook till it one day shoud leave them dry and unconsous of the thrilling joys brin[g]ing anxiety and restless cares which it had created and the praise and censures which I shall leave behind me   I knew nothing of the poets experience then or I shoud have remaind a labourer on and not livd to envy the ignorance of my old companions and fellow clowns   I wish I had never known any other   tho I was not known as a poet my odd habits did not escape notice   they fancied I kept aloof from company for some sort of study   others believd me crazd and some put more criminal interpretations to my rambles and said I was night walking assosiate with the gipseys robbing the woods of the hares and pheasants because I was often in their company and I must confess I found them far more honest then their callumniators whom I knew to be of that description   Scandal and Fame are cheaply purchasd in a Village   the first is a nimble tongued gossip and the latter a credoulous and ready believer who woud not hesitate but believd any thing   I had got the fame of being a good scholar and in fact I had vanity enough to fancy I was far from a bad one my self while I coud puzzle the village schoolmasters over my quart for I had no tongue to brag with till I was inspird with ale with solving algebrai[c] questions   for I had once struggld hard to get fame in that crabbed wilderness but my brains was not made for it and woud not reach it   tho it was a mystery scarcly half unveild to my capacity yet I made enough of it to astonish their ignorance for a village schoolmaster is one of the most pretending and most ignorant

of men – and their fame is often of the sort which that merit droll
genius Peter Pindar[30] describes – Whats christend merit often wants
a auth[or]
[A25, 1–2]

I gave up gardening and workd with a lime burner name gordon who
came from kings[t]ho[r]p near northampton
[A25, 29]

    I now left home and went with a brother of Gordons to burn
lime for Wilders of Bridge Casterton were we workd at first from
light to dark (and in some emergencys all night) to get some money to
appear a little descent in a strange place having arivd pennyless with
but a shabby appearence   in the bargain we got lodgings at a house
of scant fame a professd lodging house kept by a man and his wife of
the name of Cole and we was troubld at night with threble fares in
each bed an inconvinence which I had never been usd too   they took
in men of all descriptions the more the merrier for their profits and
when they all assembled round the evening fire the motly co[u]nte-
nances of many characters lookd like an assembledge of robbers in
the rude hut dimly and my[s]teriously lighted by the domestic savings
of a farthing taper and I remember a droll mistake in a stranger on my
first coming there which created a deal of merriment among the
lodgers tho too serious in the strangers feelings to be laughd at – at an
Election some were in Lincolnshire or Yorkshire one of the contend-

66

ing MPs decoyd a great many of his canvassers from London who
was brought down at their decoyers expence and left to go home at
their own   one of these unfortunates a delicate looking man with
manners and habits bordering on genteelity wandered back with the
pass of providence for his only friend somtimes walking and some
times riding as chances fell out by the way and he arrived in the
evening at the new Inn just soon enough to learn that all the beds
were occupied by more successfull travellers and just late enough to
make his dissapointment a nessesity to keep it or do worse so he was
reccomended to our lodging house and being a thorough bred
Londoner his simple wonderings at every thing he saw started the
titter among the other lodgers who fanc[i]ed that such simple
enquireys bespoke the man a runaway from bedlam

he on the contrary not thinking it possible that his serious
enqu[i]reys coud be construed into any thing laughable fancyd as the
fears in his co[u]ntenance easily decypherd that we had mystical
designs about us and felt for his safty no doubt enough to wish him
self at home   one of his mistakes was a startling one to be sure   on
walking in the garden in the evening he pulld up a flower of the white
nettle by the wall and admird it as one of the finest flowers he had
ever seen in a count[r]y garden   there might be some affectation of
cockney ignorance mixd up with it but I never forgot it and fancyd
that the man had been bro[u]ght up out of the world and the laugh
and whisper went round the cottage fire and made him dream of
danger so instead of going to bed he begd leave to sit up in his chair
till morning when he gladly started and told the people at the Inn that
he were in great danger of loosing his life among a gang of robbers
over the way and that in the middle of the night he verily believd
some one had been murderd in the chamber above his head so he
took care to keep awake till morning.   the noise he mistook for
murder was the groans and noise of a man that was troubled with the
nightmare – When we first went we workd hard to save money and
tryd to be saving   in which we succeeded for a time as I got a about
50 shillings in about 6 weeks with which I intended to purchase a
new olive green coat a color which I had long aimd at and for which I
was measured already ere I left home expecting to be able to pay for it
in a short time but a accident happend in the way which prevented
me   the gipseys etc [*incomplete*]   [B7, 79–80]

It was a pleasant liv[e]ly town co[n]sisting of a row of houses on each side the turnpike about a furlong long   the river gwash ran its crooked course at the back of them on the south side and washd the foot of the gardens till it crossd the turnpike under a modern looking bridge and wound along a sloping meadow northward loosing its name and its waters into strangers streams as there is some beautiful spots on its banks particularly towards the little village of Tikencoat southward were the bank on the field side rises very stunt in some places from the edge of the river and may by a fancy usd to a flat country be easily imagind into mountains   the whole prospect is diversified by gently swelling slopes and easy sunny vallys

at the back of Wilders house is a beautiful encampment or trench very perfect in the shape of a half moon   and the common name of it is 'the dykes'   wether it be roman or Saxon I know not one corner comes in the yard at the back of a stable and the other curves away to the edge of the river near the bridge   it is the widest in the middle of the curve and the highest the bank is throw up on the south side which commands the sight of another hill about a short mile distant on which there is said to be a similar encampment

[A32, 12]

the[re] was some literary assosiations too belonging to this spot   it was the place were Tycho Wing[31] the celebrated astronomer was born and lived and the hall of his Ancestors is still to be tracd by a heap of ruins and moats and fish ponds of black melancholy looking water partly in a close and partly in a wood calld 'wood head'   the moat and fish ponds are open and the water looks black and deep the ruins of the hall appear to be large and part of them is overgrown by bushwood among which a great many wild goosberry bushes lingers yet and wears the memory of its former domestic assosiations

In a large farm house were Tycho Wing once resided it is said that his study is still to be seen in the form he left [it] were the walls are stuck round with the old almanacks he made but I have not seen it and can say no further for its correctness

[A32, 13]

As soon as I got here the Smiths[32] gang of gipseys came and encam[p]d near the town and as I began to be a desent scraper we had a desent round of merriment for a fortnight some times going to dance or drink at the camp and at other times at the publick house

[B7, 88]

68

Once in these midnight revels we escapd a great danger very narrowly   on going for ale at the dancing a quarrel ensued when one party
determind on cheating the other by running off with the beer   I was
one and we got into an old barn to hide ourselves while we drank it
taking a lanthorn from the public house which had been open to the
weather for years and had been falling a long time   we saw no
danger and hugd ourselves over our bottle till we had finishd it when
we started and the next day when I passd the place the gable end we
had sat under was down and a heap of rubish   [B7, 91]

[*Gipseys*]

at these feasts and merry makings I got acquainted with the gipseys
and often assos[i]ated with them at their camps to learn the fiddle of
which I was very fond   the first acquantance I made was with the
Boswells Crew[33] as they were calld a popular tribe well known about
here and famous for fidd[l]ers and fortunetellers   the old Father
who was calld king Boswell dyd at a great age this year by above 100
and was buried at [   ] in singular pomp 30 childern and grandchil-
dern all grown up following him to the grave   (I had often heard of
the mistic language and black arts which the gipseys possesd but on
familiar acquantance with them I found that their mystic language
was nothing more then things calld by slang names like village
provincialisms and that no two tribes spoke the same dilacet exactly
    their black arts was nothing more of witchcraft then the know-
ledge of village gossips and petty deceptions playd off on believing
ignorance but every thing that is bad is thrown upon the gipseys
their name has grown into an ill omen and when any of the tribe are
guilty of an petty theft the odium is thrown upon the whole tribe
    An ignorant iron hearted Justice of the Peace at ———— Sessions
whose name may perish with his cruelty once sitting as a judge in the
absence of a wise and kinder hearted assosiate mixd up this malicious
sentence in his condemnation of 2 Gipseys for horsestealing 'This
atrosious tribe of wandering vagabonds ought to be made outlaws in
every civilizd kingdom and exterminated from the face of the earth'
and this perescuting unfeeling man was a cler[g]yman)   I usd to
spend my sundays and summer evenings among them learning to
play the fiddle in their manner by the ear and joining in their pastimes
of jumping dancing and other amusments   I became so initiated in
their ways and habits that I was often tempted to join them   They

are very ignorant in the ways of the world and very loose in their morals   they seem by their actions to be ignorant of any forms of faith in religion and if they are questiond by a confident for they will reveal nothing to strangers they will admit the existance of a god and say that a belief that there is a god is sufficient without any more trouble to get to heaven   they keep the sabbath like catholics by indulging in all manner of sports and pastimes but they show a knowledge how it ought to be kept by desisting from them when a stranger or suspic[i]ous person dressd in the color of a parson passes bye   I never met with a scholor amongst them nor with one who had a reflecting mind   they are susceptible of insult and even fall into sudden passions without a seeming cause   their friendships are warm and their passions of short duration but their closest friendships are not to be relied on   they are deceitful genneraly and have a strong propensity to lying yet they are not such dangerous characters as some in civilized life for one hardly ever hears of a Gipsey committing murder   their common thefts are trifling depre-dations taking any thing that huswifes forget to secure at night hunting game in the woods with their dogs at night of which all are fish that come [to the] nett except foxes   but some of them are honest   they eat the flesh of Badgers and hedge hogs which are far from bad food for I have eaten of it in my evening merry makings with them   they never eat dead meat but in times of scarcity which they cut into thin slices and throw on a brisk fire till it is scorchd black when it loses its putrid smell and does very well for a make shift providence   when they can afford it they wash the meat in vinegar which takes the smell out of it and makes it eat as well as fresh meat they are more fond of vegetables then meat and seldom miss having tea in an afternoon when they can afford it   they are fond of smoking to excess both men and women   there common talk is of horses lasses dogs and sports   I have often noticd the oddness of their names such as Wisdom Do[u]ghty Manners Lotty Let[t]ice Rover Ishma[e]l   these are not half the odd names but they have come easy to the reccolection – and are the names of a well known tribe whose surnames are Smith   many of their names are Jewish but few christian are Isreal [Viney Liskey Major   ]   they seem to be names that have decended from generation to generation as the young one bears similar names to their parents not generally but almost universaly   In my first acquantance with them I had often noticd that the men had a crooked finger on one hand nor woud they satisfy my enquirys till confidence made them more familiar and then I found the secret was that their parents disabled the finger of every male child in war time when infants to keep them from being drawn for Militia or being sent for soldiers for any petty theft they might commit which woud invariably be the case if they had been able men when taken before a magistrate as they lay under the lash of the law with the curse of a bad name

They had pretentions to a knowledge of medicine but their receipts turnd more on mystic charms and spells   yet they had a knowledge of Plants – which they gave names too themselves   as I had a knowledge of wild plants I usd to be amusd with the names they calld them by   a little plant with a hard stem that grows in villages and waste places one sort bearing minute yellow flowers and another purple ones they calld burvine and reckond famous for the scurvey

Wasp weed is the water betony growing by brook sides which gaind their name by the wasps being invariably attachd to its blossoms getting therfrom a gluttinous matter for the cement of their combs   this is a celebrated plant with the gipseys for the cure and relief of deafness   Buckbane is the bogbean   husk head is the self heal a cure for wounds and furze b[ou]nd is the tormentill a cure for fevers adder bites etc

In fortune telling they pertended to great skill both by cards and plants and by the lines in the hand and moles and interpretations of dreams but like a familiar Epistle among the common people that invariably begins with 'This comes with our kind love to you all hoping you are all well as it leaves us at present   thank god for it' the preface to every bodys fortune was the same that they had false friends and envious neighbours but better luck woud come and with the young that two was in love with them at the same time one being near and one at a distance   one was a dark girl and one a fair girl and he lovd the fair girl the best etc

The credulous readily belevd them and they extorted money by another method of mutterd over their power of revenge which fright[ened] the honest huswife into charity   I have h[e]ard them laugh over their evening fire at the dupes they had made in believing their knowledge in foretelling future events and trying each others wits to see who coud make a tale that might suceed best the next day

as I said before they have no scholars amon[g]st them but I have known people write letters for them to be read as I suppose by the

same assistance   the men are very hot in their tempers and loose in
their discourse delighting to run over smutty ribaldry but the women
have not lost the modesty that belongs them so far as to sit and hear it
without blushing   the young girls are reservd and silent in the
company of men and their love affections are seeming cold and
carless of return

they sometimes marry with the villagers but its very rarely and if
they do they often take to their wandering courses again   village
clowns are oftener known to go away with the gipsey girls which
happens verry frequently   I had a great desire myself of joining the
Smiths Crew and a young fellow that I workd with at a lime kiln did
join with them and married one of the gipseys   his name was James
Mobbs and hes with them still   I usd to dislike their cooking which
was done in a slovenly manner and the dread of winters cold was
much against my inclinations   their descriptions of summer revel-
lings their tales of their yearly journeys to Kent and their rendevouses
at Norwood were they got swarms of money by fiddling or fortune
telling and them that coud do neither job a rich harvest by hop
pulling which work they describd as being so easy were tickling
temptations to my fancy   [A25, 11–13]

The gipseys in matters of religion are no[t] so unfeeling as may be
imagind   instruction seems to be all they want   a friend of mine
told me last night that some methodist preacher preachd to a great
company of them on Ketton heath a few miles distant when some few
paid a disregard to his exhortations but the rest listend with attention
and some even shed tears

There is not so many of them with us as there usd to be   the
inclosure has left nothing but narrow lanes were they are ill provided
with a lodging   Langley Bush is the only place were they frequent
commonly   they are very troublesome to those who are frequented
with them always calling to see them and never leaving the house
without begging somthing   [A25, 14, 15]

Memorys of Love [Chapter 6]

As I grew up a man I mixd more in company and frequented dancings
for the sake of meeting with the lasses for I was a lover very early in
life my first attachment being a school boy affection but Mary
————[34] who cost me more ballads then sighs was belovd with a

romantic or platonic sort of feeling   if I coud but gaze on her face or
fancy a smile on her co[u]ntenance it was sufficient   I went away
satisfied   we playd with each other but named nothing of love   yet I
fancyd her eyes told me her affections   we walkd together as school
companions in leisure hours but our talk was of play and our actions
the wanton innosence of childern   yet young as my heart was it
woud turn chill when I touch her hand and tremble and I fancyd her
feelings were the same for as I gazd earnestly in her face a tear woud
hang in her smiling eye and she woud turn to whipe it away   her
heart was as tender as a birds but when she grew up to womanhood
she felt her station above mine   at least I felt that she thought so for
her parents were farmers and Farmers had great pretentions to
somthing then so my passion coold with my reason and contented
itself with another tho I felt a hop[e]full tenderness that I might one
day renew the acqua[in]tance and disclose the smotherd passion
she was a beautiful girl and as the dream never awoke into reality her
beauty was already fresh in my memory   she is still unmarried

[A25, 7]

That number three seems to have brought many things to a conclusion with me in love   I me[t] th[r]ee full stops or three professions of
sincerity – my first was a school affection – Mary J[oyce] – I am
ashamed to go on with the name   I felt the disparagement in our
situations and fearing to meet a denial I carried it on in my own
fancies to every esteem writing songs in her praise and making her
mine with every indulgence of the fancy   I cannot forget her little
playful form and witching smile even now
    I remember an accident that roused my best intentions and hurt
my affection unto the rude feelings of imaginary cruelty when
playing one day in the church yard I threw a green walnut that hit her
on the eye   she wept and I hid my sorrow and my affection together
under the shame of not showing regret lest others might laugh it into
love – my second was a riper one   Elizabeth N[ewbon][35] who laid
open her own fancys or affections by writing an unfinished sentence
with chalk on a table at a lone cottage where young people used to
meet on sundays – I guessed the rest in my own favour and met the
confession of her esteem by not caring to deny it – this went on for
years with petty jealousies on both sides   at length giving ear to the
world she charged me with sins of changing affections and rambling
fancys – I felt the accusations as insults and my temper mastered my

affections – a short time after I met Patty by accident, fell in love by accident, married her by accident and esteemed her by choice and sure enough had I not met her I should have at this day been a lonely solitary – feeling nothing but the worlds sorrows and troubles and sharing none of its happiness – as it is in the midst of trouble I am happy in having a companion whom I feel deserves my best esteem

[A53]

After mixing into the merrymakings of Wakes Weddings House warmings and Holliday [celebrations] I lost that lonely feeling and grew dissapated   not that I was over fond of drink but I drank for the sake of company and to stifle unpleasant feelings which my follys often brought on me   perhaps the word house warmings needs an explanation to be understood   it is a custom common in villages and is this   when a person shifts from an old habitation to a new one the gossips then old neighbours meet to have a tea drinking with any others that chuse to go and the men join them at night to drink ale and the young one[s] make up a dance and then they warm the new house as they call it by drinking and singing and other merriment   I spoke of follys   they were love follys that often made the heart ach a pain well known to lovers causd by rejected addresses to some one whom I felt a sudden affection for and who on my disclosing it woud affect to sneer and despise me   my first love reallity was with a girl of Ashton whose name was Elizabeth Newbon   she was no beauty but I fancyd she was every thing and our courtship was a long one   I usd to meet her on sundays at a lodge house on Ashton Green at first and then went to her home   her father was a Weelwright and an old man who professd to be learned in the bible and was always trying my wisdom were such and such passages might be found   my silence generaly spoke my lack of religion and he shook his head at my ignorance   he thought that religion consisted of learning such scraps as a sort of curiosity by heart   he knew one book in the bible in which God was not once mentiond   it was Ezra   and he knew the name of the Mountain were noahs ark rested and other bible curositys and he read it to search for these things to be able to talk about them and thought himself a religious man tho he never went church and he was so for he was happy and harmless   he possesd a Large bible with notes which he took in Numbers when a young man   it was Wrights Bible and he often spoke of the pleasure he felt in reading the first number one sunday night in a terrible thunder storm he had another book on which he set a great value   it was Lord Napier[s] Key to the revelations[36]   he believd the explanations there given as the essence of truth and every newspaper occurence that happend in war and political governments he fancyd he coud find there and Boneyparte [   ] and the comet   he believd in Moors Almanack[37] too with great reverence and unlockd its mystical herigliphic with his revelation key yearly tho it was not so suitable a key as Moors who waited the events of the year and explaind it afterwards   [A25, 7–8]

My fondness for study began to decline and on mixing more into company [of] young chaps of loose habits that began by force and growing into a custom it was continued by choice till [I] became wild and irregular and poetry was for a season thrown bye   these habits were gotten when the fields were inclosd mixing among a motly set of labourers that always follow the News of such employments   I usd to work at setting down fencing and planting quick lines with partners whose whole study was continual contrivances to get beer and the bottle was the general theme from weeks end to weeks end and such as had got drunk the oftenest fancied themselves the best fellows and made a boast of it as a fame but I was not such a drinker as to make a boast of it and tho I joind my sixpence towards the bottle as often as the rest I often missd the tott that was handed round for my constitution would not have bore it – Saturday nights usd to be what they calld randy nights which was all meeting together at the public house to drink and sing and every new beginner had to spend a larger portion then the rest which they calld colting a thing common in all sorts of labour   [B7, 91]

We usd to go on Sundays to the Flower pot a little public house at Tikencoat a neighboring village and in [one] of these excursio[n]s I first saw patty going across the fields towards her home   I was in love at first sight and not knowing who she was or were she came from I felt very ill at rest and clumb on the top of a dotterel to see which way she went till she got out of sight but chance quickly thro her again in my way a few weeks after one evening when I was going to fiddle at Stamford   I then venturd to speak to her and succeeded so far as [to] have the liberty to go home with her to her cottage about 4 Miles off and it became the introduction to some of the happiest and unhappiest days my life has met with   after I left her to return home I had taken such a heedless obsever[an]ce of the way that lead over a cowpasture with its thousand paths and dallied so long over pleasant shapings of the future after I left her that twilight with its doubtful guidance overtook my musings and led me down a wrong track in crossing the common and as I coud not correct my self I got over a hedge and sat down on a baulk between a wheat field were my ryh[m]ing feelings again returnd and I composd while sitting there the ballad inserted in the village minstrel and the song of all the days etc*   when the moon got up I started agen and on trying to get over the same hedge as I thought to cross the common I saw somthing shine very bright on the other side   I fancyd it to be bare ground beaten by the cows and sheep in hot weather but doubting I stoopd down to feel and to my terrord supprise I found it was water and while in that stooping posture I saw by the lengthy silver line that stretchd from me that it was the river   if I had take a step with out this caution my love [would have met a sudden end]

    I was frighted and sat under the hedge till daylight   what a many times do a mans follys meet with those dangers and death scapes in his heedless pleasure haunted youth   my reccolection can turn many in mine from boyhood   [B7, 81]

I usd to go on evenings in the week and every sunday to the lodge[38] not at all times on love errands merely but to get out of the way for the lodging house was generaly cumberd with inmates and the Inn was continualy troubling me with new jobs   the solitudes around the Lodge was plentiful and there were places were the foot of man had not printed for years perhaps   the scenery all round were beautiful   heaths and woods swelled their and free vari[e]tys to the edges of the orison   I usd to wander about them with my artless and interesting companio[n] in more then happiness   a large wood in summer usd to be coverd with Lillys of the valley of which she usd to gather handfulls for her flower pots and I helpd her to gather them in these woods were larg[e] caverns calld swallow pits by the woodmen of an imense depth so that if a stone was thrown in one might wait [a] while befor one heard it echo   [B7, 83]

---

* The ballad would appear to be 'When nature's beauty shone complete' (*The Village Minstrel*, vol. I, p. 143) and the song, 'Of all the days in memory's list' (vol. II, p. 46).

Casterton cowpasture which I usd to pass thro on my visits to patty very frequently was a very favourite spot and I pland and wrote some of the best of my poems in the first volume* among its solitudes

[A34, 3]

After I had burnt lime in the kiln awile Mrs Wilder of the New Inn hearing that I had been at Burghley gardens got me to work in the garden were I had a good time of it but the place led me into all sorts of company   I workd here till the autumn and then went with my old companion to Pickworth

Pickworth is a place of other days   it appears to be the ruins of a large town or city   the place were we dug the kiln was full of foundations and human bones   we was about a stones throw from the spot were the church had been which was entirely swept away excepting a curious pointed arch perhaps the entrance to the porch that still remains a stout defiance to the besiegings of time and weather   it now forms a gateway to a stackyard   A new church has been built on the cite of the old one since I was there at the sole expence as I have heard of the Revd Mr Lucas of Casterton [A32, 13]

---

* *Poems Descriptive of Rural Life and Scenery*

March to Oundle in the Local Militia

When the country was chin deep in the fears of invasion and every mouth was filld with the terrors which Bouneparte had spread in other co[u]ntrys a national scheme was set on foot to raise a raw army of volunteers and to make the matter plausible a letter was circulated said to be written by the prince regent   I forget how many was demanded from our parish but I remember the panic which it created was very great – no great name rises in the world without creating a crowd of little mimics that glitter in borrowd rays and no great lye was every yet put in circulation with[out] a herd of little lyes multipl[y]ing by instinct as it were and crow[d]ing under its wings

the papers that were circulated assurd the people of england that the French were on the eve of invading it and that it was deemd nessesary by the regent that an army from 18 to 45 shoud be raisd immediatly   this was the great lye and then the little lyes was soon at its heels which assurd the people of Helpstone that the french had invaded and got to London and some of these little lyes had the impudence to swear that the french had even reachd northampton – the people got at their doors in the evening to talk over the rebellion of 45 when the rebels reachd Derby and even listend at intervals to fancy they heard the french rebels at Northampton knocking it down with their cannon   I never gave much credit to popular storys of any sort so I felt no consern at these storys tho I coud not say much for my valour if the tale had provd true   We had a cross graind sort of choise left us which was to be forcd to be drawn and go for nothing or take on as Volunteers for the bounty of 2 guineas   I accepted the latter and went with a neighbours son W. Clark to Peterbro to be swore on and prepard to join the regiment at Oundle   the morning we left home our mothers parted with us as if we was going to Botany Bay and people got at their doors to bid us farewell and greet us with a sort of Jobs comfort that they doubted we shoud see helpstone no more – by times when we got to Oundle the place of quarters [we] was drawn out into the fields and a more motly multitude of lawless fellows was never seen in oundle before and hardly out of it   there was 1300 of us   we was drawn up into a line and sorted out into companys   I was one of the shortest and therefore my station is evident   I was in that mixd multitude calld the batallion which they nick namd 'bum tools' for what reason I cannot tell   the light Company was calld 'light bobs' and the granadeirs 'bacon bolters'

these were names given to each other who felt as great an enmity against each other as ever they all felt for the french   some took lodgings but lodgings were very expensive   the people took advantage of the tide and chargd high so I was obligd to be content with the quarters alloted me which was at the Rose and Crown Inn kept by a widow woman and her 2 daughters which happend to be a good place   the girls were modestly good naturd and the mother a kind hearted woman behaving well to all that returnd it   our company was the 5th and the Captain was a good sort of feelow using his authority in the language of a friend advising our ignorance when wrong of what we ought to do to be right and not in the severity of a petty tyrant who is fond of abusing those beneath him merely for the sake of showing authority   I was never wonderful clean in my dress at least not clean enough for a soldier for I thought I took more then nessesary pains to be so   I was not very apt at learing my exercise for I then was a rhymer and my thoughts were often absent when the word of comand was given and for this fault I was terribly teazd by a little louse looking coporal who took a delight in finding fault with me and loading me with bad jests on my awkardness as a soldier as if he had been a soldier all his life   I felt very vext at the scurroulus coxcomb and retorted which only added more authority in his language   he fou[n]d fault with me when it belongd to others merely to vex me and if I venturd to tamper with his mistake he woud threaten me with the awkard squad for speaking   I grew so mad at last with this fool that I realy think I shoud have felt satisfaction in shooting him and I was almost fit to desert home and then agen I though[t] my companions woud laugh at me so I screwd up my resolution to the point at last and determind if he accusd me wrongfully for the time to come I woud certanly fall out of the ranks and adress him be the consequence what it woud   I had no great heart to boxing but I saw little fear in him for he was much less in strength then I was and the dread of the dark hole or awkard squad was but little in comparison to the teazing insults which this fellow daily inflicted so I was determind to act up to my vengance be the consequenc[e] what it might and I soon found an oppertunity for he was present[l]y at his pert jests and sneering meddling again madness flus[h]t my cheek in a moment and when he saw it he rapt me over my knees in a sneering sort of way and said that he woud learn me how such fellows as I was dealt with by soldiers   I coud stand it no longer but threw my gun aside and seizing him by the throat I twisted him down and kickd him when he was down which got the fellow fame for those that had been against him before lifted him up and calld him a good fellow and calld me a coward while they led me to the black hole but the captain enqu[i]rd into the frey and the black hole was dispensd with in serving an addition on guard in its stead   the fellow th[r]ew a mortified eye on me ever after and never found his tounge to tell me of a fault even when I was in one

[B7, 98–7]

I was threatend with the [b]lack hole by one and even the tying up to the halbert by others who said the drummers were exce[rcis]ing themselves and being able to use the whip with punishment   I thought I possest common sense in a superior degree as not to feel fear at threatend sirmises of any sort for I always look'd on such things as mere tampering for childern but I confess my common sense was overcome and I felt fearful that somthing was in the wind till it blew over and got too late to [require me a flogging]   [B7, 96]

I once got into the awkard squad not for my own fault but that of others which shows that bad company is not very commendable one morning an old pieman came up and taking as he fancyd an advantage of our hunger like a crafty politician he askd an increasd price for them thinking our nessesitys woud urge us to buy   [B7, 94]

The officers were often talking about Bounaparte in the field and p[r]aising each other in a very redicilous manner very often   I will repeat one anecdote   having found out that the common men were more expert in making nightly plunders in orchards then learing their exercise by day and as they coud not come at the offenders being those who slept in out houses that coud go in and out as they chusd they determind on a plan to harass them as they calld it by taking them out in the field two additionel hours in the morning from 6 to 8 but they was not aware that 6 was a late hour with ploughmen who was usd to get up before the sun all the year round so instead of harrising the men they quickly harassd themselves and the scheme was dropt   in one of these early exercises one of the Officers ladys whose fears for her husbands safty seemd very great even in little things sent the servant maid after him with his breakfast and as she came simpering along making her timid enquireys the captains of companys declard that they thought M^r xxx had been too much of a soldier to stand this and others swore upon their honours that he woud not stand it   at length the enquiring maid found out her noble master who sneeringly disdaind to take it the maids only reasons for bringing it being that her mistress was afraid he woud take cold by being out of doors in such unusual hours which to be sure was a mortifying disclosure to the pin featherd soldier   'Go home and teach your mistress to know better girl' was the gallant replye and his brother officers who were on the look out to watch the event when they saw the maiden depart hastend up and congratulated his valour and shake hands with him as a brother worthy the name of a soldier

the very clowns coud not help seeing this as rediculous and burst into a hearty laugh as the farce ended   the others got into a bye word and I itchd to do somthing with it and wrote a ballad which I venturd to offer one evening at Bells the printers for publication when a young man behind the co[u]nter read it and laughd heartily saying he had heard of the circumstance but it was too personal to print and returnd it   I felt fearful of being found out so I quickly destroyd it tearing it into very small pecies as I went along and threw them away but I heard nothing more of the matter   I can[n]ot remember much of it now but I thought little of it when I wrote and more after it was destroyd   [B7, 95]

On the last time we was calld up there was a fresh bounty set on foot of a further 2 guineas to those who woud enlist for extended service as they calld it to be sent so many miles out of the county to guard barracks castles or any other urgengys that might happen five shillings of which was to be paid down and the rest to be given when they were wanted   I did not much matter an extent of service but I felt purposes enew for the 5 shillings and when it was offerd me I took it without further enquirey and never heard further about it

[B7, 94]

My first feelings and attempts at Po[etry]

I cannot say what led me to dabble in Ryh[me or] at what age I began to write it but my first r[ude attempts took the form of] imitations of my fathers Songs for he knew and sung a great many and I made a many things before I venturd to comit them to writing for I felt ashamd to expose them on paper and after I venturd to write them down my second thoughts blushd over them and [I] burnt them for a long while but as my feelings grew into song I felt a desire to preserve some and usd to correct them over and over till the last copy had lost all kindred to the first even in the title   I went on some years in this way wearing it in my memory as a secret to all   tho my parents usd to know that my leisure was occupyd in writing yet they had no knowledge of what I coud be doing for they never dreamd of me writing poetry   at length I venturd to divulge the secret a little by reading imatations of some popular song floating among the vulgar at the markets and fairs till they were common to all but these imatations they only laughd at and told me I need never hope to make songs like them   this mortified me often and almost made me desist for I knew that the excelling such doggerel woud be but a poor fame if I coud do nothing better but I hit upon an harmless deception by repeating my poems over a book as tho I was reading it   this had the desird effect   they often praisd them and said if I coud write as good I shoud do   I hugd myself over this deception and often repeated it and those which they praisd as superior to others I tryd to preserve in a hole in the wall but my mother found out the hurd and unconscously took them for kettle holders and fire lighters when ever she wanted paper not knowing that they were any thing farther then attempts at learning to write for they were writing upon shop paper of all colors and between the lines of old copy books and any paper I coud get at for I was often wanting tho I saved almost every penny I had given me on sundays or holidays to buy it instead of sweet meats and fruit and I

82

usd to feel a little mortified after I discoverd it but I dare not reveal the
secret by owning to it and wishing her to desist for I feard if I did she
woud have shown them to some one to judge of ther value which
woud have put me to shame so I kept the secret dissapointment to
myself and wrote on suffering her to destroy them as she pleasd but
when I wrote any thing which I imagind better then others I preservd
it in my pocket till the paper was chafd thro and destroyd by a
diff[er]ent and full as vain preservation   [A34, 10]

My mother brought me a picturd pocket hankerchief from Deeping
may fair as a fairing on which was a picture of Chatterton and his
Verses on Resignation[39]   chance had the choice of it   she was
mentioning the singular circumstance to me yesterday be asking me
wether I rememberd it and saying that she little thought I shoud be a
poet then as she shoud have felt fearful if she had for Chattertons
name was clouded in mellancholly memorys which his extrodinary
Genius was scarcly know[n]   the common people knew he was a
poet and that was all   they know the name of Shakespear as one but
the ballad monger who prints and supplys hawkers with their ware
are poets with them and they imagine one as great as the other   so
much for that envied emenence of common fame   I was fond of
imatating every thing I met with and therefore it was impossible to
resist the oppertunity which this beautiful poem gave me   I am not
certain that this is the name of the poem   my memory was freshend
some few years ago to believe so in reading the life of Chatterton by (I
think) someone of the name of Davy   as I have the poem by me I will
insert it   [A34, 9]

The Resignation

Supposed to be written by the unfortunate Chatterton just before he took the
deadly draught that put a period to his existence

> Since disappointment and despair
> The vainness of all hopes declare
> Since toss'd upon this restless main
> I strive 'gainst wind and waves in vain
> The more I struggle for the shore
> Misfortunes overwhelm the more
> Then since I struggle to maintain
> And strive alas to live in vain

Ill hope no more – Since prov'd and tried
The feeble light she once supplied
Resembled but the taper's ray
That only burns to die away
And leave one lost in endless night
(My follies but expos'd to sight)
Then come misfortunes as ye will
Oppressions sink we lower still
Haste keen despair and urge my doom
And all that haunt the wretched come
Fate from my heart all fears expunge
I stand resolv'd to take the plunge

       *   *   *

O thou great Being who resides
Far above where yon ether glides
Whose power almighty piercing eye
Marks all on earth in air and sky
Who oft (such care we ought to praise)
This sand grain call'd a world surveys
Nor deems unworthy of thy care
Vain Men as worthless as we are
Who oft with liberal hands bestows
Thy guiding mercy here below
And while our sins so multiply
Like mountains heap'd before thee lie
So loath – so tempted to chastize
And then to bless us in disguise
To disappoint our restless schemes
Our airy hopes and foolish dreams
Is but to prove the empty shew
Of painted happiness below
O thou that hears the wretched call
Thou universal friend to all
I own thy goodness feel they pow'r
And humbl'd in this trying hour
Affecting as my troubles seem
I prove thy mercy was extream
But O thou universal lord
Some shelter to the wretch afford

84

Forgive the sin if sin it be
To sink beneath adversity
Prest down O God – thou knowest all
I am but mortal and must fall

Ye grisley ghosts that seem to rise
And swim before these frantic eyes
My blood runs chill – your hollow screams
But serve to terrify my dreams
And make this hopeless heart of mine
Desist and shrink from its design
But hush ye fears ye lengthen pain
Here fancy may imagine vain
No terrors need the soul attend
When we are gone our sorrows end
Or why (my kindred fortunes hate
These victims sacrifis'd to fate)
Did they the self-same road pursue
Unless they thought and hop'd it true
And since that last resource is mine
Stern fate resolve – and I resign

[1, 227]

I always wrote my poems in the fields and when I was out of work I usd to go out of the village to particular spots which I was fond of from the beauty or secre[c]y of the scenes or some assosiation and I often went half a days journey from home on these excursions   in one of these rambles I was in a narrow escape of being taken up as a poacher   it was a fine day and I went to wander on wittering heath with the double intention of ryhming and seeking wild plants – I found a beautiful spot on the side of a rivulet that ran crooking and neglected among the yellow furze and misty green sallows that met on both sides   I sat down nearly conseald in the furze and tall downy grass and began to ryhme till I insensibly fell asleep and was awakend by muttering voices on the other side of the thicket   I lookd thro and saw they were keepers and the men made a stop as if they suspected somthing was in it   I felt very fearful but it was soon over for they passd on   I was far away from any road and my account of myself woud have seemd but an idle one   it woud have only raisd their suspicions and I shoud have been taken up as a poacher undoubtedly

85

so as soon as they were safe off I made the best of my way out of danger for the part I was enclosd with a wall and belongd to the Marquis [A32, 6]

I always wrote my poems in great haste and generaly finished them at once wether long or short for if I did not they generaly were left unfinishd   what corrections I made I always made them while writing the poem and never coud do any thing with them after wards [A25, 10]

There was an Elegy also on an old Cart Horse an early poem which I alterd and made a tollerable thing of   the old Horse was in great fame in the Village for his gentleness and strength and readiness at all sorts of jobs   Another was a Tale of the Lodge house [B6, 81R]

The Death of Dobbin

Old Dobbin now I sing a mournful theme
The noted horse of many a farmers team
Who in the Glory of his youthful days
Near faild to reap his driver's daily praise
Who too the hero of each story prov'd
Of weights he carried and of loads he moved
But ah the praises of the world abide
Long as a buble on a floating tide
Poor worn-out Dobbin good as he had prov'd
In spite of all the loads he bore and mov'd
And sp[i]te of all his worthy labours past
Fell like the rest a cumber ground at last
Ah poor old injur'd Dobbin well might we
Be warn'd to know the world[s] deceits from thee
Thou an Example both to horse and man
Show how we've served when we've done all we can
But tho thy loss old dobbin boy was hard
For such real merit to meet such reward
Tho by thy master used so unkind
The rural Muse is glad at heart to find
'Mong thy old friends thy memory still survive
Where worthy deeds are sure to keep alive
Those old companions of thy former time
That knew thee well and knew thee in thy prime

When thou out match'd by none to none would yield
That often geard thee in their team to field
Those old Companions of thy former prime
That yok'd thee out to field full many a time
And many a day and many a weary morn
That have with thee the lengthening furrow drawn
And through each tim[e]ly season as they roll'd
The summers heat and winters cutting cold
Have stood with the[e] as pastures spar'd
The toiling slaves to those that better far'd
These were thy friends and these thy friends well knew
A horses worth that might be trusted too
And this they every day could p[r]ove and see
The value dobbin of a horse like thee
They by experience taught knew how to prize
That worth which unexperienced fools despise
And treat thy memory with that due respect
Which thy self loving master does reglect
Never through him by handy works attain'd
And last no longer then his ends are gain'd
Sway'd by self interest – when thy best was o'er
As he could profit by thy strength no more
When courage left thee and old age came on
And all the hopes of an amendment gone
When willing still weak effort prov'd too true
That thou hadst done the utmost thou coulds do
Then merits past and praises all adieu
His profits vanish'd and his praises too
Ah merits past he cou'dn't tent to call
Nor spare a praise where merits past was all
But turn'd the[e] out in yon bare ground to feed
To pine or die as future fate decreed
And happy future fate did so ordain
To see thy sufferance and to ease thy pain

The Lodge house of my mothers [I] put into ryhme   it was a current
one in the village and the place were it was said to have happend was
a lone house calld the 'heath house' about 2 miles from the Village
it stood in a lone hollow in the ground northward below the present
new one called Milton Farm   it was disinhabited and in ruins when I

was a boy   it had been a farm house and one of the barns was kept
up were my father used to thresh in winter for several years – there
were several dismal storys afloat of midnight murders done in this
place in the days of its prosperity and of course a great many
accounts of shrieking women and groaning men heard and seen near
the spot by passing shepherds and feast goers in the night   I
remember with what fearful steps I usd to go up the old tottering
stairs when I was a boy in the dinner hours at harvest with other
compainons to examine the haunted ruins   the walls were riddeld
all over with names and dates of shepherds and herdsmen in their idle
hours when the[y] crept under its shelter from showers in summer
and storms in winter and there were mysterious stainings on the old
rotting floors which were said to be the blood of the murderd
inhabitants – it also was the haunt of Gipseys and others who pulld
up every thing of wood to burn till they left nothing but the walls –
the wild cat usd to hide and raise its kittens in the old roof an animal
that usd to be common in our woods tho rather scarce latly – and the
owls usd to get from the sun in its chimney and at the fall of evening
usd to make a horrid hissing noise that was often taken for the
waking noise of the hanting spirits that made it a spot shund desolat
and degected   [A34, 2]

The Lodge house A Gossips Tale

On a heath stood a farm house as lone as coud be
Let em look where they woud nothing els coud they see
But here an odd furze bush and there an odd tree
   Green corn field and fallow land brown
More lonsomly too in a hollow it lay
The hermit like tennants no neighbours had they
To pop in and chat a few hours of the day
   Twas two mile or more from a town

The farmer was wealthy as many coud tell
He managd wi care and he ploughd his land well
And card not for living in such a lone cell
   If he coud get crops to his will
Of servants for labour he kept a good clan
Stiff chaps five or six and a sturdy headman
A house keeping maid and a under want man
Who had in a dairy good skill

Who lives at a lodge but gen dangers prepard
So wealthy and lonly he kept a good guard
And four mettle bull dogs turnd loose in his yard
   And guns ready chargd for alarms
Twas nothing unlikley for rogues coming here
So noted for hurded up wealth as he were
The towns round about him for miles far and near
Had heard of his dogs and his arms

Tho nothing to scare em as yet hadnt been
Of any one tempting down right to get in
But folks hanging round it at night time was seen
Which left em suspisions of fear
And maids often sed when the rest were gone church
That stagger-down fellows theyve seen on the lurch
That tryd at the front door and then at the porch
   And begd in excuse bread or beer

– O dear what sensations from solitude rise
What trifles she loves that a town woud despise
Een the squeakings of mice now the maidens woud prize
And thus when alone theyd sit down
And listen the chirp of the sparrows to hear
And think em then songs of the linnet more dear
And all those fine singers in solitude drear
   As they put em in mind of a town

One day as it rather gets dusk at the hour
When the winters days done all it can about four
The thresher gave in and had cleard up his floor
And took out the straw to the stock
When three lusty fellows peept into his barn
And the right road for somwhere requested to learn
Tho drest like three clowns twas a blackis[h] concern
   And the thresher was struck like a rock

They gun force discourse bout the master and men
What servants and dogs hed in keeping and then
Theyd squint in the yard and gin talking agen
   Poor michael he quakd like a leaf

He answerd their questions wi hah and wi no
But hinted on dogs and the guns for a show
For he had the deepness about him to know
    That such like woud frighten a thief

They then lungd away wi out bidding good night
Such tokens confirmd that his notions was right
Pleasd enough too were he to get out of their sight
    And instantly shut up his barn
And went to the servants and told 'em his doubt
Who cast their opinions and then gave it out
That men at that hour for no good came about
    Twas surely a hidden conscern

Be't een as it woud they got ready for work
To guard agen danger if peace shoud be broke
They hunted up cutting knife cudgel and fork
    And drove all the dogs in the house
Thus armd they were fixt let it be as it might
And doors they lockd up hard the windows shuts tight
Each waited ast were upon thorns all the night
    And listnd as still as a mouse

Besure now and then mutterd hints went about
And fis'es were shook to note somthing without
Some fancyd a whistle some heard a shill shout
    And some heard their steps in the yard
Poor hog serving hodge frit to dead as it where
A'most dreaded the supper job going to draw beer
And dursnt go down 'the cellar for fear
    Wi out hed a dog for his guard

The wind whistld hollow the weather was foul
Round the jaumbs of the cottage the tempest did howl
The dog rather restles gun grumble and growl
    And wagged their tails at the door
The candle curld winding sheets dismal to view
And tokening danger the fire burned blue
And plump to the maidens the coffin sparks flew
    Which made em neer sink on the floor

Footsteps pass the window! the bull dogs all bark
Theres one shouts for cudgel and one for a fork
And he take the gun who can best hit the mark
    And thus they are fixt for alarm
Some'at sorrowful calls and the door gis a tap
Twas a voice like a womans – agen a small rap
Poor hodge he woud have it twas nought but a trap
    Tho the voice sed it meant em no harm

'Who ever ye be' said the master 'begone'
Some bawld for the gun to let know they had one
And some tapt the bull dogs to harden em on
    And bragd of their savagness too
The door haunter wouldnt wi little be scar'd
But still to come in beggd terrible hard
It told em theyd little need keeping a guard
Twas small harm a woman coud do

'The storm gatherd deep and my road got unseen
'Lost on the dark heath for an hour have I been
'My limbs are most stiffnd it freezes so keen
    'Id be thankful to lye in yer barn'
The master was tender it melted his breast
Who coudnt but pity a woman distrest
He instant called counsil to give her some rest
    Lord knows twas a shocking conscern

But hodge still presisted she meant em no good
The maidens both backd him 'keep safe while they coud'
And vowd were they them let her wowl as she woud
She neer shoud set foot i the lodge
'Most votes the day carried' wi caution and guard
A tall woman enterd the house the boy stard
The stranger een smiled to see him so scard
    And hard ran the jest upon hodge

Still he eyed her all over from top to the toe
And jogd wi his elbow the maids to let know
That her voice were to gruff – women never talkd so
    Let the others consiet as they might

Quere fancys he coudnt get out of his head
As in crossing the house she seemd heavy to tread
'Sides her foot looked large – well he might go to bed
    But hed neer shut his eyes for the night

They questiond the stranger she answerd em well
Where bin and where going far as questions compell
But whod any sense in his head coud soon tell
    She were little to talking inclind
She wouldnt go bed and good reasons were shown
Her fatherless childern all sleeping alone
She 'tended to start soon as first cock had crown
    For she couldnt be easy in mind

The head man knew well bout the place whence she came
And knew too as well there was none of her name
Had hodge or the maidens bin up to the same
    Theyd blobbd out the matter of course
He answerd her nothing but kept up his eye
And found hidden mistery lapt up in the eye
And wisperd his master the hint by and bye
    Who resolvd to scheme matters no worse

Bed time cometh on man and master set up
The womans but vainly intreated to sup
Poor hodge spite or fear begun drowsy and droop
And she beggd theyd all go to their beds
For her part she wisht cause no trouble at all
The things that she begd of their kindness was small
And if she got worser she easy coud call
    – Excuse freshnd doubts in their heads

So now left on garrison master and will
The woman they thought got uneasier still
But she said twas the thoughts of her babes made her ill
As the youngest of four suckt her breast
What leave sucking infants! – the clock tung eleven
She wisht that the capons first signal was given
The master and man wisht em sens was in heaven
    New lies added dangers exprest

She dozd now and then on her chair she woud lye
And they found like the cat she coud doze wi one eye
Nigh as fourpence a groat is the watches coud spy
　　The plot were a rougish conscern
And they wisperd of fire arms in each others ear
But wisperd as loud as the stranger shoud hear
And talkd of their guns as a store house it where
　　As she all her perrils might learn

Then to see what she woud do they made a mock sleep
Dogs close to their master did watchfully keep
The woman play[d] chances and off did she creep
　　As soft as she coud to the door
The way that she vent'd made anyone dread
She seemd as she wisht to have lightnd her tread
As one strimes and steps where sick folks lye a bed
　　Her feet scarcly prest on the floor

Doubts now were all cleard – out of doors she had got
A shrill whistle blew – and the master he shot
And will like an arrow brusht up to the spot
　　And agen turnd the key on their guest
'All keep out as is out' in triumph sed will
A groan murmurd help a weak call faint and chill
Foot steps tramped gently – agen all were still
　　Save the dogs who woud not be at rest

The rout soon disturbd all the lodge of its rest
The wenches for saftey rund nearly undrest
And hodge sorely frightend wi what he had guest
　　Bawld out to know what were amiss
And soon as he heard twas his prophesied trick
And the thief were lockt out – then he took up his stick
And bragd wi the best hadnt skulls a bin thick
　　They might a seen easy in this

The master calld silence to listen if aught
Still tokend near danger but they coud hear nought
Save hodge who heard groans now and then as he thought
　　And his stick was prepard in his fist

Some proposd take the gun and go see if they coud
Execution if twas done or not be as twoud
But as now matters stood – hodge he votes for some good
   And they from his caution desist

First cock shouted morning aloud from his shed
And minded em all what the stranger had sed
And they deemd it rare luck as they didnt go bed
   To leave the guisd rogue to her sen
The maids offerd prayers for thus being preservd
The master reflected how theyd a been servd
And hodge in a moment most drily observd
   Theyd none a seen daylight agen

And oft they calld silence now and then the dogs growl
But nothing was heard save the woop of an owl
And winds in the chimney – the weather was foul
   That mournfully wisperd alarm
Hodge coudnt help heaving a whistle and groan
But night and its terrors thank God they were flown
The morning thro cracks of the window shuts shown
   And light woud soon free em of harm

The scales now was turnd and in triumph hodge sed
What scores of opinions he had in his head
Which fearing theyd laugh at him worse then they had
   He kept em all in to his sen
He knew very well that her bosom was flat
Coud mark on her chin hairs as black as his hat
Saw her pull down her bonnet to hide it and that
   And scarce coud help hinting agen

The woman too slung herself back in her chair
And hodge sed he vain gogged well to look there
Blue stockings she wore as to that he woud sware
   Which he neer saw on woman before
And once in her rocking she tosst up her feet
He thought he saw breeches but kept it discreet
And thought as none else saw – his fears might consiet
   So he woudnt pretend to no more

94

Hodge sed he thought much what he dare not express
Twas a good for nought rouge in disguisd womans dress
His wit pleasd the master who coudnt say less
   Then a worthy reward he shoud have
And all bragd of courage what each would have done
How that woud a servd em how this wi his gun
Woud a rallied down two at a level like fun
   As all out of danger are brave

When darkness grew thin and the twilighting red
Like beauty thro veils began dimly to spread
They took up their weapons the stoutest hearts led
   And venturd to see what they coud
The door soon as opend the dogs rushed out
And tracked the caus way and snufted about
And soon was the masters shot provd wi out doubt
   The dogs lap'd a puddle of blood

Good god they was sorry and felt for her pain
The groans which they heard thus did quickly explain
And they called the dogs up to track her again
   To be sure shed lye dead further on
They searched the yard under cribs did they peep
And rooted the straw where it seemd in a heap
As to dye out of sight any where she woud creep
   But the wounded encroacher was gone

Holes and corners they hunted for hours round and round
But nothing of rogues dead or living was found
Tho sure enough some one had got a deep wound
   And the living helpd off wi the lame
The morn past opinions but nothing was heard
All day the[y] expected but nothing appeard
Hodge went to the village conjectures he heard
   But nothing for truth never came

This friend and that wi opinions ran over
Wi tidings of this that and tother hurt sore
They knew they was hurt but they knew nothing more
   Suspicion might think as she woud

The farmer such stories did little regard
But trebld the strength of his guns and his yard
And thought to be stronger gen dangers prepard
   Were the only best means for his good

And he thankd all his men for the courage theyd shewn
And he gen em that day from their labour a boon
And in reason what ale they likd drink morn and noon
   Keeping guard for the nighttime in view
As to hodge for his service – the master declard
He merited honour as well as reward
And he placd him from thence the head boy in his yard
   And a bran spanking whip gave him too

And still he continued to live at the lodge
And if by a woman rogue playd such a dodge
He vowd to remember the caution of hodge
   And think em to trapping inclind
And when a chap lay awaken in bed
And heard the first crow of the cock from his shed
He thought what the woman drest robber had sed
   And brought it all fresh in his mind

I had often thought of colecting my best poems in a book and I went
to Hensons to enquire the price of one   he told me 8 shillings and on
being alowd to pay for it as I woud I had one   (this book is now in
the possesion of Ned Drury)   he seemd puzzled to imagine what use
I was going to make of it   he had know[n] me before by binding
books for me taken in No^s and by seeing me often at the chappel at
Helpstone for I was then fond of hearing the Independants and was
much happier then perhaps then I have been since – but his knowledge of me only served to darken the riddle of my purchase for my
ignorant appearance and vulgar habits had nothing of literary
[manners] about them   he urgd many side wind enquireys to pump
and wide guesses but I had kept the secret too long to be so easily
perswaded as to let it go – but it was the fair day and getting a little
bold with ale on my going for the book before I started home I lost
my sho[y]ness and dropt a few hints as to the use I intended it and it
wakend his guesses into the suppose that I dabbled in ryhme   I
acknowledged it and he wishd to see them   I told him he shoud but it

passd on with out any further conversation about the matter till
now*   [B3, 80; A31, 214]

He [J. B. Henson] was a bookseller and printer in a small way at
Market Deeping one of the lowest market towns in england and as
full of ignorance of books as a village – he came to Deeping as a
school master   he then turnd to a bookbinder and bought and sold a
few second hand books and finally he set up printing Auction Bills
and songs and pamphlets for travellers and at last he ventured to
print books   his first trial was the 'history of Joseph'[40] which was
badly done   the next was Bunyans Pilgrims Progress Heavenly
footman etc which he sold in sixpenny Numbers   these was done
much better nay tolearably well so as to procure him employment for
the London Booksellers and he printed several religious books for
one Baine a London Puplisher and the last things I know of which he
printed on his own account was The Golden Treasury – a small book
of Arithmetic by a ––– Pousnell a schoolmaster of Deeping and a
political pamphlet of wooden ingeniuty by a Northamptonshire
Farmer – he then broke and contented himself with his smaller
beginnings of hunting Ballads and Auction bills till last year when he
left the place on the experement at adventuring of finding a better –
when he first came to deeping he was a religious man belonging to the
congregational dissenters or Independants and then did some dirty
doings with sathan or at least the doings were exposd by accident for
they are worldly doings and tho preachd and reprobated every
sunday be religious of all persuasions the[y] are common to her every
family – tho the poluted stream flows by a secret passage – like the
muddy one that emptys itself in the Thames – proffession in all
religious opinions is a very meek pretending good lady clamourous
against the world and its ways and always busy to abuse it – but in
pra[c]tice of good she is a dead letter – he was turnd off from his
profession of clerk to the Independants
    The current coin that carrys a man at self interest thro the world
is fair pretentions hollow friendships and false promises which are all
of one value and but the reverse and transvers of a counterfit
                                                        [A31, 216–17]

I wrote several of my poems while I was here and formd a resolution
of publishing them for I was over head and ears in embarassments

---

* A parallel passage to this occurs at A25, 10.

and knew not which way to get out   I had shown some to my first acquaint[a]n[c]e in the matter J. B. Henson of Market Deeping Among which was the Sonnet to the Setting Sun and the one to the Primrose two of the earliest I ever wrote and these two he approvd of very much and also a poem on the death of Chatterton which he wanted to print in a penny book to sell to hawkers but I was doubtful of its merits and not covetous of such fame so I declind it   he seemd very anxious to publish my poems   he said he woud write to his London booksellers to hear if they woud assist us or take a share in the matter   I forget their names   and we proposd to do it by subscription and as soon as an hundred subscribers was gotten he was to begin to print it and on our starting he was to print 300 prospectuses for one Pound and I wishd him to write the thing but he declind and urgd me to it   I was very loath and had a worse opinion of my prose abilitys then my poetry for I had never written a letter excepting the silly love epistles aluded [to] but I tryd what I coud do

we lodgd at a public house still if a mellancholy sign swinging in the wind by a solitary clump of some five or six houses coud give it a licence to be calld so that stood as if no passenger could ever be supposd to find it and as tho the road had forgotten the few fragments of the town that mea[s]urd it   it seemd to stand out of the worlds eye yet there was occasional droppers in that made it any thing but a place fit for study so I usd to think over it in my morning and night journeys too and from work   in one of the mellancholy mornings I wrote the two first verses of what is life   having another lime kiln at royal about 2 miles off and at this place I sat down one day on a coal shuttle and wrote my address to the Public on a piece of paper which I kept for the purpose   it gave me a deal of trouble and I was ill satisfied with what I had written but I wanted to do somthing to get out of debt so I wrote it and Directed it with a pencil and in the want of sealing wax seald it with pitch and took it to Stamford but my heart was in a thousand minds ere I got there   somtimes I thought I woud give up all though[t]s of poetry and again my hopes returnd and I resolvd to try the experiment thinking that if I got laughd at and reapd scorn instead of profit in the publication of my poems it woud only be a cure to all foolish fancys and scribbling follys for the future so I sat down upon a stone heap before I got into Stamford and lookd over it again to correct it and I felt as I went on as if every body knew my errand and my face reddend at the gaze of a passer bye   the post office was shut up when I got there and they wanted a penny with the letter but I had not got one so they took [it] with a loath kind of [attitude] an[d] bye and bye a letter returnd from Henson stating that he woud meet me at Stamford with 100 of the prospectuses and arrange for further matters   I accordingly went and for the first time saw a sonnet of mine in print and I scarcly knew it in its new dress and felt a prouder confidence then I had hither too done thinking it got merit by its dress   his mind was rather changd when I got there   he did not seem so urgent to print them and instead of a pound he had got 5 or 6 shillings more one for his journey etc   I was not aware that promises was a current coin among booksellers of all sizes from Henson the sale bill printer to the city professor   I met him at the Dolphin Inn   I found that he did not come on purpose of my errand but he had two old books to dispose of them and left some prospectuses   he wanted to go into Thompsons shop but I declind as I owd him a small debt which I coud not discharge and while we was drinking together a dull looking fellow in a genteelish dress came in to whom Henson gave one of the papers offering at the same time as a sort of apology a little account of [my] profession etc but the fellow just threw his eyes over it then lookd at me and walkd out of the room without saying a word   the next person that came in was of a milder disposition tho his profession is not a common assosiate at such places yet in spite of his foibles he was a good fellow   Henson begd him to peruse one   he did and made enquires to me which I answerd in a shoy [manner] but he wishd me success and gave the sonnet some praise askd me to drink with him and bade Henson set his name down as a subscriber wishing at the same time that he was able to give me further assistence   this gave me heart and did me more good then all I ever met with before or after   I felt it deeply and never forgot the name of the Rev^d M^r Mo[u]nsey[41]   a short [while] after I left pickworth and returnd home wher Henson proposd to print the work as soon [as] he shoud have 100 Subscribers   the[n] after I had got a good many things ready for him to begin with he said he coud not do it unless I coud borrow £15 of any friend in the village but there was not a friend in the village friendly enough to lend me fifteen shillings and I told him so   then he proposd £10 and in this shuffling from one proposal to another I got very uneasy and my confidence in his promises shrunk to nothing   I wishd then that I had never engagd in the matter and felt ashamd as I went down the street scarcly daring to look any one in the face for the prospectuses had filld every bodys

mouth with my name and prospects most of which was Jobs
comforters and the cry was against me (see etc)   [A32, 14–15]

at the situation I found myself in after I had printed and distributed
all my papers – I found not one subscriber and my hopes seemd lost –
I knew not what course to take   I had got no work to go too and I
hardly dare show my face to seek for any – every body seemd to jeer
me at my foolish pretentions and seemd showing shony at my fallen
hopes – enquirey stood on tiptoe with question go were I woud and I
hated to hear them and evaded them as well as I coud   I felt
uncommonly uneasy and knew not what to do   I sometime thought
of running away and leaving home were I might be at peace among
strangers (for my dissapointment was fast growing into a bye word)
– and I went to Stamford twice to enlist in the attillery which was
recruiting there but my variety of minds prevented me besides my
love matters and was a strong tether that I coud not easily break – I
went so far at one time as to take the money for a recruit but the
sergant was a better man then such usually are and said he took no
advantage of a man in liquor for I was fresh at the time and let me off
with paying the expences of the drink – but I was wanting in height
which might be a better plea then the sergants honesty   [A32, 5]

in the midst of this dilemma a bookseller name Thompson sent in a
bill for 15 shillings which he desird I woud pay him as he was going to
leave the place   I was very willing to pay him but I was not able so I
wrote a few lines to tell him the situation I was in sending at the same
time a few prospectuses and wishing he woud do somthing to assist
me while I promisd to pay the debt as soon as ever I was able which I
hopd to be ere long   I got my companion T Porter of Ashton to take
the letter but he treated all with contempt and abusd him   the debt
was ran for some numbers of the boston enquirer which I never
finishd – Ned Drury had enterd on the shop then and on seeing one of
the prospectuse[s] he took it as a matter of profit and paid the 15
shillings for me before he enquird further   this matter he has
translated into a lye in the Introduction which has another lye in it
not of his insertion as he says and that is of my selling the poems for
26 Pounds   I never sold them at all is the fact of the matter   I once
signd an agreement of Drurys which alowd me a quarters profit   I
was fresh at the time but it got wind and others heard of it that knew
better then I did who calld it a villanous trick so he sent it up to

London to be destroyd as they say   I know nothing   this I know
that I have never signd an agreement of any kind since and never will
    when my friend Porter told me of his success I was in a tetherd
perplexity and knew not what to do but Ned Drury with his friend R
Newcomb publisher of the Stamford Mercury they calld at a farmers
of the name of Clerk to dine and enquire into my character and
merits as a poet   the former was open to every meddler but the latter
was a secret so they came to enquire more about it with me   I was
at a neighbours house at Billings the bachelors hall when they came
and my sister ran for me and on telling me two gentlemen wanted to
see me I felt hopful and timidly went home when I found them talking
to my parents   Drury said little or nothing but Newcomb asked
some questions as to how my writings was disposd of and when I told
him that I had made proposal to henson to print them he said they did
not wish to take them out of his hands but that instead of desiring
money to print them they woud let me have money for my nessesitys
so I thought the difference of advantage a good one and readily
engagd to get my MSS from Hensons   Mr Newcomb invited me to
dine with him on the monday as he prepard to start but cautiously
opend the door again to remind me that unless I brought the MSS I
need not come   I felt insulted with his kindness and never accepted
the invitation   [A32, 16, 18]

tho I took some of them the next day when Drury lookd over them
and gave me a guinea as a sort of earnest I suspect and promisd to pay
my debts   I remaind with him the whole day and he gave me a poem
in my hands to read of Lord Byrons   I think it was the G[i]a[o]ur
and the first time I had ever seen any of them   I promisd to take him
more of my poems when I got them from Hensons (he making it a
matter of speculation and trying to be sure of his bargain before he
enterd too far in it   so far he was right) so I wrote to him and sent it
by my mother to deliver up my poems as [he] had broken the
engagments by wishing me to borrow £15   I told him that this was
an impossib[ili]ty all along and mentiond my better prospects in the
new engagment I had made with Mr Drury   he gave them up with
some reluctance and I took them to Drury   [he] showd them to the
Revd Mr Towpenny of Little Casterton who sent them back with a
cold note stating that he had no objection to assist in raising the poor
man a small subscription tho the poems appeard to him to posses no
merit to be worthy of publication   Drury read this presious thing to

me and as I fancyd all men in a station superior to me as learned and wise especialy parsons I felt my fortune as lost and my hopes gone and tho he tryd to cheer me I felt degected a long time and almost carried it too far   after 'prosperity shone out upon me' I rememberd it keenly and wrote the following lines on his name and a letter which I never sent

Towpenny his wisdom is and towpenny his fame is
Towpenny his merit is and towpenny his name is
And as twopence is a trifle I well may do without him
Ill sing in spite of twopenny and not care towpence about him

Soon after Twopenny sent his note Drury showd them again to Sir English Dobbin[42] who expressd a different opinion and left his name as a subscriber   this heartend me again and I ryhmd on and became pacified   in this winter I finis[h]d all the fragments that I thought worth it for most of what I had done hitherto was unfinishd

the earliest of such were Helpstone which I had intended for a long poem in the manner of Goldsmith and the fate of amy Address to a Lark*   the address to a Lark was made one cold winters morning on returning home from raking stubble as the ground was so froze that I coud not work   I frit the lark up while raking and it began to sing which suggested the poem that was written in a mellancholy feeling – the Lost Greyhound was made while going and returning from Ashton one winters day

the fate of Amy was begun when I was a boy   I usd to be very fond of hearing my friend J O Sim read the ballad of Edwin and Emma[43] in weeding time and as Ameys story was popular in the village I thought it might make a poem so tryd it and imitated the other as far as the ideas of it floated on my memory

Evening was alterd from a very early one of a great length made one evening after I had been cowtending on the common . . . Noon which I wrote very early and composd on a hot day in summer while I went to fill my fathers bottle with water at round oak spring and Evening etc and the sonnets to the Setting Sun the Primrose the

---

* The subsequent passage from 'the address to a Lark' down to 'on the common' also appears at A32, 7 but it is there followed by:

some of the sonnets a short poem or two are early   the rest was written at later periods and most of them while at Casterton   the one on the Fountain was written one sunday evening while sitting bye a brook in Casterton cowpasture with patty

Gipseys evening blaze and a Scene etc   these were begun when I was 14 or 15 and finishd and in some cases alterd throughout   I began to write Sonnets at first from seeing two very pretty ones in an old news paper   I think they were by charlotte Smith[44]   the rest in the first vol was written the next summer and winter while the book was going thro the press or at the latter end

Crazy Nell was taken from a narative in the Stamford Mercury nearly in the same manner it was related   I was very pleasd with it and thought it one of the best I had written and I think so still   the next spring my master Wilders sent for me to work in the Garden and I started when I renewd my acquantance with Patty which had rather broken off   I usd to seize the leiseur that every wet day brought me to go to Drurys shop to read books and to get new tunes for my fiddle which was a pleasure of a pastime   when ever I wrote a new thing I usd to take it to Drury very often on Sunday morning to breakfast with him and in one of these visits I got acquanted with Dr Bell[45] a man of odd taste but a pleasant acquantance   he was fond of books and had edited a droll one Entitld the banisher of the blue devils a jest book   he usd to cut out all the curious and odd paragraphs out of the news papers and paste them on sheets of paste board he had a great many of these things which [he] had collected for many years   he had been a docter in the army and in the east or west Indias [and] became acquainted with Peter Pindar then in the same capacity some of whose early poems he possesd which had never been publishd   he wrote to earl Spencer respecting me and succeeded in getting me a salary of £20 per Annum —   I was full of hopes at my present success but my money matters were still precarious for Drury objected at times to paying all my bills tho he did it afterwards   my mistress wishd to see some of my pieces and usd to be anxious to introduce me to strangers whom she would talk too about me and who woud express a curosity to see me but I usd to get out of the way when I coud   one of these who stopd there a day or two saw some of them and said that the poem of evening was an imitation of somthing which has slipt my memory now   I thought the man shoud say somthing if he knew nothing and seeing we displayd but a bookeless appearnace he hazarded his make shift for learning as heedless as he pleasd   I know nothing of who or what he was — Drury told me now that my poems was crownd with the utmost success I coud wish for as they were in the hands and met the favourable opinion of a gentleman who coud and woud do them justice but he woud not tell me his name and a painter of profiles was in the town whom he engagd to take my likness   these things were trifle[s] to remember but they were great at their beginings   they made me all life and spirits and nothing but hopes and prosperity was before me – (Pattys friends who rather lookd coldly on my acquainter with her and who seemd to take my [attentions] as more of intrusions then visits now began to be anxious after my [welfare] and courted my acquaintance while I on the contrary felt their former slights and now I felt my self on advantage ground I determind to take my revenge and neglected to go or but slightly heeded their urgent invitations and while I was at home in the winter I renewd my acquaintance with a former love and had made a foolish confidence with a young girl at Southorpe[46] and tho it began in a heedless flirtation at Stamford fair from accompanying her home it grew up in to an affection that made my heart ach to think it must be broken for patty was then in a situation that marriage coud only remedy   I felt awkardly situated and knew not which way to proceed   I had a variety of minds about me and all of them unsettld   my long smotherd affections for Mary revivd with my hopes and as I expected to be on a level with her bye and bye I thought then I might have a chance of success in renewing my former affections   amid these delays pattys emergencys became urgent   she had reveald her situation to her parents when she was unable to conseal it any longer who upbraided her with not heeding thier advice and told her as she had made her bed hard she shoud lye on it for on my first arrival at Casterton a young shoemaker paid his address to her whose visits were approvd off more by her parents then her self and when I had disinherited him of his affections they encouragd him to come on and tryd and urgd to win her mind over to his and their wishes   when I reflected on these things I felt stubbornly disposd to leave them the risk of her misfortunes but when she complaind of their coldness towards her I coud stand out no longer and promisd that my prosper[i]ty shoud make me her friend and to prove that I was in earnest I gave her money to [bolster her] independance till we shoud be married   this behaviour pacified them and left her at peace – they were poor tho they had known better days and fancyd that the memory of these things aught to be accou[n]ted for and make them above the level in the vulgar occupations of life like my profession   their friends too still enjoyd prosperity and woud fancy it a stain to [unite] their family with a lime burner   such was the tide that bore strongly against us on our first acquaintance but when my book was publishd the wind changd and all were on my side courting my acquaintance and things will fall in their season wether they are wanted and expected or not   Autum seldom passes away without its tempest and friendship began upon speculation and self interest is sure to meet with a shock as chances and changes fall out   the man that built his house upon the sand was run down by the tide – my friendship is worn out and my memorys are broken

I held out as long as I coud and then married her at Casterton church   her uncle John Turner was father and gave her the wedding dinner

I workd on at the New Inn till the winter and then returnd home on a disagreement in the wages as he promisd me nine shillings a week the year round and then wanted to put me off with seven   he was an odd man but a good Master and the place on the whole was one of the best I ever met with   I left it with regret and rather wishd to return as I liked the town and the fields and solitudes were wild and far better then the fenny flats etc that I had been usd to but circumstances fell out to prevent me

I left Casterton on the Bullruning day at Stamford and on calling on Drury I fell in with John Taylor whom I found was the Editor of my poems then in the press and nearly ready for publishing   he was visiting at Mr Gilchrists and in the evening they sent one of the servant maids to Drurys to invite me to go   I felt loath but on his persuasion I started and he showd me the door and felt very irksome while I stayd   Mr Gilchrist read an account of Woodcroft Castle from Woods Historys[47] and Taylor talkd over some sayings and doings of the living authors   I stopt a short time and when I got back to Drurys I wrote some ryhmes which was publishd in the first [volume]   [A32, 18–22]

most of the Poems which I destroyed* were descriptive of Local Spots about the Lordship and favourite trees and wild flowers   one of these 'On the Violet' was inserted by Taylor in the Village Minstrel and the 'Walk to Burghley Park' is of the same date   There was another on 'Round Oak Spring' as good as either of these which has not been published†   Chauncy Hare Townsend[48] saw the Book in

* This passage amplifies a statement in *Sketches in the Life of John Clare* (see p. 12 before).

† The poem is printed here immediately after this passage.

Drurys possesion and told me he was particularly pleased with this poem which made me think more of them afterwards then I had done
the encouragment my first Volume met with lifted me up into heartsome feelings and ryhming was continually with me night and day   I began the Village Minstrel a long while before attempting to describe my own feelings and love for rural objects and I then began in good earnest with it after the trial of my first poems was made and compleated   it was little time but I was still unsatisfied with it and am now and often feel sorry that I did not withold it a little longer for revision   the reason why I dislike it is that it does not describe the feelings of a ryhming peasant strongly or localy enough   I began a second part to effect this and got a good way in it and sent Taylor a specimen but he said nothing in return either for it or against it and as I found the verses multiplied very fast and my intended correction of localitys growing very slow I left off and destroyd a good part of it
the rest remains as they were – all the poems in the Village Minstrel save the early ones above mentioned were written after the publication of the first Vol and a many more unpublished yet   most of the Poems now written were written in the three years preceding the first publication   I have written nothing since I was taken ill march was a twelvemonth in ryhme   I had many ryhming projects in my head and often felt anxious to write a dramatic Poem but perhaps the prevention by illness has been the means of saving the fame I have gotten as they might have been by a failure in such matters have forfieted all   [B6, 81R]

The Lamentations of Round Oak Waters
Oppress'd wi' grief a double share
Where round oak waters flow
I one day took a sitting there
    Recounting many a woe
My naked seat without a shade
    Did cold and blealy shine
Which fate was more agreeable made
    As sympathysing mine

The wind between the North and East
    Blew very chill and cold
Or coldly blew to me at least
    My clothes were thin and old

The grass all dropping wet wi dew
   Low bent their tiney spears
The lowly daisy bended too
   More lowly wi mi tears

(For when my wretched state appears
   Hurt friendless poor and starv'd
I never can withold my tears
   To think how I am sarv'd
To think how many'd men delight
   More cutting than the storm
To make a sport and prove their might
   O' me a fellow worm)

With arm reclin'd upon my knee
   In melancholy form
I bow'd my head to misery
   And yielded to the storm
And there I fancied uncontrould
   My sorrows as they flew
Unnotic'd as the waters roll'd
   Were all unnotic'd too

But soon I found I was deceived
   For waken'd by my woes
The naked stream of shade bereaved
   In grevious murmurs rose

'Ah luckless youth to sorrow born
   Shun'd son of poverty
The worlds made gamely sport and scorn
   And grinning infamy
Unequall'd tho thy sorrows seem
   And great indeed they be
O hear my sorrows for my stream
   You'll find an equal there

'I am the Genius of the brook
   And like to thee I moan
By Naids and by all forsook
   Unheeded and alone

Distress and sorrow quickly proves
   The friend sincere and true
Soon as our happiness removes
   Pretenders bid adieu

'Here I have been for many a year
   And how my brook has been
How pleasures lately flourish'd here
   Thyself hast often seen
The Willows waving wi the wind
   And here and there a thorn
Did please thy melancholy mind
   And did my banks adorn

'And here the shepherd with his sheep
   And with his lovely maid
Together where these waters creep
   In loitering dalliance playd
And here the Cowboy lov'd to sit
   And plat his rushy thongs
And dabble in the fancied pit
   And chase the Minnow throngs

'And when thou didst the horses tend
   Or drive the ploughmans team
Thy mind did naturally bend
   Towards my pleasing stream
And different pleasures fill'd thy breast
   And different thy employ
And different feelings thou possessd
   From any other boy

'The sports which they so dearly lov'd
   Thou couldsnt bear to see
And joys which they as joys approvd
   Neer seem'd as joys to thee
The joy was thine could thou but steal
   From all their gambols rude
In some lone thicket to conceal
   Thyself in Solitude

'There didst thou joy and love to sit
   The briars and brakes among
To exercise thy infant wit
   In fancied tale or song
And there the insect and the flower
   Would court thy curious eye
To muse in wonder on that power
   Which dwells above the sky

'But now alas my charms are done
   For shepherds and for thee
The cowboy with his green is gone
   And every bush and tree
Dire nakedness o'er all prevails
   Yon fallows bare and brown
Is all beset wi' post and rails
   And turned upside down

'The gently curving darksome bawks
   That stript the cowfields o'er
And prov'd the shepherds daily walk
   Now prove his walks no more
The plough has had them under hand
   And over turn'd them all
And now along the elting land
   Poor swains are forc'd to maul

'And where yon furlong meets the lawn
   To ploughmen Oh! how sweet
When they had their long furrow drawn
   Its Edlings to their feet
To rest 'em while they clean'd their plough
   And light the loaded shoe
But ah there's ne'er an edding now
   For neither them nor yow

'The baulks and eddings are no more
   The pastures too are gone
The greens the meadows and the moors
   Are all cut up and done

Theres scarce a greensward spot remains
    And scarce a single tree
All naked are thy native plains
    And yet they're dear to thee

'But O my brook my injur'd brook
    'Tis that I most deplore
To think how once it us'd to look
    How it must look no more
And haply fate thy wanderings bent
    To sorrow here wi' me
For to none else could I lament
    And mourn to none but thee

'Thou art the whole of musing swains
    That's now residing here
Thou one ere while did grace my plains
    And he to thee was dear
Ah – dear he was – for now I see
    His name grieves thee at heart
Thy silence speaks that misery
    Which language cant impart

'O T—L T—L* dear should thou
    To this fond mourner be
By being so much troubled now
    From just a naming thee
Nay I as well as he am griev'd
    For oh I hop'd of thee
That hadst thou stay'd as I believ'd
    Thou wouldst have griev'd for me

'But ah he's gone the first o' swains
    And left us both to moan
And though art all that now remains
    With feelings like his own
So while the thoughless passes by
    Of sence and feelings void
Thine by the Fancy painting eye
    On by-gone scenes employ'd

    * 'Turnill, Turnill' – Clare's boyhood friend.

'Look backward on the days of yore
    Upon my injur'd brook
In fancy con its beauties o'er
    How it had us'd to look
O then what trees my banks did crown
    What willows flourish'd here
Hard as the axe that cut them down
    The senceless wretches were

'But sweating slaves I do not blame
    Those slaves by wealth decreed
No I should hurt their harmless name
    To brand 'em 'wi the deed
Altho their aching hands did wield
    The axe that gave the blow
Yet 'twas not them that own'd the field
    Nor plan'd its overthrow

'No no the foes that hurt my field
    Hurts these poor moilers too
And thy own bosom knows and feels
    Enough to prove it true
And o poor souls they may complain
    But their complainings all
The injur'd worms that turn again
    But turn again to fall

'Their foes and mine are lawless foes
    And l—ws them s—s* they hold
Which clipt wingd justice cant oppose
    But forced yields to g—d†
These are the f—s‡ of mine and me
    These all our ruin plan'd
All tho they never fell'd a tree
    Or took a tool in hand

---

* 'laws them selves'. Clare is even afraid to name the law.
† 'gold'
‡ 'foes'

'Ah cruel foes with plenty blest
    So ankering after more
To lay the greens and pastures waste
    Which profited before
Poor greedy – souls – what would they have
    Beyond their plenty given
Will riches keep 'em from the grave
    Or buy them rest in heaven?'

Old favourite tree art thou too fled the scene
    Could not the axe thy 'clining age delay
And let thee stretch thy shadows o'er the green
    And let thee die in picturesque decay
What hadst thou done to meet a tyrants frown
    Be drag'd a captive from thy native wood
What was the cause the rage that hew'd thee down
    Small value was the ground as which thou stood
So sweet in summer as thy branches spread
    In such gay cloathing as thy boughs were drest
Where many a shepperd swain has laid his head
    And thy cooling fragrance sunk to rest

Adieu old friends ye trees and bushes dear
    The flower refresh'd with morning dews
Hopeful blooms in azure skies
    Under the noontide heat ensures
It hopeless withers droops and dies
    O cruel change of love like mine
To bid me hope one only day
    And ere that worst of days decline
To snatch that only hope away.

[N4, 159–71]

A pro[p]het is nothing in his own country

Envy was up at my success with all the lyes it coud muster
some said that I never wrote the poems and that Drury gave money
to father them with my name   others said that I had stole them out
of books and that parson this and Squire tother knew the books from
which they were stolen   pretending scholars said that I had never

112

been to a grammer school and there fore it was impossible for me to write any thing and our parson[49] industriously found out the wonderful discovery that I coud not spell and of course his opinion was busily distributed in all companys which he visited that I was but a middling success of a poet but his opinion got its knuckles rapt – and then he excusd the mistake by saying he did not read poetry and consequently knew little about it   there he was right – one sunday the same prophet caught me working a common problem in geo- metry with the scale and compasses in which I was fond to dabble and after expressing his supprise at my meddlings in such matters he said we do these things different at colledge   we make a circle without compasses and work a problem without a scale – the solution of this problem was somthing like a round lye – an old leistershire farmer and his family in a neighboring vill[a]ge was uncommonly against me   they declard it was impossible for me to do anything and dis believd every thing but that which was against me – thus every kind loves its own color and on that principal the Indian believes the devil a white sprit and the europea[n]s a black one – the old man had a lubberly son whom he fancied to make a learned one by sending him to school till he was a man and his ten years wisdom consisted of finding that 2 and 2 makes 4 that a circle was round and a triangle had 3 corners and that poetry was nothing in comparison to such knowledge   the old men believd it and though[t] like wise   [B7, 90]

The Critics speaks their guesses or opinions with such an authourity of certainty as tho they were the fountain of truth   some of them said I had imitated the old poets Raleigh Drumond etc and several of them complaind at my too frequent imitations of Burns   now the fact is that when my first poems was written I knew nothing of Burns not even by name for the fens are not a literary part of england   nay my ignorance was not only a wide guess from all these but they had no existance with me – and I knew nothing of Drummond etc further then the name even now   I had an odd volume of Ramsey a long while and if I imitated any it should be him to which I am ready to acknowledge a great deal   [B3, 81]

I have been accused of being a drunkard and of being ingratful towards my friends and Patrons by a set of meddling trumpery to whom I owe none who never gave me furether notice then their scandal which is too weak or foolish for me either to notice or replye to   they are a set of little curs without teeth whose barkings can do no harm and whose busy meddling rather serves to create laughter then anger   the utmost breath of their satire tho blown up to bursting has not sufficient strength to bear up a soap bubble so let them rail   most of them have known me from childhood and coud never find that I had any faults till now – I possesd their good word for 18 years and it did me no service – and if I shoud live to wear their bad one as long it will do me no harm so I care nothing about them tho their meddlings get the ears of some that believe them – I have felt all the kindness I have received tho I did not mak[e] a parade of it   I did not write eternal prases and I had a timidity that made me very awkard and silent in the presence of my superiors which gave me a great deal of trouble and hurt my feelings   I wishd to thank them and tell them that I felt their kindness and remained silent   neither did I trumpet the praises of patrons eteranly werever I went – I had found that great talkers were always reckond little liars and that eternal praisers in public were alowd to be whisperers of slander in secret so I thought that if I was always speaking of myself and patrons among such company I shoud be suspected and reckond as one of them – I was never utterly cast down in adversity   I st[r]uggled on   neither was I at any time lifted up above my prosperity   I never attempted to alter my old ways and manners   I assumed no proud notions nor felt a pride above my station   I was courted to keep company with 'the betters' in the village but I never noticed the fancied kindness   the old friends and neighbours in my youth are my friends and neighbours now and I have never spent an hour in any of the houses of the farmers since I met with my [success] or mixd in their company as equals   I visit none but an old neighbours with whom I was acquainted in my days of labour and [hardship]   I keep on in the same house that we always occupied   I have never felt a desire to have a better – tho it has grown into a great inconvenience since my father first occupied it 35 years ago   it was as roomy and confortable as any of our neighbours and we had it for 40 shillings rent while an old apple tree in the garden generaly made the rent   the garden was large for a poor man and my father man[a]ged to dig it night and morning before and after the hours of labour and lost no time   he then did well – but the young farmer that succeeded our old Landlord raised the rent and the next year made four tennements of the house leaving us a corner of one room on a floor for 3 Guineas a year and a little slip of the garden which was divided into 4 parts but as my father had been an old tennant he gave him the choice of his share as he retaind our old apple tree   tho the ground was good for nothing yet the tree still befrended us and made shift to make up the greater part of our rent till every misfortune as it were came upon him to crush him at once for as soon as hee was disabled from work the old tree faild to bear fruit and left us unable to get up the rent and when Drury found me out we owd for 2 years and was going to leave it the next year   my father was going to a parish house and I was at Casterton in service were I intended to remain and when I met with unexpected prosperity I never felt a more satisfied happiness then being able to keep on the old house and to put up with all its unconven[i]enc[e]s and when I was married the next door occupier happend to leave his tenement so I took it and remaind on – I have often been urged and advised to leave it and get a more roomey and better looking house by visitors who gave me no better encouragement then their words and whom I did not expect woud be of any service to me in case their advice happend to lead me into greater inconvenences in the end so I took no notice of them and lived on in the same house and in the same way as I had always done following my old occupations and keeping my old neighbours as friends without being troubled or dissapoi[n]ted with climbing ambitions that shine as fine as they may only tempt the restless mind to climb so that he may be made dizzy with a mockery of splendor and topple down headlong into a lower degradation then he left behind him –

and as soon as he went to the parish for relief they came to clap the town brand on his goods and set them down in their parish books because he shoud not sell or get out of them   I felt utterly cast down for I coud not help them sufficient to keep them from the parish so I left the town and got work at Casterton with Gordon   I felt some consolement in solitude from my distress by letting loose my revenge on the unfeeling town officer in a Satire on the 'Parish' which I forbore to publish after words as I thought it [   ]

and they remaind quiet spectators of my success and ceased to meddle with my father when I did not care for their kindness [nor] fear for the[ir] resentment   [B3, 85–6]

In the beginning of January my poems was publishd after a long waiting anxiety of nearly two years and all the reviews excepting

Philips waste paper Mag: spoke in my favour   in the course of the publication I had venturd to write to Lord Milton to request leave that the vol might be dedicated to him but his Lordship was starting into Italy and forgot to answer it so it was dedicated to nobody which perhaps might be as well   as soon as it was out my mother took one to Milton when his Lordship sent a note to tell me to bring 10 more copys on the following sunday   I went and after sitting awhile in servants hall were I coud eat and drink nothing for thought his Lordship sent for me and instantly expland the reasons why he did not answer my letter in a quiet unaffected manner which set me at rest   he told me he had heard of my poems by parson Mossop who I have since heard took hold of every oppertunity to speak against my success or poetical abilitys before the book was publishd and then when it came out and others praisd it instantly turnd round to my side   Lady Milton also askd me several questions and wishd me to name any book that was a favourite expressing at the same time a desire to give me one but I was confou[n]ded and coud think of nothing so I lost the present   in fact I did not like to pick out a book for fear of seaming overeaching on her kindness or else Shakespear lay at my tongues end   Lord fitzwilliam and lady fitzwilliam too talkd to me and noticd me kindly and his Lordship gave me some advice which I had done well perhaps to have noticed better then I have   he bade me beware of booksellers and warnd me not to be fed with promises – on my departure they gave me an handfull of money the most that I had ever possesd in my life together   I almost felt that I shoud be poor no more   there was seventeen pound

Af[ter]wards I was visited by the Hon^{bl} Mr Pierpoint^{50} with an invitation to go to burghly on the sunday but when sunday came it began to snow too unmercifully for a traveller even to ventur thus far so I coud not go till the monday tho it was not the weather that prevented me   I felt fearful that my shoes woud be in a dirty condition for so fine a place   when I got there the porter askd me the reason why I did not come before and when I spoke of the weather he said 'they expected you and you shoud stand for no weathers tho it rained knives and forks with the tynes downward   we have been suspected of sending you away'   this was a lesson that I afterwards took care to remember   after awhile his Lordship sent for me and went upstairs and thro winding passages after the footmen as fast as I coud hobble almost fit to quarrel with my hard naild shoes at the noise they made on the marble and boarded floors and cursing them

to myself as I set my feet down in the lightest steps I was able to utter
his Lordship recieved me kindly askd me some questions and
requested to look at the MSS which Mr Pierpont wishd me to bring in
my pocket   after I had been about half an hour eyeing the door now
and then looking at my dirty shoes and wishing myself out of the
danger of soiling such grandeur he saw my embarassments as I
suspect and said that I sho[u]ld loose my dinner in the servants hall
and said I had better go but it was no use starting for I was lost and
coud not stir a foot   I told his Lordship and he kindly opend the
door and showd me the way when he sudde[n]ly made a stop in one
of the long passages and told me that he had no room in his gardens
for work at present but that he woud alow me 15 gineas a year for life
which woud enabale me to pursue my favourite studys at least two
days in a week (this bye the bye was far better)   I was astonishd and
coud hardly believe that he had said it   he then calld a servant and I
went off scarcly feeling the ground   I went on and almost fanc[y]ing
myself as rich a man as his Lordship   that night I calld at
O Gilchrists and he scarcly belie[v]d it and I thought I was mistaken
[A55, 7; A32, 1]

good luck began to smile from all quarters and my successes made me
almost beside myself   Lord Radstock wrote to me with the most
feeling affections and has acted to me more of a father then a friend
Blairs Sermons[51] accompanied the letter and Mrs Emmerson[52] about
the same time wrote with kind encouragments and accompanied it
with a Youngs Night thoughts but the first letter I ever recievd was
from a disguisd Name A.B. supposd to be Dawson Turner of
Yarmouth seasond with good advice which I did not heed as I ought
and Captain Sherwell[53] wrote to me early and kindly   it was thro his
friendship that I recievd the present from Walter Scott of 2 Guineas
and the Lady of the Lake which was wrongly and sadly mistated in
the gossip that appeard in the London Mag: intitld a Visit etc   I felt
disapointed when I heard it was a present from the author but I said
nothing   C.S. made an apology for the omission by saying that
Walter Scott enjoyd such a high literary character that he did not
wish to hazerd an opin[i]on or insert his name in the Vol   I cannot
exactly say what the words were without refering to the letter but a
little slip of paper was inserted in the vol by CS stating that Walter
Scott presented the Lady of the Lake to John Clare with the modest
hope that he woud read it with attention   it was a foolish modesty

at best – I told a friend of mine about the matter [and he] laughd and said* that he rememberd the time when the author of the lady of the lake hazarded his reputation in a matter by courting the favour of the critics in stating that his livelihood consisted in his writings   wether this be true or false it rests in my mistake for Octave Gilchrist was the man that told me and I believe him –   [A32, 1–2; B3, 75]

[Visitors and Visits]

I was now wearing into the sunshine and the villagers that saw caraiages now and then come to the house filld with gossiping gentry that was tempted by curosity more then any thing else to seek me from these I got invitations to corespond and was swarmd with promises of books till my mother was troubld and fancied that the house woud not hold them but the trouble was soon set aside for the books never came and one letter generally worded with extravagant praise courting a quick reply I replied warmly and there the matter ended   I had nothing but my dissapointment in return but I soon felt expierenc[e] growing over these deceptions and when such matters was palmd on me again I never answerd them   I had two or three of these things nay more from parsons – amid these successes I went to work as usual but was often tormented and sent for home to satisfye the gaze of strangers – Lord Radstock started a subscription that filld me with astonishment at his account of its success   Taylor and Hessey inserted a hundred pounds in there names at the top of the List and the good Lord Fitzwilliams gave me a hundred pounds from a letter which Taylor sent who took the [opportunity] to kill two birds with one stone and mentiond Keats in his letter to whom his Lordship gave 50 pound and a short time after a tirade [was published in the] London Magazine   [A32, 2–3]

the first publication of my poems brought many visitors to my house out of a mere curiosity to expect to know wether I realy was the son of a thresher and a laboring rustic as had been stated and when the[y] found it realy was so they lookd at each other as a matter of satisfied supprise askd some gossiping questions and on finding me a vulgar fellow that mimicd at no pretentions but spoke in the rough ways of a th[o]rough bred clown they soon turnd to the door and dropping their heads in a good morning attitude they departed – I was often

* Insertion from a slip of paper attached to B3, 75 but formerly part of A32, 2.

annoyd by such visits and got out of the way when ever I coud and my wife and mother was often out of temper about it as they was often caught with a dirty house then which nothing was a greater annoyance   [B7, 93]

some of them askd me if I kept a book to insert the names of visitors and on my answering in the negative they woud often request to insert them on my paper and many of them left promises which they never performd so I soon learnd that promises was a good seed time but pefromances brought a bad harvest forgetfulness coming in between the pharoahs lean kine and swallowing them up*   I had the works of Lord Byron promisd by 6 different people and never got them from none of them   [B7, 93]

Among the many that came to see me was a dandified gentleman of uncommon odditys of character that not only borderd on the ridicilous but was absully† smotherd in it   he made pretentions to great learning and knew nothing   on his first coming he began in a very dignified manner to examine the fruits of experience in books and said he hoped I had a fondness for reading as he wished to have the pleasure to make me a present of some   he then begd my walking stick and after he had got it he wanted me to write my name on the crook   I really thought the fellow was mad   he then asked me some insulting libertys respecting my first acquaintance with Patty and said he understood that in this country the lower orders made their courtship in barns and pig styes and asked wether I did   I felt very vext and said that it might be the custom of high orders for aught I knew as experience made fools wise in most matters but I assured him he was wrong respecting that custom among the lower orders here   his wife said he was fond of a joke and hoped I shoud not be offended but I saw nought of a joke in it and found afterwards that he was but a scant remove from the low order himself as his wife was a grocers daughter   after he had gossiped an hour he said well I promised to give you a book   but after examining your library I dont see that you want any thing as you have a great many more then I expected to find   still I shoud make you an offer of somthing

* At B7, 90 Clare has the couplet:
    a lean mouthd fellow whose dead visage seems
    Akin to pharoahs hunger hanted dreams
† Clare presumably intended to write 'absurdly' or 'absolutely'.

have you got a Bible   I said nothing but it was exactly what my Father had long wanted and he instantly spoke for me and said we have a bible sir but I cannot read it the print is so small so I shoud thank you for one   the man lookd very confused and explaind by his manner that he had mentiond the very book which he thought we had to escape giving it   [A33, 1]

[*Preston*]

his name was Preston[54] and he made me believe that he was a very great Poet and that he knew all the world and that almost all the world knew him   he had a vast quantity of M.S.S. he said by him but had not published much at present tho he had two rather important works in the press at that time whose publication he anxiously awaited and on pressing him hard about their size and contents he said that one was an Elegy on the death of the Queen and some anecdotes that he had pickt up in India which the religious tract society was printeing for him   he said he thought that the first would be about 9^d and the other 3^d price but his grand work for he calld it so himself was yet to be tried   it was 'The Triumph of Faith'   he had met with one patron at Cambridge by accident as it were who admird a hymn which had been sung and enquiring after the Author Mr Preston presented himself and the person invited him to sup with him were he heard his himny again sung to the Pianaforte with excessive gratification as him self expressd it – he had been a sailor and pretended to be familiarly acquainted with Ireland the Shakespear Phantom[55] whom he described as a great and unfortunate Genius – he was for ever quoting beautys from his own poetry and he knew all the living poets in England and Scotland as familiar as his own tongue – he was a living hoax – he had made two or three visits to Bloomfield and talkd of him as familiar as if he had been his neighbour half a life time   he calld him 'brother bob'
            he was one who was very fond of asking questions and answering them him self by guesses before those whom he was talking had time to replye   'how large will your new book be – say about 5 shillings   who is your first Patron   shall we say Lord Radstock
            how many are printed at an edition   we'll say a thousand eh' and these he woud utter and reply too in one breath without a break or hesitation to wait your reply or to know the correctness of his guesses and between the intervals of his discourse he woud repeat some lines

from Byron in mouthing drawl somthing like the growl of a mastiff – he askd me wether I was a good reader of poetry and on my saying that I was not he woud say come to London sir by all means 'come to London' we have sporting clubs Lectures and all manner of [exercises] to make you a perfect reader and reciter of poetry – he knew all the Painters and Royal Academicians and coud critis[iz]e their various excellences and defects with great dexterity of tongue he praised Hilton[56] and two or three others as the tops of the tree while a stood abusing a sketch of my head that hung by the wall and finding a thousand faults with it   I let him go on and then told him it was done by Hilton   he turnd himself round on his heel blamed his eyesight and discoverd nothing but beautys afterward

with 'well friend John you must give me so and so' he utterd a prayer expounded a chapter in the bible sung a hymn told a smutty story and repeated one of Mores Songs in quick succession   I felt quite wearied with his officious company for I had him the whole day and some months after he wrote me word that urgent busness had brought him to Peterbro and that if I wanted to see him I shoud write a welcome to tell him so   I thought this was an easy oppertunity to let silence inform him he was not welcome so I never wrote and he never came   [A33, 8; A18, 275]

Another impertinent fellow of the Name of Ryde[57] who occupys a situation which proves the old Farmers assertion that the vilest weeds are always found in the richest soil   [A18, 269]

Hopkinson

Mr Hopkinson[58] of Morton the magistrate sent an odd sort of invitation for he was an odd sort of man   he sent a note saying that a horse woud be at my door at helpstone on such a morning at such a time of the clock leaving me no option wether I chused to go or not it was harvest and I was busy reaping wheat   I told the man I was reaping for about the matter and he said I had better go so accoudringly the poney came and I started   the day after I got in his wife took me round the town to walk as she told me but I found it was to sho me to her parishioners   I felt very much anoyd at the awkard situation it led me in for I found they did not want to be troubled either with one or the other   her impertinent enquireys were often evaded with a carless indifference and a pretending business at their

domestic labours   they woud scarcley wait to hear her speak ere the weel was started into a quicker twirl or the pots and pans scoured with a more bustleing hand   she was going to take me regularey round from door to door but I was obliged to tell her that I was not fond of such visitings so she desisted but not without seeming to be offended – she was one of the oddest and most teasing ca[r]ds in her fancied kindness that I ever met with – as soon as I got in she took me up stairs to show me a writing desk which she told [me] to consider as my own and showd me at the same time all the draws and their contents of Paper Pens ink sealing wax sticks saying that she expected I shoud make use of it and hoped I woud write somthing every day as she woud find me plenty of paper but when the up shoot came and after I had exhausted my whole budget of thanks and compliments for the present she begd to caution me that I shoud not take it away that it was mine every time I came and as long as I staid but she coud not part with it out of the house as it was an old favourite – she proposed reading my poems over leaf by leaf to give her opinions of them and make observations etc etc for my benefit and advantage to correct in a second edition and she began with the introduction   she read a few lines and then preached over an half hours comment   she said the introduction was very well written but I must now think of improving it as I had met with many friends whom it woud be very rude of me not to mention as they certainly woud look for some compliment from me for the notice they had taken and she thought that I coud do it better in ryhme   when she got to the poems she woud remark this is a pretty poem but why did you not dedicate it some one of your friends as you did the woodman
    she read in a loud confident voice like the head boy in a school who is reckond a good reader and whos consiet thinks he is so g[ood] and tho she met with words frequently in reading other books that she did not understand she woud jar them over with an unmeaning mutter as if she thought you woud take no notice or did not understand it – she woud often lift up her eye from her book to see if I was attentive and on finding my attention occupied with other things she gave up the critisismes after commenting on a few pages   she appeard to be a woman of very little understanding and less learning to help it out – there were two daughters that were well read in books and of quiet and amiable disposition but they had quarreld with her and did not come down stairs while I stayd – the man was one of odd taste and habits and I found that tho a magistrate he woud tell lies –

he had written a book with a design of instructing his parishoners in a pompous and long winded style   he never wishd to be seen ignorant of any[thing] not even in the gossip or news of the village – he woud not bear contradicting and therefore was well quallified for a country magistrate   if you told any thing at dinner as an interesting story or fact of any kind it woud not seem to move his attention to listen a moment but the next day he woud repeat your story word for word as his own and tell it to you with as much gravity as if you had been a stranger to it and never heard it before

He askd me some pointless questions about my patrons in a carless manner as if he did not need enquireys when one day or two after wards he woud talk about them as if he had been a familiar acquaintance and knew much more about them then I did nay he woud tell me about them as if I knew nothing   he askd about the way in which Lord Milton and Exeter behaved and after I had told him he said he woud mention me to them as if they had never known or noticed me – he said he was acquainted with Lord Waldgrave and showd me a vol of my poems which he said Lady Waldgrave had given him – he took me with him to see Falkingham joal a good distance from Morton and everyone we met gentle or simple he woud stop to speak too and almost ask their business nay he woud question those that appeard his inferiors as if they were under going an examination in a court of justice – once when we were going to see Belvoir Castle while walking by a plantation a labourer happend to break out into a brisk loud whistle of a song tune and he instantly stopt to listen and swore they were poachers and bade me go on the other side to watch which way they started   I tryd to convince him that the whistle was a song tune but it was no use – and as soon as the fellow heard or perhaps saw that he was suspected tho hid from us I expect he felt fearful and stopt his whistle   this convinced the other that his opinion was right – so after watching awhile the fellow made his appearance and met us to know if we was waiting for him   He askd him his business there and he said he was putting down fencing which satisfied the magistrate – who I verily believe mistrusted every stranger for thieves or vagabonds   [A25, 20–29]

I had several kind and gentlemanly visitors came to see me

Chauncy Hare Townsend came to see me   it was one evening in summer and asked me if John Clare lived there   I told him I was he and he seemd supprised and askd agen to be satisfied for I was shabby

and dirty   he was dissapointed I dare say at finding I had little or
nothing to say for I had always had a natural depression of spirits in
the presence of strangers that took from me all power of freedom or
familarity and made me dull and silent for [if] I attempted to say any
thing I coud not reccolect it and made so many hums and hahs in the
story that I was obliged to leave it unfinished at last   I often tryd to
master this confusion by trying to talk over reasonings and argu-
ments as I went about in my rambles which I thought I did pretty well
but as soon as I got before any body I was as much to seek as ever –
C.H.T. was a little affecting with dandyism and he mimicked a lisp in
his speech which he owd to affectation rather then habit   otherwise
he was a feeling and sensible young man   he talkd about Poets and
poetry and the fine scenery of the lakes and other matters for a good
while and when he left me he put a folded paper in my hand which I
found after he was gone was a sonnet and a pound bill   he promised
and sent me Beatties Minstrel[59]   some letters passd between us and
I sent him a present of my Village Minstrel when I never heard of
him afterwards[60]   he has since published a Volume of Poems

[B6, 86R]

I met with notice from the Bishop of Peterbro[61] who sent me a
beautifully bound copy of Miss Aikins Elizabeth[62]   his Lady came
to see me twice with the Rev[d] M[r] Parsons[63] and a young lady who
presented me with a vol of sermons on the christian religion   M[r]
Parsons gave me a copy of the Oxford missale   they talkd awhile
about my poems and then lookd in the garden at my flowers and
started – Drury usd to be very fond of introdusing me to strangers
when I was at his house and I went there very often and at one of
these calls General Birch Reynardson[64] came into the shop to buy
some books and made some enquireys about me   Drury told him I
was at hand and he expressd a desire to see me when he invited me to
come to Holywell and expressd a regret that Lady Sophia his sister
coud not see me being very ill and having sat up too long the day
before on expecting my coming   I felt vext I did not go but it was no
use (her Ladyship gave me the pleasures of hope) which I did in the
beginning of April   it was a pleasant day for the season and I found
the scenery of Holywell very beautiful   he showd me his library
which was the largest I had seen then and he pulld out of the crammd
shelves a thin Quarto beautifully bound in red morrocco   he said
they were Love Elegys written by his father and of course in his mind

124

were beautiful   I just glancd over them and fanc[i]ed they were
imitations of Hammond   at the end were some in MS which I
suspected to be written by himself. I then went to see the garden and
strolld a little about the park   a little river ran sweeping along and in
one place he was forming a connection with it to form an Island   in
one sunny spot was a large dial and near it under the shadows of
some evergreens was a bird house built in the form of a cage glass all
round and full of canarys that were fluttering about busily employd
in building their nests – in looking about these places with the general
a young lady the governess to the child[e]r whom accompanyd us
whom I mistook for his wife neither of whom unriddeld my mistake
till I found it out and I felt ashamd and vexd   when I started home
the young lady wishd to see me again
         after dinner the young lady came and requested I woud write a
copy of Verses for her and an elderly woman wanted me to write an
address to her son in imitation of Cowpers Lines on his mothers
Picture   [A32, 3–4]

after looking about the gardens and the library I was sent to dinner in
the Servants Hall and when it was over the housekeeper invited me
into her room were the governess came and chatted in a free manner
and asking me to corespond with her gave me her address   the house
keeper wishd me to write an address to her son in imitation of
Cowpers lines on his mothers picture – the governess was a pretty
impertinent girl and mischevously familiar to a mind less romantic
then my own   I felt startled into sudden supprises at her manner and
in the evening on my return home I was more supprisd still when on
getting out of the park into the fields I found her lingering in my path
and on coming up to her she smiled and told me plainly she was
waiting to go a little way home with me   I felt evil apprehensions as
to her meaning but I was clownish and shoy* and smiling threatnd
no advantages to interpret it   she chatted about my poems and
resumed the discourse of wishing me to correspond with her which I
promised I woud   when we came to the brink of the heath that
stands in view of Pattys cottage I made a stop to get rid of her but she
lingerd and chatterd on till it grew very late when a man on
horseback suddenly came up and askd the road we had came from
when she thinking it was the General hastily retreated but on finding

* At this point Clare has tried to obliterate the words by writing 'John Clare' in
bold letters over them.

her mistake she returnd and resumd her discourse till it grew between the late and early when I wishd her good night and abruptly started without using the courage of taking her by the hand – I felt excessive[l]y awkard all the way home and my mind was filld with guesses and imaginings at her strange manner and meanings – I wrote one letter too her and intended to be very warm and very gallant in it but fearing that she only wanted me to write love letters to have the pleasure to talk about them and laugh at them so my second mind wrote a very cold one in which I inserted the second address to a Rosebud in humble life in which I requested no Answer nor hinted a second adventure so there the matter or mystery ended for I never unriddeled its meanings tho it was one of the oddest adventures my poetical life met with   it made me rather consieted as I sometimes fancied the young lady had fallen in love with me and I expected [   ] – she came from Birmingham   I shall not mention her name here   [A25, 19]

I now recieved invitations to go to Milton not to visit Lord Milton but his servants but they were the first rate of the house and well informed men not unacquanted with books and I never met with a party of more happy and hearti[e]r fellows in my life   There was Artis up to the neck in the old Norman Coins and broken pots of the Romans and Henderson[65] never wearied with hunting after the Emperor Butterfly and the Hornet Sphinx in the Hanglands wood and the Orchises on the Heath and West an upright honest man tho his delight in reading extended little further then the prices that fat sheep and bullocks fetchd and the rise of corn every week in the news paper – 'the mans the man for a that' and Roberts who sung a song of Moor[e]s and admired his poetry as clever and as stoutly as most ametuers and Gull the Cook   he was a french man and possesd a fund of patient good humour and a countenance inimitable in england   his visage was a Ciracature in good earnest and woud heartily repay Cruikshanks a journey from London to take it   Artis drew an outline often of his countenance but they want the spirit of the origional   they are only outlines – and there was Hague the wine Butler whose library consisted of one solitary book 'Browns reflections on a summers day'   he was an odd good sort of fellow – there were two young maidens – Mrs Procter and M[rs] Byron who had not the womanly affectation about them of even attempting showing some affinity of kindred from the coinsidences of their names with

two popular poets   they were above pardonable vanity and one of
them was a lover of poesy   [A18, 273]

John Taylor came to see me merely I suppose to make up an
article for the London Mag: for he never came afterwards   he was to
have met a friend who came from the same place a hearty fellow that
called the day before – I was a going to Stamford and met Taylor on
the road   he spent most part of the day with me in walking about the
fields   Taylor is a man of very pleasant address and works himself
into the good opinions of people in a moment but it is not lasting for
he grows into a studied carlessness and neglect that he carries into a
system till the purpose for so doing becomes transparent and reflects
its own picture while it woud hide it – he is a very pleasant talker and
is excessive fluent on Paper currency and such politics   he can talk
on matters with a superficial knowledge of them very dexterously
and is very fond of arguing about the latin and Greek poets with
Reverends and the cambridge [scholars] that drop in to his waterloo
house   he assumes a feeling and fondness for a poetry and reads it
well – not in the fashionable growl of mouthing spouters but a sort of
whine – he professed a great friendship for me at my first starting and
offerd to correct my future poems if he did not publish them so I sent
all my things up as I wrote them and neither got his opinion or the
poems back again his only opinion being that he had not time to
spare from other pursuits to revise and correct them for the press and
when I sent for the poems agen he was silent – he wrote the
Introductions to both my Vols of Poems – his manner is that of a
cautious fellow who shows his sunny side to strangers
      he has written some pamphlets on polotics and The identaty of
Jun[i]us a very clever book and some very middling papers in the
London Magazine and bad sonnets   Gilchrist told me that he first
displayd the schoolboy prodogy of translating some of Horaces odes
into ryhme which he sent to the Mirror that hot bed of Indications –
he askd me to correspond with him which I did very thickly as I
fancied he was the greatest frend I had ever met with but after he had
publishd 3 vols of my poems his correspondence was laid by and I
heard nothing more from him
      he never asks a direct question or gives a direct reply but
continualy saps your information by a secret passage coming at it as
it were by working a mine like a lawyer examining a witness and he
uses this sort of caution in his common discourse till it becomes

tedious to listen or reply   he sifts a theory of truth either true or false with much ingenuity and subteltly of argument and his whole table talk is a sort of Junius Identified but his patience carrys it to such lengths in seeming consistency till the first end of the ravelled skein which he winds up at the begining is lost again and unwound in looking for the other – to sum up his character he is a clever fellow and a man of Genius and his Junius Identified is the best argument on circumstantial Evidence that ever was written   [B6, 85R–86R]

Opinions in Religion

I have not yet mentiond any thing about my opinions on religious matters and I am sorry to say I am much wanting   in my younger days I inclined to deism but on reading Pain[e]s Age of Reason lent me by a companion instead of hardening my opinion it broke it and I was doubtful of pain[e]s sub[t]eltys for he seemd determined to get over every obstacle with the opinion he set out with

after this I turned a methodist but I found the lower orders of this persuasion with whom I assosiated so selfish narrow minded and ignor[ant] of real religion that I soon left them [and] sank into m[ethodist] sects agen   they believed every bad [opi]nion [except abou]t themselv[es] [Henson] the preacher then of [Market Deeping]*   [D2, 8]

if every mans bosom had a glass in it so that its secret might be seen what a blotted page of christian profession and false pretentions woud the best of them display

My mind was always hung with doubts   I usd to fancy at times that religion was nothing and woud say to myself if there is a god let him dry up this pond of water or remove this stone and then I will believe and then on seeing things remain as they were I concluded that my doubts were true but after reflection upbraided my foolish presumption and my conscence woud struggle to correct my errors   [A25, 17]

* Incomplete reference to Henson, the bookseller; see p. 97 above. Clare regarded him as an arch hypocrite and may have been thinking of him when he wrote the sentence that follows. A further reference to methodists occurs at B3, 81; it may refer to a brother of Stephen Gordon of Kingsthorpe: 'Insert account of Oliver who woud not suffer a book to be in the house unless the name of Lord or God was in it'.

I feel a beautiful providence ever about me as my attendant deity she casts her mantle about me when I am in trouble to shield me from it   she attends me like a nurse when I am in sickness puts her gentle hand under my head to lift it out of pains way and lays it easy by laying hope for my pillow   she attends to my every weakness when I am doubting like a friend and keeps me from sorrow by showing me her pictures of happiness – and then offering them up to my service she places herself in the shadow that I may enjoy the sunshine and when my faith is sinking into despondency she opens her mind as a teacher to show me truth and give me wisdom when I had it   [A53]

First Visit to London*

My Gilchrist often asked me if I shoud like to see London and as I felt an anxiety he said I shoud go up with him the next time he went which was early in March and I started with him in the old Stamford Coach   my mind was full of expectations all the way about the wonders of the town which I had often heard my parents tell storys

about by the winter fire and when I turnd to the reccolections of the past by seeing people at my old occupations of ploughing and ditching in the fields by the road side while I was lolling in a coach the novelty created such strange feelings that I coud almost fancy that my identity as well as my occupations had changd that I was not the same John Clare but that some stranger soul had jumpd into my skin – when we passd thro Huntingdon Mr G. shewd me the House at this end of the town were Oliver Cromwell was born and the parsonage with its mellancholy looking garden at the other were Cowper had lived which was far the most interesting remembrance to me tho both were great men in the annals of fame   I thought of his tame hares and Johnny Gilpin   as we glided along in the heavy sweeing coach I amusd myself with catching the varying features of the scenery   I

* There is a similar passage at A46, 153.

remembere the road about Royston was very dreary   the white chalk like hills spread all round the cir[c]le and not a tree was to be seen   on[e] mellancholy thorn bush by the road side with a bench beneath it was all that my eye caught for miles   as we approached nearer London the coachmen pointed out 3 large round hills close by the road side and told a superstition about them which I forget

[A33, 9]

on the night we got into London it was announcd in the Play Bills that a song of mine was to be sung at Covent garden by Madam Vestris[66] and we was to have gone but it was too late   I felt uncommonly pleasd at the circumstance   we took a walk in the town by moonlight and went to westminster bridge to see the river thames   I had heard large wonders about its width of water but when I saw it I was dissapointed thinking I shoud have seen a fresh water sea and when I saw it twas less in my eye then Whittlesea Meer   I was uncommonly astonishd to see so many ladys as I thought them walking about the streets   I expressd my suprise and was told they were girls of the town as a modest woman rarely venturd out by her self at nightfall

[A33, 10]

I had often read of the worlds seven wonders in my reading Cary at school but I found in London alone thousands   Octave took [me] to see most of the curiositys   we went to see westminster abbey to see the poets corner and to both Play houses were I saw Kean and Macready and Knight and Munden and Emmery[67] the two latter pleased me most of all but the plays were bad ones   they were [*incomplete*]

[A31, 58]

When I was in london the first time Lord Radstock introduced me to Mrs Emmerson   she has been and is a warm kind friend of tastes feelings and manners almost romantic   she has been a very pretty woman and is not amiss still and a womans pretty face is often very dangerous to her common sense for the notice she recevd in her young days threw an affectatious [air] about her feelings which she has not got shut of yet for she fancys that her friends are admirers of her person as a matter of course and acts accordingly which appears in the eyes of a stranger ridiculous enough but the grotesque wears off on becoming acquanted with better qu[a]litys and better qualitys she certanly has to counterballance them   she [was] at one word the best friend I found and my expectations are looking no further   her correspondence with me began early in my public life and grew pretty thick as it went on   I fancyd it a fine thing to corespond with a lady and by degrees grew up into an admirer some times writing as I felt somtimes as I fancyd and sometimes foolish[l]y when I coud not account for why I did it   I at length requested her portrait when I reccolect ridic[il]ous enough alluding to Lord Nelsons Lady Hamilto[n]   she sent it and flatterd my vanity in return   it was beautifuly done by Behn[e]s the sculpter but bye and bye my knowledge [of] the world sickend my roma[n]tic feelings   I grew up in friends[hip] and lost in flattery afterwards so she took to patronizing one of Colridges who had written a visionary ode on Beauty in Knights quarterly Magaz[in]e in whom she discoverd much genius and calld him on that stake one of the first Lyric poets in England – she then whisht for her picture agen and I readily agreed to part with it – for the artificial flower of folly had run to seed   [B3, 82]

On my first visit to London I met with [Edward Villiers] Rippengille the painter and we have been acquainted ever since   a good sort of a odd fellow with a desire [to] be thought one and often affects [to] be so for the sake of singularity   he is a man of great genius as [a] painter [but] what [is] better he has not been pufft into notice like the thousands of farthing rush lights in all professions that have glimmerd their day and are dead   I spent many pleasant hours with him while in London   he is a pleasant fellow over [a] bottle and a strong dealer in puns   what a many jokes have we crackt together and what a many of life farces have we acted over together in London
    that was the first time I knew [him]   we once went to Offleys the Burton alehouse and sat till morning   [A31, 54]

he has some pretentions to rhyme and wrote An Address to Eccho which was inserted in the London Mag   most of his 'Trifles' in that way are satirical   I was to have gone over to Bristol to see him but illness prevented me   he affected to be little taen with worldly applause and was always fishing for it – he was very carless of money and squanderd it away as a thing of no other use but to spend
                                                                [B3, 56]

and from him I had learnd some fearful disclosures[68] of the place he usd to caution me if ever I happend to go to be on my guard as if I once lost my way I shoud [be] sure to loose my life as the street Ladys woud inveigle me into a fine house were I shoud never be seen agen and he described the pathways on the street as full of trap door[s] which dropd down as soon as pressd with the feet and sprung in their places after the unfortunate countryman had fallen into the deep hole as if nothing had been were he woud be robd and murderd and thrown into boiling cauldrons kept continualy boiling for that purpose and his bones sold to the docters – with these terrible jealousys in my apprehensions I kept a continual look out and fanci[e]d every lady I met a decoyer and every gentleman a pick-pocket and if the[y] did but offer any civility my suspicions were confirmd at once and I felt often when walking behind Gilchrist almost fit to take hold of his coat laps [A31, 59]

Burkhardt[69] took me to Vauxhall and made me shut my eyes till I got in the midst of the Place and when I opened them I almost fancyd myself in a fairey land but the repetition of the round about walk soon put the Romance out of my head and made it a faded reality – these were the scenes that he delighted in and he wishd to take me sometime to see the Beggars Opera[70] a public house so calld the resort of [thieves] but we had no time   I had a romantic sort of notion about authors and had an anxious desire to see them fancying they were beings different to other men but the spell was soon broken when I became acquainted with them but I did not see many save at Taylors Dinner partys were Charles Lamb and young Reynolds and Allan Cunningham[71] and Carey with Wainwright the painter[72] often met and I saw Hazlitt [A31, 58]

One of my greatest amusments while in London was reading the booksellers windows   I was always fond of this from a boy and my next greatest amusment was the curiosity of seeing litterary men   of these all I have seen I shall give a few pictures just as they struck me at the time   some of them I went purposely to see   others I met in litterary partys that is the confind contributors dinners at Taylors and Hesseys   I had no means of meeting the constellation of Genius in one mass   they were mingld partys   some few were fixd stars in the worlds hemisphere   others glimmerd every month in the Magazine   some were little vapours that were content to shine by the light of others   I mean dabling critics that cut monthly morsels from genius whose works are on the waters free for all to catch at that chuses these bye the bye I coud observe had a self satisfaction about them that magnified molehills to mountains I mean that little self was in its own eye a giant and that every other object was mere nothings I shall not mention names here but it is evident I do not alude to friends

[I have heard it asserted that all critics are dissapointed ryhmsters there attempts for a name turning bankrupt as soon as they began business this may be because of their general abuse of the trade this general opinion to the extent of my knowledge holds good of every critic I know were they were not poets by profession I have found they had been ryhmers in their boyish days and their librarys generaly conseald in one corner the lover of poetry and of consequence a poet this little great pretending volume with its unasuming pretentions pleasd the circle of friends for whom it was printed at the authors expence and on getting no further they found it was easier to talk about a book then make one so they turnd critics and sold their brain dress of praise and abuse at market price]*

Reynolds[73] was always the soul of these dinner partys he was the most good natured fellow I ever met with his face was the three in one of fun wit and puning personified he woud punch you with his puns very keenly without ever hurting your feelings for if you lookd in his face you coud not be offended and you might retort as you pleasd nothing coud put him out of humour either with himself or others if all his jokes and puns and witticisms were written down which were utterd at 2 or 3 of these dinner partys they woud make one of the best Joe Millers that have ever passd under that title he sits as a carless listner at table looking on with quick knaping sort of eye that turns towards you as quik as lightning when he has a pun joke or story to give you they are never made up or studied they are the flashes of the moment and mostly happy he is a slim sort of make som thing as you may conscieve of an unpretending sort of fashionable fellow without the desire of being one he has a plump round face a nose somthing puggish and a forehead that betrays more of fun then poetry his teeth are always looking through a laugh that sits as easy on his unpuckerd lips as if he was borne laughing he is a man of genius and if his talents was properly applied he woud do somthing I verily believe that he might win the favours of fame with a pun but be as it will wether she is inclind to

* I have chosen to insert this paragraph from D2, 3 into the discussion of writers meeting at John Taylor's.

smile or frown upon him he is quite at home wi content   the present
is all with him   he carrys none of the Author about him   an hearty
laugh which there is no resisting at his jokes and puns seems to be
more reccompence then he expected and he seems startld into
wonder by it and muses a moment as if he turnd the joke over agen in
his mind to find the 'merry thought' which made the laughter   they
drop as it were spontaniously from his mouth and turn again upon
him before he has had time to conside[r] wether they are good or bad
    he sits in a sort of supprise till another joke drops and makes him
himself again*. . .   [B3, 68]

Reynolds is a near kin to Wainwright in openheartedness and
hillarity but he is a wit and a punster and very happy and entertaining
in both pretentions for with him they are none for they come
naturally from his discourse and seem rather to flow from his ink in
his pen in writing then from his mind   there is nothing studied about
them — and be the pun as severe as it may his pleasant arch manner of
uttering it forbids it to offend and it is always taken as it is intended —
he has written a great deal in Magazines and periodicals of all names
and distinctions and is an author of no mean pretentions as to
quantity tho he has never acknowledged any with his name   he
wrote the Poem called the Naiad in imitations of the old scotch
ballad called the Mermaid of Galloway The Remains of Peter
Cocoran The Garden of Florence and a mock Parody on Peter Bell all
full of wit fun and real Poetry with a good share of affectation and
somthing near akin to bombast
    He is one of the best fellows living and ought to be a Poet of the
first order   himself is his only hinderance at present   Lord Byron
was his first Patron and corrected a poem and praised it which has
not been published   [B3, 58]

    . . . Hazlit[t] is the very reverse of this   he sits a silent picture
of severity   if you was to watch his face for a month you woud not
catch a smile there   his eyes are always turnd towards the ground
except when one is turnd up now and then with a sneer that cuts a
bad pun and a young authors maiden table talk to atoms were ever it
is directed   I look upon it that it carrys the convi[c]tion with it of a

---

* I have interrupted this passage which, in the original MS, continues uninter-
rupted with 'Hazlitt is the very reverse of this' below, to include two further
paragraphs headed 'Reynolds' occurring at B3, 58.

look to the wise and a nodd to the foolish   he seems full of the
author too and I verily believe that his pockets are crambd with it
he seems to look upon Mr This and Mr Tother names that are only
living on Cards of Morning calls and Dinner Invitations as upon
empty chairs as the guests in Macbeth did on the vacancy were
Banquo's ghost presided   they appear in his eye as nothings too thin
for sight and when he enters a room he comes stooping with his eyes
in his hands as it were throwing under gazes round at every corner as
if he smelt a dun or thief ready to seize him by the colar and demand
his money or his life   he is [a] middle sizd dark looking man and his
face is deeply lind with a satirical character   his eyes are bright but
they are rather turned under his brows   he is a walking satire and
you woud wonder were his poetry came from that is scatterd so
thickly over his writings   for the blood of me I coud not find him out
that is I shoud have had no guess at him of his ever being a scribbler
much more a genius   they say she is an odd lady and sure enough in
him her odditys are strongly person[i]fied – then there is Charles
Lamb a long remove from his friend hazlett in ways and manners
he is very fond of snuff which seems to sharpen up his wit every time
he dips his plentiful finger into his large bronze colord box and then
he sharpens up his head thro[w]s himself backward in his chair and
stammers at a joke or pun with an inward sort of utterance ere he can
give it speech till his tongue becomes a sort of Packmans shop turning
it over and over till at last it comes out wetted as keen as a razor and
expectation when she knows him wakens into a sort of danger as bad
as cutting your throat but he is a good sort of fellow and if he offends
it is innosently done   who is not acquanted with Elia and who woud
believe him otherwise   so soon as the cloath is drawn the wine and
he become comfortable   his talk now doubles and trebles into a
combination of repitition urging the same thing over and over again
till at last he – leans off with scarcly 'good night' in his mouth and
dissapears leaving his memory like a pleasant ghost hanging about
his vacant chair and there is his sister Bridget a good sort of woman
tho her kind cautions and tender admonitions are nearly lost upon
Charles who like an undermined river bank leans carlessly over his
jollity and recieves the gentle lappings of the waves of womans
tongue unheedingly till it ebbs and then in the same carless posture
sits and recieves it again tho it is all lost on Charles   she is a good
woman and her cautions are very commendable for the new river
runs very near his house and the path for a dark night is but very

precar[i]ous to make the best of it and he jeanty fellow is not always blind to dangers so I hope the advice of his Sister Bridget will be often taken in time to retire with the cloth and see home by daylight

and there sits Carey the translator of Dante[74] one of the most quiet amiable and unasuming of men   he will look round the table in a peacful silence on all the merry faces in all the vacant unconser[n]-ment imaginable and then he will brighten up and look smilingly on you and me and our next hand neighbour as if he knew not which to address first and then perhaps he drops a few words like a chorus that serve all together   his eyes are not long on a face   he looks you into a sort of expectation of discoursing and starts your tongue on tiptoe to be ready in answering what he may have to start upon when suddenly he turns from you to thro[w] the same good naturd cheat of a look on others   he is a tallish spare man with a longish face and a good forhead   his eyes are the heavy lidded sort whose easiest look seems to meet you half closd   his authorship and his priesthood sit upon him very meekly   he is one of those men which have my best opinions and of whom I feel happy with every oppertunity to praise

on my second visit to London I spent 2 very happy days with him at Chiswick (I was then in good health)   his wife is a good sort of person and of so young a look in his company that I mistook her a long while for his daughter   he lives [in] the house once occupied by Thorn[h]ill the painter and he showd me the window thro which Miss Thornill elopd with Hogarth and over the chimney piece were some heads sketchd on the wall by Hogarth but the servants being left to themselves to white wash the room in Mr Careys absan[c]e from home utterly defacd this precious relic and he greatly regretted the loss when he told me   I also saw Hogarth[s] painting room at the end of the garden which is now a hay loft   you asend to it by a broad stept ladder   it has no prepossesing appearance about it and you almost feel to doubt memorys veracity when she whispers you this is the spot were Hogarth sat and painted pictures for the royal academy of fame but proofs as strong as holy writ meet your eye in a corner of the Garden were two narrow slips of stones stand close to the wall one [to] the memory of a bird with an inscription on it by Hogarth himself and the other to the memory of a dog with an inscription taken from Churchills poetry by M[rs] Hogarth 'Life to the last enjoyd here Pompey lies'   the Arbour of honey suckles or creepers hangs shadowy silence above them and in this corner M[r] Carey pointed out the spot were Hogarth usd to play skittles and if my memory wears right impressio[n]s the frame is there still and then to wind up the curosity that such objects had excited we went to see the monument of Hogarth in the Church yard   I coud not help fancying when I walkd about the garden that the roses and cloves and other flowers were old tennants that knew Hogarth and his lady as well as their present occupants   bye the bye the translator of Dante will not deminish the classical memorys of the old mansion with his pos-sesion of it   Poetry and painting are sisters – There was Col[e]ridge at one of these Partys   he was a man with a venerable white head fluent of speech not a 'silver tong[ue]d hamilton'   his words hung in their places at a quiet pace from a drawl in good set marching order so that you woud suppose he had learnt what he intended to say before he came   it was a lecture parts of which [*incomplete*]

[B3, 68–69–70–61, 62]

A little artless simple seeming body somthing of a child over grown in a blue coat and black neckerchief for his dress is singular with his hat in his hand steals gently among the company with a smile turning timidly round the room – it is De Quincey the Opium Eater that abstruse thinker in Logic and Metaphysics XYZ

Then there is Allan Cunningham (Reynolds calls him the dwarf) comes stalking in like one of [Scott's] black knights but his counte-nance is open and his look is hearty   he hates puns and is fond of scotch ballads scotch Poets and every thing scottish down no doubt as far as scotch snuff – well he is a good fellow and a good poet and when the companys talk is of poetry he is ready to talk 2 ways at once but when puns are up his head is down over his glass musing and silent and nothing but poetry is the game to start him into hillarity again

[B3, 64]

Southey

I never saw him but I heard somthing about him by meeting in company with 2 of his wifes sisters at Mrs Emmersons those 'Pretty milliners of Bath' as Byron calls them but I cannot say much for his judgment if these sisters are to be taken as a sample for the rest   they are sharp ready witted girls but rather plain   I learnd from them that Southey was a livly sort of man always in gay spirits who wrote both in prose and verse with a great deal of ease but the Number of his publications woud almost tell us that this is the fact   he writes amid

the noise of his childern and joins in their sport at intervals
Wordsworth on the contrary cannot bear a noise and composes with
great difficulty   I shoud imagine he prefers the mossy seat on the
mountains to the closet for study   at least his poems would lead one
to think so

Southy presents a copy of every work he publishes to his wife
and he wrote a copy of Roderic on french green paper on purpose to
present to her   [B3, 84]

I stopt about a month in London and spent my time very pleasantly
visiting about the town with those former wonders of Poets Painters
and authors of most denominations that had worn out of my
wonders into common men   I visited Hilton and [went] to Wainwright Lamb [ ] with Taylor   Wainwright is a very comical sort of
chap   he is about 27 and wears a quizzing glass and makes an excuse
for the ornament by complaining of bad eyes   he is the Van Vink
booms James Weathercock etc of the Magazine   he had a picture in
the exebition of 'Paris in the chamber of Helen' and the last time I
was in London he had one there of 'the Milk maid' from Waltons
angler both in my opinion very middling performances but my
opinion is but of it self a middling one in such matters so I may be
mistaken – he is a clever writer and some of his papers in the
Magazine are very entertaining and some very good particulary the
beginging of one a description of a Churchyard   [B3, 54]

[Second Visit to London]

When Taylor came to see me he invited me to come to London and I
took his invitation and started a second time   I spent most of my
time at Taylors and Mrs Emmersons – I went up by myself as poor
Gilchrist was very ill and coud not start just then tho he came up
afterwards   he took me to see Gifford[75] who the first time we went
up was too ill to see us but this time he was rather getting near
neighbour to health and gave me welcome with a hearty shake of the
hand and congratulated me on my last poems (the Village Minstrel)
then just published which he said were far better then my first   he
also bade me beware of the booksellers and repeated it several times

he was getting on his sofa surrounded with books and papers of all
sorts   he chatted awhile to Gilchrist about Books and Authors and
Pope and lent him a New Satire to read called the 'Mohawks'[76] in

which he said he was mentioned   he supposed Lady Morgan was the author and after Gilchrist had dipt into it here and there he prono[u]nced it worthless – the next day we went to call on Murray[77] in Albemarle street who flatterd me with some compliments on my success and hoped that I woud always call on him when ever I came to London   he is a very pleasant man   he showed us the English Bards and Scotch Reviewers illustrated with Portraits which we turned over and departed and as we got at the door Giffords carriage drove up and on leaving the shop he gave each of us a copy of his Translation of Persius   [B3, 88]

altho I had conquered the old notion of kidnappers or men stealers being a common trade in London and staid long enough to find that this was a tale on my first visit I found that another very near kin to it on my second visit that I had not expected to find in the places were it was most practised was very common among all professions – they are a sort of genteel Purse knappers that tho they do not want the carcass will quickly lighten the pockets in exchange for bad bargains and they seem to know and pounce on a countryman as a raven on carrion – I wanted several things while there as curoisitys or presents to take home with me and I used to think that by going into the best looking shops in the most thorough fare streets I shoud stand the least risk to be cheated so in I went and gave every farthing they set upon the article and fancied I had got a good bargain till experience turned out to the contrary   when I first got up being rather spare of articles of dress I went into a shop in fleet street and purchased as a first article a pair of stockings for which the man asked 3/6 and on my giving it without a word of contrariety he made a pause when I asked him the price of another article and told me as he kept nothing but first rate articles they were rather high in the price and laying a redy made shirt on the counter he says that is 14 Shillings   I told him it was too high for me and with that he instantly pretended to reach me another which was the very same article agen   this was 6^s/6^d I paid it and found afterwards that the fellows fine cloth was nothing but callico – I obse[r]ved it was always a custom in most shops that when you went in to ask for an article the thing they first shew you was always put a one side and another recommend[e]d as superior which I found was always to the contrary – so experience taught me always in future to take the one they did not reccommend – on my last visit to London I wanted to take somthing home for

Patty and thinking that Waithman[78] had been a great stickler for
freedom and fair dealing among the citizens his news paper notoriety
reccomended me to his shop at the corner of Bridge street as the hope
that I might come in for a fair bargain but here I was more decieved
then ever for they kept the best articles aside and reccomen[de]d the
worst as soon as they found out their customer was of the country
when I took the things home I found that they were a bad bargain still
and a great deal dearer then they might have been bought for at home
– so much for Patrons of Liberty and news paper passports for honest
men – I saw more in the way of wonders this time then I did at first
but they did not leave such strong impressions on my memory as to
be worth remembrance – I usd to go with Thomas Bennion Taylors
clerk or head porter about the city when he went out on errands and
very often went into each curosity that came in our way such as [   ]
A[nd] [   ] and other hard names claptraps to ease the pocket of its
burthen   I remember going into Bullocks Mexico[79] with the Editors
Ticket that Taylor gave me and the fellows at their several posts of
money catching fancying I dare say that I was the critisizing editor
looked with much supprise at my odd clownish appearance and
asked me so many pumping questions that I was glad to get out agen
without paying much attention to the wonder of the show – Tom was
very fond of introducing me to the booksellers were [he] had business
who were too busily occupied in their own conserns to take much
head of me   [D2, 2; B3, 55]

I did not know the way to any place for a long while but the royal
academy and here I used to go almost every day as Rippingille the
painter had told the ticket keeper who I was and he let me come in
when ever I chose which I often made use of from nessesity   [B3, 54]

I do not know how the qualms of charity come over those who have
plenty of riches to be charitable but I often feel it so strongly myself
when objects of compassion pass me that is the only thing that makes
me oftenest wish I had plenty for the pleasure of relieving their wants
and when I was in London I often parted with my little money so
freely that I was often as bad off as those I relieved and needed it
perhaps as bad that is I felt as bad or worse inconvenience then they
from the want of it   I remember passing by Sr Pauls one morning
where stood a poor African silently soliciting charity but the sincerity
of his distress spoke plainer then words   I felt in my pockets but I

had only fourpence in all and I felt almost ashamed to recieve the poor creatures thanks for so worthless a pittance and passed him but his looks spoke so feelingly that even a trifle woud be acceptable that I ran back a long way and put the fourpence into his hand and I felt worse dissapointed when I saw the poor creatures heart leap to thank me and the tears steal down his cheeks at the gratification of the unlooked for boon for his thanks and supprise told me he had met with little of even such charity as mine – and I determined the next day to get my pocket recruited if possible and give him a shilling and my first walk was to St Pauls but the poor affrican was gone and I never saw him again

[B5, 93]

My [Third] Visit to London

'Nothing set down in malice'

A journey for pleasure is a precarious sympathy soon robd of its enjoyments by unforeseen dissasters but a journey for the improvment of ill health undertaken by that smiling encourager hope hath little to make it palatable tho the joys of the one are as much to be relied on as the other

Upon this last matter my Journey to London was made   I went for the benefit of advice to a celebrated scotch phisic[i]an Dr Darling[80]   the complaint lay in my head and chest   I was very ill when I first went but I gradualy recievd benefit   some reccolections of this visit shall be the subject of this chapter   they are observations of men and things thrown together in a myscellaneous manner   this was the third time I had been up so the vast magnitude that human ant hill that strikes every stranger with wonder had lost its novelty the first time I went up was in company with a first friend of old long syne memory Octavius Gilchrist now gone to the land of uncertainty   poor Octave   I still remember how we went sweeing along the road on the heavy reeling coach   London was no novelty with him but with me ever thing was a wonder   I had read in my reading easy of the worlds seven wonders but I found in london alone thousands   as we approachd it the road was lind wi lamps that diminishd in the distance to stars   this is London I exclaimd   he laughd at my ignorance and only increasd my wonder by saying we were yet several miles from it   when we got in it was night and the next morning every thing was so uncommon to what I had been usd to

that the excess of novelty confou[n]ded my instinct   every thing hung round my confusd imajination like riddles unresolvd while I was there   I scarcly knew what I was seeing and when I got home my remembrance of objects seemd in a mass one mingld in another like the mosaic squares in a roman pavement   on my second visit things became more distinct or separate on the memory and one of my greatest wonders then was the continual stream of life passing up and down the principal streets all the day long and even the night and one of my most entertaining amusments was to sit by Taylors window in Fleet Street to see the constant successions throng this way and that way and on this my last visit I amusd my illness by catching the most beautiful women['s] faces in the crowd as I passed on in it till I was satiated as it were with the variety and the multitude and my mind lost its memory in the eternity of beautys successions and was glad to glide on in vacancy with the living stream   one of the greatest curiositys I saw then was Devilles the Phrenologists[81] collections of heads himself excepted   he is a kind simple hearted good humourd man   Phrenology is with him somthing more then a System   it seems the life and soul of his speculations   he is never weary of talking about it or giving 'Lectures on heads'   Strangers of all exceptions Poets Philosophers Mathematicians and humble un-known beings that with the world have no name are all welcomd up his stairs and led to his matchless head gallery while he with smiling politness satisfys ever eager enquirey as readily as it is askd for   they have only to pull off their hats and drop half hints and then the lecture on heads commencing he mostly begins with 'Why Sir I shoud say heres order very strong – or wisa wersa the want of it   heres plenty of constructivness – I shoud say your fond of mathematics and heres ideality   I shoud say that you have a tallent for poetry   I dont say that you are a poet but that you have a tallent for it if applied heres the organ of collor very strong   I shoud say you are fond of fine colors and wisa werse   were theres the organ of form with out color nothing showy is likd of   here is benevolence wery prominent
    I shoud say you seldom pass a beggar or street sweeper without dropping a copper   heres weneration very high   I shoud say you are religious   (the subject perhaps is worldly minded and remains silent)   I dont say your a christian mind but you have a veneration for the deity   heres combativness very large   I shoud say you are not slow at revengeng an insult particulary if it be offerd to a female for the armorous propensitys are large also   I shoud say you have a

love for the fair sex but not so as to make it troublsome   aye aye sir
    now I look agen heres order very strong sure enough   I shoud say
that things being put out of order displeases you very much and that
you are often tempted while at table to put a spoon or knife and fork
in its place   I shoud say its the most likly thing to create disturbances
in your family   heres form very strong   I shoud say you are a
painter or that you have talents for painting if applied   heres
construction very large   I shoud say you are fond of mathematics
and I shoud say you have a great talent that way if the mind was
turnd to it   heres ideality too   (he is a poet)   no I shoud not say
that   he has a talent for it if put into action   are you a poet Sir
(yes)   aye aye the systems right but I shoud not venture so far as to
decide upon that as a many heads develop poetry very stron[g]ly
were it has never been applyd   well sir you see the system is correct'
    he then in smiling silence waits your de[c]ision of his remarkable
prophecy and hard and earthlike is that soul who can return an harsh
and unbelieving opinion on the system but I believe his is seldom paid
so unkindly for his good naturd trouble   his perdictions are so
cautiously utterd with so many causes for the liklihood of failures in
nice points that even failings them selves in his lectures strike as
convictions   when he lecturd on my head I coud not help likening
him to a boy (perhaps he had no existance but in my friends Reynolds
fancy for it was he that told the story) who was so cautious as not to
be out in any thing   he was once askd wether the earth went round
the sun or the sun round the earth   the boy said he believd they took
it by turns one going round one day and the other the next – Deville
then leads your eye to his collection [and] points out on particular
heads the most convincing proof of his system in the characteristics
of Murderers Poets Painters Mathematicians and little actors of all
work were his wisa wersas become very frequent   he then takes you
below were the apparatus is all ways ready to bury you in plaster if
you chuse and if Literary men and Artists he politly hints that he
shoud like a cast of them   they cannot do less than comply and the
satisfaction of adding fresh materials to his gallery doubly repays
him for all his trouble   [B3, 65–8]

After I had been in London awhile Rippingille came down from
Bristol with Mr Elton[82] and as I was much improved in health under
Dr Darling I indulged in some of the towns amusments with my old

comrade for he was fond of seeking after curiosity and brancing about the town he was always for thinking that constant exercise taking all weathers rough and smooth as they came were the best phisic for a sick man and a glass of Scotch Ale only seemed to strengthen his notions the first jaunt that we took together was to see the 'Art of Self Defence' practiced at the fives court it was for the Benefit of Oliver[83] and I caught the mania so much from Rip for such things that I soon became far more eager for the fancy then himself and I watch'd the appearance of every new Hero on the stage with as eager curosity to see what sort of fellow he was as I had before done the Poets – and I left the place with one wish strongly in uppermost and that was that I was but a Lord to patronize Jones the Sailor Boy[84] who took my fancy as being the finest fellow in the Ring – I went with Rippingille and Elton to see Deville the Phrenologist and a very clever fellow in his own profession we found him after he found who I was he instantly asked me permission to take my bust in plaister which I consented to as Ripingill and Elton wanted a copy – the operation was stifling and left a strong dislike on the subject not to do it again – Rippingille also introduced me to Sir T.L.[85] who was a very polite courtouis and kind man which made the other matters sit very agreeable about him – just as we got up to the door Prince Leopold was going in to sit for his picture – and we took a turn up the Square for a while and did not offer to venture till we saw him depart Rip sent in his card and we was instantly sent up into his painting gallery were we amused ourselves till he came and kindly shook me bye the hand and made several enquireys about me he paid Rip several fine compliments about his picture of the breakfast at an Inn and told him of his faults in a free undisguised manner but with the greatest kindness after he had shown us about his painting room and chatted a considerable time we prepared to start when he followed us and said he coud not let me go without showing me a brother poet and took us into another room were a fine head of Walter Scott stood before us – I left his house with the satisfactory impression that I had never met with a kinder and better man then Sir T.L. and I dare say Rip was highly gratified with the praise he had received for S[ir] T[homas] told him that the Royal family at a private view of the Exebition before it opened to the public took more notice of his picture then all the rest – but Rip woud not own it for he affects a false appeerence of such matters – we went to F freelings[86] the same day who had expressed a desire to have a copy of his picture of the 'post office' but he was 'not at home' so I had not the pleasure of seeing him and when Rip went the next day I coud not go with him

[B3, 12]

Rip was very fond of talking and looking at things of which he understood nothing and with this feeling we went 2 or 3 times to the french Playhouse[87] somewere in tottenham court road   none of us understood a word of french and yet we fancied ourselves delighted for there was a very beautiful actress that took our fancys and Rip drew a Sketch of her in penc[i]ling for me which was somthing like her tho he stole none of her beauty to grace it still

we also went to see Astleys Theatre[88] were we saw morts of tumbling

Rip stopt about 3 weeks this time and hastened home to get ready some Lectures on painting which he intended to deliver at the Bristol Institution

[B3, 20]

I got acquainted this time with Van Dyk[89] a young man whose literary matters sat very quietly about him   he was of a very timid and retreating disposition before strangers but to a friend he was very warm hearted   he published a little vol of Poems called Theatrical Portraits   he was very ready at writing an impromtu which he woud often do very happily   he went with me to M[rs] E[mmerson]s were we met with Lord R[adstock] who was very friendly with him

[B3, 12, 18]

Etty the painter

I went with Hessey to visit a very odd sort of character at the corner of St Pauls Church yard   he was a very simple good sort of man with a troublesome sort of fondness for poetry which was continually uppermost and he wrote ryhmes himself which he thrust into any ones notice as readily as if they were anothers   he had two daughters who seemd to be very amiable girls one of which kept an album in which her fathers productions were very prominent   he seemed to be very fond of translating Davids Psalms into ryhme   he was a friend and acquaintance to Miss Williams to whom he said he had sent a copy of my poems   at his house I met with Etty the painter[90] he was a man of a reservd appearance and felt as awkardly situated I dare say as myself when M[r] Vining proposed healths and expected

145

fine speeches in reply for tho Etty replyed he did it very shortly and when mine was drank I said nothing and tho the companys eyes were expecting for some minutes I coud not say a word tho I though[t] of some several times and they were wishes that I was out of the house – Mr Vining appeard to be a sort of patron to Etty [B3, 20, 30]

for 3rd Visit to London

When I used to go any were by my self especially Mrs E[mmerson]s I used to sit at night till very late because I was loath to start not for the sake of leaving the company but for fear of meeting with super-natural [apparitions] even in the busy paths of London and tho I was a stubborn disbeliever of such things in the day time yet at night their terrors came upon me ten fold and my head was as full of the terribles as a gossips – thin death like shadows and gobblings with sorcer eyes were continually shaping in the darkness from my haunted imagi-nation and when I saw any one of a spare figure in the dark passing or going on by my side my blood has curdled cold at the foolish apprehension of his being a supernatural agent whose errand might be to carry me away at the first dark alley we came too and I have oftened contrived to catch his countenance by the windows or lamps which has only satisfied me to undergo the terrors of a fresh [apprehension]   I have often cursed my silly and childish apprehensions and woud disbelieve it tho I coud not help thinking so on – I coud not bear to go down the dark narrow street of Chancery lane   I[t] was as bad as a haunted spot to pass and one night I resolved to venture the risk of being lost rather then go down tho I tryd all my courage to go down to no purpose for I coud not get it out of my head but that I shoud be sure to meet death or the devil if I did so I passd it and tryd to find fleet street by another road but I soon got lost and the more I tryd to find the way the more I got wrong so I offerd a watchman a shilling to show me the way thither but he said he woud not go for that and asked half a crown which I readily gave him when he led me down many narrow alleys and I found myself in Chancery lane at last.

I believe I may lay this foolish night feeling to a circumstance in my youth when I was most terribly frightend   I coud never forget it nor yet be thoroughly pacified tho I always boasted of a disbelief of such matters in the day time to keep up a forced courage to keep one

from being laughd at as I often do now for the same reason
[*incomplete*]   [B3, 16]

while I was in London the melancholly death of Lord Byron was
announ[c]d in the public papers and I saw his remains born away out
of the city on its last journey to that place were fame never comes –
tho it lives like a shadow and lingers like a sunbeam on his grave it
cannot enter   therefore it is a victory that has won nothing to the
victor   his funeral was blazd forth in the papers with the usual
parade that accompany the death of great men   one ostentatious
puff said to be written by Walter Scott which I dont believe was
unmercifully pompous   Lord Byron stood in no need of news paper
praise those little wirl puffs of praise   I happend to see it by chance
as I was wandering up Oxford street on my way to Mrs Emmersons
when my eye was suddenly arested by straggling gropes of the
common people collected together and talking about a funeral   I did
as the rest did tho I coud not get hold of what funeral it coud be but I
knew it was not a common one by the curiosity that kept watch on
every co[u]ntenance   bye and bye the grope collected into about a
hundred or more when the train of a funeral suddenly appeard on
which a young girl that stood beside me gave a deep sigh and utterd
poor Lord Byron   there was a mellancholy feeling of vanity – for
great names never are at a loss for flattere[r]s that as every flower has
its insect – they dance in the sunbeams to share a liliputian portion of
its splendour – upon many countenances – I lookd up in the young
girls face   it was dark and beautiful and I coud almost feel in love
with her for the sigh she had utterd for the poet   it was worth all the
News paper puffs and Magazine Mournings that ever was paraded
after the death of a poet since flattery and hypoc[ris]y was babtizd in
the name of truth and sincerity – the Reverend the Moral and
fastid[i]ous may say what they please about Lord Byrons fame and
damn it as they list – he has gaind the path of its eterni[t]y without
them and lives above the blight of their mildewing censure to do him
damage – the common people felt his merits and his power and the
common people of a country are the best feelings of a prophecy of
futurity – they are below – or rather below* the prejudices and
flatterys the fancys of likes and dislikes of fashion – they are the
feelings of natures sympathies unadulterated with the pretentions of
art and pride   they are the veins and arterys that feed and quiken the

* Did Clare intend to write 'above'?

heart of living fame   the breathings of eternity and the soul of time are indicated in that prophecy   they did not stand gaping with suprise on the trappings of gaudy show or look on with apathisd indefference like the hir[e]d mutes in the spectacle but they felt it   I coud see it in their faces   they stood in proufond silence till it passd not enquiring what this was or that was about the show as they do at the shadow of wealth and gaudy trappings of a common great name – they felt by a natural impulse that the mighty was fallen and they mournd in saddend silence   the streets were lind as the procession passd on each side but they were all the commonest and the lowest orders   I was supprisd and gratified   the windows and doors had those of the higher [orders] about them but they wore smiles on their faces and thought more of the spectacle then the poet – tho there was not much appearance of that   it lookd like a neglected grandeur

the young girl that stood by me had cou[n]ted the carriages in her mind as they passd and she told me there was 63 or 4 in all   they were of all sorts and sizes and made up a motly show   the gilt ones that lede the procession were empty – the hearse lookd small and rather mean and the coach that followd carried his em[bers] in a urn over which a pawl was thrown thro which one might distinguish the form of the [urn] underneath and the window seemd to be left open for that purpose – I believe that his liberal principals in religion and politics did a great deal towards gaining the notice and affections of the lower orders   be [that] as it will it is better to be beloved by the low and humble for undisguisd honesty then flatterd by the great for purchasd and pensiond hypocrisy were excuses to win favours are smmuggeld on the public under the disguise of a pretended indifference about it*   [B3, 71–72]

I woud advise young authors not to be upon too close friendships with booksellers that is not to make them bosom friends – they may all be respectable men tho respectability is but a thin garment in the worlds eye of pretending claims that often 'covers a multitude of sins' – and their friendships are always built on speculations of profit like a farmer shewing his sample   if a book suits them they write a fine friendly letter to the author   if not they neglect to write till the author is impatient and then comes a note of declining to publish mixd with a seasoning of petulance in exchange for his anxiety therefore like all other matters of trade interested friendships too

* The last eighteen words appear at B3, 87 but, I believe, belong here.

close and hastily made must meet some time or other a drop in the market and leave one side dissapointed   when I first began with the world a fair promise was a sufficient pledge to trust my heart in the opinion and a warm friendship was soon kindled   as I grew older in them some of these began to dissapoint me and I regretted but leaping out of the frying pan into the fire I remain were I began

When I began with the world I felt as much worldly faith in fair words and seasoning promises as woud have loaded a car[a]van to mecca but as soon as I mixd up with it I felt the mistake and reformd a little   I knew of some little trea[c]herys in low life of mock friendships that spoke fair words to the face and soon as the back was turnd joind in the slanders against him who told lyes for a purpose and acted the hypocrite in matters of religion friendship gain or an ruling passion that might be uppermost but I was not aware that these dwarfs had grown up with fashions and other life to giants   on my first visit to London I had a glimpse of things as they are and felt doubtful   on my second I had more dissapointments and in my last I saw so much mistey shuffling that my fa[i]th of the world shrunk to a skeleton and woud scar[c]e fill a nutt shell or burthen a mouse to bear it – the vastest of wisdoms hath said 'put no confidence in men for they will decieve you'   [B7, 77–78]

near conclusion

Many people will think me a vain fellow perhaps for attaching or fancying such importance to these memoirs as to think they will repay my vanity or labour in dwelling on them to th[e] length and in many instances the manner in which they are written may draw on me a juster [criticism] for some of my remarks ar[e] very weak and some of the anecdotes very trifling and the expressions impertinent but most of the naritive was written in severe illness which may be a sufficient apology for defects *in the author not perhaps for their being thrust on the reader**   As to the humble situation I have filled in life it needs no apology for all tastes are not alike   they do not all love to climb the Alps but many content themselves with wanderings in the valleys – while some stand to gaze on the sun to watch the flight of the towering eagle – others not less delighted look down upon the meadow grass to follow the fluttering of the butterflye   in such a

* Italicized words written in a different ink.

latitude I write not without hopes of le[a]ving some pleasures for readers on the humble pages I have here written   [D2, 8]

I shoud imagine that my low origin in life will not be a mote in the eye of literature to bear against me and I will not urge it as an excuse for what I have written   [B3, 59]

Poverty has made a sad tool of me by times — and broken into that independance which is or ought to belong to every man by birthright — the travellers situation is no riddle to me now — tho I used to wonder over it when I had no friends — A traveller who had been questioned as to what he had seen and where he had been declared that [he] had been so far as to be able to get no further [to] see the greatest of wonders and being at last forced to turn back as not being able to place even a sixpence between the earth and sky

I have been so long a lodger with difficulty and hope and so often looked on the land of promise without meeting with it — that I have often felt myself in the midst of Solomons advice to his son — 'My son it is better to die then to be poor — for the honesty of a poor man is ever suspected while the rich "makes faults graces"

> And on the finger of the throned queen
> The basest jewel will be esteemed'   [A53]

some bring in a [plea] on the reader that have had an eye to modesty that they have written nothing no not even a syllable that she need even blush to read   another says that they have kindled their musings at the coals of the alter and that they breath in toto the true spirit of religion as if writing about religion was the test of Poetry another urges the persuasion of friends and quotes the proofs of their judgments praises to be sure — these are the cants and excuses of prefaces   [B6, 83R]

I might have inserted several praises from friends in extracts from their letters mentioning my poems etc but I leave the books I have published and the poems that may yet be published to speak for them selves   if they cannot go without leading strings let them fall and be forgotten   they [ha]ve gaind me many pleasures and freinds that have smoothed the rugged road of my early life and made my present lot and if they are deemd unworthy of the notice of posterity I have neither the power nor the wish to save them from the fate that awaits them   I am proud of the notice they have gained me and I shall feel a prouder gratification still if my future publications be found worthy of further [notice]   [A31, 51]

When a person finds fault with every body but himself it may be rightly infered that self is the only pleasant thing in life with him and that the credit of every body is sacrifised to mentain that opinion – but when one speaks with the same freedom of himself as of others it can never be doubted that there is any other cause or interest attached to it then the one that he writes as he feels – impartiallity is not always truth as it sometimes and often mistakes its own opinion for it but it can never be construed into pergury as uttering a false opinion for the interest of itself or others – I have attempted to do so throughout this narative   I have described things as I thought they were without feeling a dislike to this poem or a love for that – I have exposed my own faults and feelings with the same freedom as tho I was talking of an enemey   I have not hesitated about the interpretations that they may give birth too but related them as they are and were ever   if I am mistaken in my opinion of others it is my Judgment and not my will that misled me   [B3, 59]

I have provd the world and I feel disapointed   the hollow pretendings calld friendships have deadend my feelings and broken my confidence and left me nothing and perhaps the fault is not in the world but in me   every friendship I made grew into a vain attachment   I was in earnest always or I was nothing and I believd every thing that was utterd came from the heart as mine did   I made my opinions of people the same to their faces as I did behind their backs reserving nothing   I spoke as freely of their faults as I did of their merits and lovd everybody the better for serving me like wise if I tryd to disemble my real inosc[ence]ness woud break thru and betray me so I spoke as I thought and [waited] for the des[– – –] when I made a familiar friend I gave him my confidence and unbosomed my faults and failings to him without hesitation and reserve putting my all into his hands and there by making my self bare to his with out caring to enquire into his own as a holdfast or earnest to keep secrets   on the other hand I have a fault that often hurts me tho I cannot master it   I am apt to mistake some foibles that all men are subject to into breaths of friendship and therebye grow hessitant and loose my sincerity for them and when I feel dissapointed in my opinions of them I never can recover my former attachment tho I often try and I always see the silent enmity of an enemey when I can no longer feel the sincerity of a friend   I know I am full of faults tho I have improvd and temperd my self as well as I was able but these that stick to me were born with me and will dye with me   if every any body did or does me a foul barefacd wrong that memory grows with my life and break[s] out with every oppertunity and if there is a resurection quickning with the dust it is such a vivid spark in my nature that I believe I shall not forget it in my grave   [D2, 7]

JOURNEY OUT OF ESSEX

Journal Jul 18 – 1841 – Sunday – Felt very melancholly – went a walk on the forest in the afternoon – fell in with some gipseys one of whom offered to assist in my escape from the mad house by hideing me in his camp to which I almost agreed but told him I had no money to start with but if he would do so I would promise him fifty pounds and he agreed to do so before saturday   on friday I went again but he did not seem so willing so I said little about it – On sunday I went and they were all gone – an old wide awake hat and an old straw bonnet of the plumb pudding sort was left behind – and I put the hat in my pocket thinking it might be usefull for another oppertunity – as good luck would have it, it turned out to be so

July 19 – Monday – Did nothing

July 20 – Reconnitered the rout the Gipsey pointed out and found it a legible one to make a movement and having only honest courage and myself in my army I Led the way and my troops soon followed but being careless in mapping down the rout as the Gipsey told me I missed the lane to Enfield town and was going down Enfield highway till I passed 'The Labour in vain' Public house where A person I knew comeing out of the door told me the way

I walked down the lane gently and was soon in Enfield Town and bye and bye on the great York Road where it was all plain sailing and steering ahead meeting no enemy and fearing none I reached Stevenage where being Night I got over a gate crossed over the corner of a green paddock where seeing a pond or hollow in the corner I forced to stay off a respectable distance to keep from falling into it for my legs were nearly knocked up and began to stagger   I scaled some old rotten paleings into the yard and then had higher pailings to clamber over to get into the shed or hovel which I did with difficulty being rather weak and to my good luck I found some trusses of clover piled up about 6 or more feet square which I gladly mounted and slept on   there was some trays in the hovel on which I could have reposed had I not found a better bed   I slept soundly but had a very uneasy dream   I thought my first wife[1] lay on my left arm and somebody took her away from my side which made me wake up rather unhappy   I thought as I awoke somebody said 'Mary' but nobody was near – I lay down with my head towards the north to show myself the steering point in the morning

July 21 – when I awoke Daylight was looking in on every side and fearing my garrison might be taken by storm and myself be made prisoner I left my lodging by the way I got in and thanked God for his kindness in procureing it (for any thing in a famine is better then nothing and any place that giveth the weary rest is a blessing)   I gained the north road again and steered due north – on the left hand side the road under the bank like a cave I saw a Man and boy coiled up asleep which I hailed and they woke up to tell me the name of the next village*

Some where on the London side the 'Plough' Public house a Man passed me on horseback in a Slop frock and said 'here's another of the broken down haymakers' and threw me a penny to get a half pint of beer which I picked up and thanked him for and when I got to the plough I called for a half pint and drank it and got a rest and escaped a very heavy shower in the bargain by having a shelter till it was over – afterwards I would have begged a penny of two drovers who were very saucey so I begged no more of any body meet who I would

* Baldeck [Clare's footnote; i.e. Baldock].

N

Northborough
Glinton
Helpston
Werrington
Walton
Peterborough

Norman
Cross
Stilton

NORTHAMPTONSHIRE

HUNTINGDONSHIRE

Bugden *or*
Buckden

Ram Inn
St Neots

CAMBRIDGESHIRE

Potton

BEDFORDSHIRE

Shefford +
Church

Baldock

Stevenage

HERTFORDSHIRE

ESSEX

High Beach
*Epping
Forest*

Enfield

0   5   10 miles

MIDDLESEX

JOURNEY OUT OF ESSEX

— I passed 3 or 4 good built houses on a hill and a public house on the road side in the hollow below them   I seemed to pass the Milestones very quick in the morning but towards night they seemed to be stretched further asunder   I got to a village further on and forgot the name   the road on the left hand was quite over shaded by some trees and quite dry so I sat down half an hour and made a good many wishes for breakfast but wishes was no hearty meal so I got up as hungry as I sat down — I forget here the names of the villages I passed through but reccolect at late evening going through Potton in Bedfordshire where I called in a house to light my pipe in which was a civil old woman and a young country wench making lace on a cushion as round as a globe and a young fellow all civil people — I asked them a few questions as to the way and where the clergy-man and overseer lived but they scarcely heard me or gave me no answer*

I then went through Potton and happened with a kind talking country man who told me the Parson lived a good way from where I was or overseer I do'n't know which so I went on hopping with a crippled foot for the gravel had got into my old shoes one of which I had now nearly lost the sole   Had I found the overseers house at hand or the Parsons I should have gave my name and begged for a shilling to carry me home but I was forced to brush on pennyless and be thankfull I had a leg to move on — I then asked him wether he could tell me of a farm yard any where on the road where I could find a shed and some dry straw and he said yes and if you will go with me I will show you the place — its a public house on the left hand side the road at the sign of the 'Ram'[2] but seeing a stone or flint heap I longed to rest as one of my feet was very painfull so I thanked him for his kindness and bid him go on — but the good natured fellow lingered awhile as if wishing to conduct me and then suddenly reccolecting that he had a hamper on his shoulder and a lock up bag in his hand

---

* Note. On searching my pockets after the above was written I found part of a newspaper vide 'Morning Chronicle' on which the following fragments were pencilled soon after I got the information from labourers going to work or travellers journying along to better their condition as I was hopeing to do mine in fact I believed I saw home in every ones countenance which seemed so cheerfull in my own — 'There is no place like home' the following was written by the Road side:—
1st Day — Tuesday — Started from Enfield and slept at Stevenage on some clover trusses — cold lodging
Wednesday — Jacks Hill is passed already consisting of a beer shop and some houses on the hill appearing newly built — the last Mile stone 35 Miles from London got through Baldeck and sat under a dry hedge and had a rest in lieu of breakfast [Clare's note].

cram full to meet the coach which he feared missing – he started hastily and was soon out of sight – I followed looking in vain for the country mans straw bed – and not being able to meet it I lay down by a shed side under some Elm trees between the wall and the trees being a thick row planted some 5 or 6 feet from the buildings   I lay there and tried to sleep but the wind came in between them so cold that I lay till I quaked like the ague and quitted the lodging for a better at the Ram which I could hardly hope to find – It now began to grow dark apace and the odd houses on the road began to light up and show the inside tennants lots very comfortable and my outside lot very uncomfortable and wretched – still I hobbled forward as well as I could and at last came to the Ram   the shutters were not closed and the lighted window looked very cheering but I had no money and did not like to go in   there was a sort of shed or gighouse at the end but I did not like to lie there as the people were up – so I still travelled on   the road was very lonely and dark in places being overshaded with trees   at length I came to a place where the road branched off into two turnpikes one to the right about and the other straight forward and on going bye my eye glanced on a mile stone standing under the hedge so I heedlessly turned back to read it to see where the other road led too and on doing so I found it led to London   I then suddenly forgot which was North or South and though I narrowly examined both ways I could see no tree or bush or stone heap that I could reccolect I had passed so I went on mile after mile almost convinced I was going the same way I came and these thoug[h]ts were so strong upon me that doubt and hopelessness made me turn so feeble that I was scarcely able to walk yet I could not sit down or give up but shuffled along till I saw a lamp shining as bright as the moon which on nearing I found was suspended over a Tollgate[3]   before I got through the man came out with a candle and eyed me narrowly but having no fear I stopt to ask him wether I was going northward and he said when you get through the gate you are; so I thanked him kindly and went through on the other side and gathered my old strength   as my doubts vanished I soon cheered up and hummed the air of highland Mary[4] as I went on   I at length fell in with an odd house all alone near a wood but I could not see what the sign was though the sign seemed to stand oddly enough in a sort of trough or spout   there was a large porch over the door and being weary I crept in and glad enough I was to find I could lye with my legs straight   the inmates were all gone to roost for I could hear them turn over in bed as I lay on the stones in the porch – I slept here till daylight and felt very much refreshed as I got up – I blest my two wives and both their familys when I lay down and when I got up and when I thought of some former difficultys on a like occasion I could not help blessing the Queen* Having passed a Lodge on the left hand within a mile and half or less of a town I think it might be St Ives but I forget the name† I sat down to rest on a flint heap where I might rest half an hour or more and while sitting here I saw a tall Gipsey come out of the Lodge gate and make down the road towards where I was sitting when she got up to me on seeing she was a young woman with an honest looking countenance rather handsome I spoke to her and asked her a few questions which she answered readily and with evident good humour so I got up and went on to the next town with her – she cautioned me on the way to put somthing in my hat to keep the crown up and said in a lower tone 'you'll be noticed' but not knowing what she hinted – I took no notice and made no reply at length she pointed to a small tower church which she called Shefford Church[5] and advised me to go on a footway which would take me direct to it and I should shorten my journey fifteen miles by doing so I would gladly have taken the young womans advice feeling that it was honest and a nigh guess towards the truth but fearing I might loose my way and not be able to find the north road again I thanked her and told her I should keep to the road when she bade me 'good day' and went into a house or shop on the left hand side the road I have but a slight reccolection of my journey between here and Stilton for I was knocked up and noticed little or nothing – one night I lay in a dyke bottom from the wind and went sleep half an hour when I suddenly awoke and found one side wet through from the sock in the dyke bottom so I got out and went on – I remember going down a very dark road hung over with trees on both sides very thick which seemed to extend a mile or two I then entered a town and some of

* Clare has the following note:

The man whose daughter is the queen of England is now sitting on a stone heap on the highway to bugden without a farthing in his pocket and without tasting a bit of food ever since yesterday morning – when he was offerd a bit of Bread and cheese at Enfield – he has not had any since but If I put a little fresh speed on hope too may speed tomorrow – O Mary mary If you knew how anxious I am to see you and dear Patty with the childern I think you would come and meet me.

This was presumably written late on Wednesday, 21st. Bugden was an accepted variant of Buckden.

† It was St. Neots [Clare's note].

the chamber windows had candle lights shineing in them – I felt so
weary here that I forced to sit down on the ground to rest myself and
while I sat here a* Coach that seemed to be heavy laden came rattling
up and stopt in the hollow below me and I cannot reccolect its ever
passing by me   I then got up and pushed onward seeing little to
notice for the road very often looked as stupid as myself and I was
very often half asleep as I went   on the third day I satisfied my
hunger by eating the grass by the road side which seemed to taste
something like bread   I was hungry and eat heartily till I was
satisfied and in fact the meal seemed to do me good   the next and last
day I reccollected that I had some tobacco and my box of lucifers
being exausted I could not light my pipe so I took to chewing
Tobacco all day and eat the quids when I had done and I was never
hungry afterwards – I remember passing through Buckden and going
a length of road afterwards but I dont reccolect the name of any place
untill I came to stilton where I was compleatly foot foundered and
broken down   when I had got about half way through the town a
gravel causeway invited me to rest myself so I lay down and nearly
went sleep   a young woman (so I guessed by the voice) came out of a
house and said 'poor creature' and another more elderly said 'O he
shams' but when I got up the latter said 'o no he don't' as I hobbled
along very lame   I heard the voices but never looked back to see
where they came from – when I got near the Inn at the end of the
gravel walk I met two young women and I asked one of them wether
the road branching to the right bye the end of the Inn did not lead to
Peterborough and she said 'Yes' it did so as soon as ever I was on it I
felt myself in homes way and went on rather more cheerfull though I
forced to rest oftener then usual   before I got to Peterborough a man
and woman passed me in a cart and on hailing me as they passed I
found they were neighbours from Helpstone where I used to live – I
told them I was knocked up which they could easily see and that I had
neither eat or drank any thing since I left Essex   when I told my story
they clubbed together and threw me fivepence out of the cart   I
picked it up and called at a small public house near the bridge were I
had two half pints of ale and twopenn'oth of bread and cheese
   when I had done I started quite refreshed only my feet was more
crippled then ever and I could scarcely make a walk of it over the

* The Coach did pass me as I sat under some trees by a high wall and the lumps
lasshed in my face and wakened me up from a doze when I knocked the gravel out of
my shoes and started [Clare's note].

stones and being half ashamed to sit down in the street I forced to
keep on the move and got through Peterborough better then I
expected   when I got on the high road I rested on the stone heaps as I
passed till I was able to go on afresh and bye and bye I passed Walton
and soon reached Werrington and was making for the Beehive[6] as
fast as I could when a cart met me with a man and woman and a boy
in it when nearing me the woman jumped out and caught fast hold of
my hands and wished me to get into the cart but I refused and
thought her either drunk or mad but when I was told it was my
second wife Patty I got in and was soon at Northborough but Mary
was not there neither could I get any information about her further
then the old story of her being dead six years ago which might be
taken from a bran new old Newspaper printed a dozen years ago but
I took no notice of the blarney having seen her myself about a
twelvemonth ago alive and well and as young as ever – so here I am
homeless at home and half gratified to feel that I can be happy any
where

> Mary none those marks of my sad fate efface
> For they appeal from tyranny to God
> > Byron

July 24th 1841 Returned home out of Essex and found no Mary – her
and her family are as nothing to me now though she herself was once
the dearest of all – 'and how can I forget'

[Northampton MS 6, 2]

To Mary Clare – Glinton

Northborough July 27 1841

My dear wife
    I have written an account of my journey or rather escape from
Essex for your amusement and hope it may divert your leisure hours
– I would have told you before now that I got here to Northborough
last friday night but not being able to see you or to hear where you
was I soon began to feel homeless at home and shall bye and bye feel
nearly hopeless but not so lonely as I did in Essex – for here I can see
Glinton church and feeling that Mary is safe if not happy and I am
gratified   though my home is no home to me my hopes are not

entirely hopeless while even the memory of Mary lives so near me   God bless you My dear Mary Give my love to your dear and beautifull family and to your Mother – and believe me as I ever have been and ever shall be

My dearest Mary

Your affectionate Husband

John Clare

APPENDIX
Clare's Notes for his Autobiography

Carrying fathers dinner to the hayfield – filling his bottle at the fountain
house warmings – E.C.
Weddings
[Pilf]ering the sticking etc
living a year at Gregorys
refusing to be a shoe maker
tending horses of a sunday
getting peas to boil
old bibles
muddying ponds out for fish in meadow
Bathing
chalking names under brig arch with firsticks
Playing at soldiers – nine peg Morris
making cockades etc of corn poppys and blue bottles
Buying Isaac Walton at Stamford
Buying Leonidas Cue
childish games
making house of sticks clay and stones
gathering broken pots   getting mallow seeds and calling them cheeses when
playing
at feasts

Playing soldiers
Mallows etc   Mallow prizes Berys etc for keeping sunday well and going
church
Love Memorys
Acquaintance with Mary at school
Going to T Porters Cottage at Ashton every sunday
Meeting E Newbon there – her fathers bible
– meeting with E: Sells at Stamford fair – going to Southorp living at
Casterton

Acquaintance wi patty   going to work at Casterton – living
Burning lime at Pickworth   at Wilders – acquaintance with Patty
Playing the fiddle –   first acquaintance with Henson Deeping
Gardening at Wilders etc
Pattys Lodge   Drury   Lincoln
Beautiful Scenery   Taylor   London
Huge caverns in the woods there   Gilchrist   Stamford
                                  Revd Holland – Mrs Emmerson London
My first visit to London   Lord Radstock

Marriage etc etc

Going to Lord Milton to get him to   cutting pictures from books
    procure me a writers place   Pomfrets poems etc
his failure
his long enduring kindness to my father
the wish to dedicate my first poems to his Lor[d]ship
the reasons for not doing so
first Visit to Milton
Visit to Burghley

Old Hopkinson and wife – Morton
their characters

'Rumour and the popular voice'
'Some look to more then truth and so confirm Opinion'

Carey's Dante

first visit to London – going to Mr Carys church – Visiting Thompsons grave
    at Richmond church – Wainwright
Visit to holliwell house   mistake in a young governess spending sundays in
    woods
fetching bags flower maxey
robbing orchards nights
love affairs
Trip to Oundle
Local Militia

Visit to Wisbeach
Garden boy at burghley
Runaway to Newark
Return home
Old B . . . Journey from London wi 4$^{d\,1}$ [B3, 75–76]

Waithmans shop   Sir M. B. Clare[2]
Visit to Carys   West Indies

Drury and Songs by Crouch[3]   Sir T. Lawrence
Dedications
etc Writing for Every day book and for Receptacle   [B3, 88]

Pooty Hunting
Visiting favorite spots
Hopkinson   Morton
Boyish reccolections
French girl[4]   [A18, 273]

NOTES

Sketches in the Life of John Clare

1   *John Cue of Ufford*: He died on Wednesday, 2 February 1825, as we are told in Clare's *Journal* for that date. He had been head gardener for Lord Manners of Ufford Hall. Clare worked with him for some seasons at turnip-hoeing. From him (see p. 162) Clare acquired a copy of Leonidas.

2   *old Nixons Prophesies*: Robert Nixon, *A True Copy of Nixon's Cheshire Prophecy* (London, 1715). A chapbook of the same kind as *Mother Shipton's Legacy*, see below. Such books were published by the Aldermary Churchyard Press, owned by the Dicey family. Mentioned by Clare at B5, 82. Several editions are in the Harding Collection, Bodleian Library, Oxford.

   Mother Bunches Fairey Tales: See G. L. Gomme (ed.), *Mother Bunch's Closet Newly Broke Open and The History of Mother Bunch of the West* (London, 1885). *Mother Bunch's Fairy Tales*, printed for S. Maunder, 10 Newgate St. Price Sixpence, 1830, and many other editions, several in the Harding Collection, Bodleian Library, Oxford.

   Mother Shiptons Legacy: See W. H. Harrison, *Mother Shipton Investigated*, 1881: also K. M. Briggs, *A Dictionary of British Folk Tales*, 1970, Part A, vol. 2, p. 549 and Part B, vol. 2, pp. 690–1. Mentioned by Clare at B5, 82. See also *The History of Mother Shipton* [Ursula Sonteil], Coventry, 1815. There are several editions in the Harding Collection, Bodleian Library, Oxford.

3   *the sister that was born with me*: There is no mention of her baptism at Helpston but such an occurrence was not uncommon. She was called 'Bessey' by Clare. See 'To a Twin Sister who Died in Infancy', *London Magazine*, August 1821.

4   *adam and Eve*: This Bible story was always of very great significance to Clare's writing.

5   *a master at a distance*: John Seaton of Glinton.

6   *the flower of honour*: Admiral the Hon. William Waldegrave, second son of the third Earl Waldegrave, later Baron Radstock, had been a friend of Nelson, quelled a mutiny on HMS *Latona* at the mutiny of the Nore. He was an ardent evangelical and became Clare's patron. See pp. 43–4.

7   *the bible*: Clare's work is deeply marked by his knowledge of the Bible. In particular he wrote many verse-paraphrases of biblical passages. See E. Robinson and D. Powell, *The Later Poems of John Clare* (Oxford, 1983).

8   *Sixpenny Romances*: See G. Deacon, *John Clare and the Folk Tradition*, 1983. These pamphlets sold by hawkers were an important part of Clare's literary tradition. Some of the books to which Clare refers, e.g. Thomson's *Seasons*, Defoe's *Robinson Crusoe* and Kirke White's *Remains*, were published in chapbook editions and it may be to these that he refers.

   'Zig Zag': Probably refers to the story entitled 'The Man with a Long Nose' (see Briggs, op. cit., Part A, vol. 1, pp. 408–9) in which occurs the rhyme:

> Did you see a maid running zigzag
> And in her hand a long leather bag

With all the gold that e'er I won,
since the time I was a boy yet?

'*Prince Cherry*': The same story as 'Prince Darling'. See A. Lang, *The Blue Fairy Book* (New York, 1966), pp. 278–89.

9   *Bonnycastles Mensuration*: J. Bonnycastle, *An Introduction to Mensuration and Practical Geometry*, 10th edn., 1807.

   Fennings Arithmetic and Algebra: D. Fenning, The British Youth's Instructor; or, a . . . Guide to Practical Arithmetic, 2nd edn., 1754: D. Fenning, *The Young Algebraist's Companion*, 1750.

10   *John Turnill*: Elder brother of Richard Turnill, Clare's schoolfellow and first close friend. They were the sons of a neighbouring farmer for whom both Clare and his father worked at various times. There are other testimonies (see pp. 28 and 40) to John Turnill's intellectual aspirations.

11   *a shoemaker*: Will Farrow, see pp. 10, 49, and 53.

12   *Francis Gregory*: Proprietor of the Blue Bell Inn, kept a few animals and had about six acres of land under the plough. See pp. 54–5 and 60.

13   *Thompsons Seasons*: James Thomson's *Seasons*, 1730.

14   *the words Lord and God*: See note, p. 128.

15   *Burghly Park*: Burghley House, just South of Stamford, the home of the Marquis of Exeter, one of Clare's patrons.

16   '*the morning walk*': 'A Morning Walk: Ah, sure it is . . .' See Peterborough A23.

17   *the evening walk*: 'Recollections after an Evening Walk: Just as the even-bell rang . . .' See J. W. Tibble, *The Poems of John Clare*, 1935, vol. 1, pp. 75–6.

18   *the Master of the Kitchen Garden*: See pp. 61–3.

19   *on this ramble*: See pp. 63–4.

20   *Pomfrets 'Love triumphant over reason*': Revd John Pomfret, *Poems on Several Occasions* (London, 1746), pp. 15–33.

21   '*Abercrombies Gardiners Journal*': John Abercrombie, *The Gardener's Pocket Journal* or *Every Man his own Gardener*. In Clare's library, items 89 and 90 are Abercrombie's *The Gardener's Companion*, 1818, and his *Practical Gardener*, 1823.

   '*Wards Mathematics*': E. Ward, *The Elements of Arithmetic . . . In five parts* (Liverpool, 1813).

   Fishers 'Young mans companion': George Fisher, *The Instructor: or Young Man's Best Companion*, 1763.

   '*Robin Hoods Garland*': This was a popular chapbook containing songs and had many publishers. One copy is no. 29 in the John Johnson collection in the Bodleian Library. It was published at price 6d. by Dicey who also published the *Northampton Mercury*. His distribution-routes for chapbooks ran through Peterborough, Stamford, and Boston.

   '*Death of Abel*': S. Gessner, *Death of Abel*, trans. F. Shoberl, n.d. but probably 1814. Much of Clare's Eden imagery may have derived from this work. Selections from Gessner were also published as a chapbook.

   '*Joe Millers Jests*': Another famous chapbook, e.g. *Joe Miller's Jest Book; forming a rich Banquet of Wit and Humour*, 1834. It dates from the Elizabethan period.

'*Collection of Hymns*': Perhaps John Wesley, *A Collection of Hymns, for the use of people called Methodists*, 1825. Item 393 in Clare's Library. See D. Powell, *Catalogue of the John Clare Collection in the Northampton Public Library* (Northampton, 1964), p. 33.

22 *grammer*: See p. 28.

23 '*Universal Spelling Book*': Daniel Fenning, *The Universal Spelling Book; or, a New and Easy Guide to the English Language*, 1756, was a popular textbook and reached its 71st edition in 1823.

24 *Mr Arnold M.D.*: Arnold attended Clare at John Taylor's request in spring, 1824. See Tibble, *Letters of John Clare*, p. 159.

25 *Thomas Porter*: See also pp. 21, 61, and 162. Letter from Clare to Charles Clare, 1 June 1849: '. . . how is Thomas Porter of Ashton he used to be my Companion in my single Days when we loved Books and Flowers together' (Northampton MS 30).

26 *a Bookseller*: J. B. Henson of Market Deeping. See pp. 98–100. He was also a preacher and a publisher of chapbooks, though I have not been able to find surviving specimens of his work. There was a Henson, printer of broadsides (see Northampton Public Library and Maddon Collection, Cambridge University Library), of 81 Bridge St., Northampton, but he seems to have been George Henson, possibly a relation of Clare's would-be publisher.

27 *Ryhall*: Clare sometimes spells this name 'Royal'.

28 '*Enquirer*': The *Boston Enquirer*: this subscription is mentioned, p. 100. The copies are item 199 in Clare's Library. See Powell, op. cit., p. 27.

29 *Mr Drury*: Edward Drury of Lincoln, bookseller, publisher, friend of Peter De Wint and William Hilton and cousin of John Taylor.

30 *the Setting Sun*: See Tibble, *Poems*, vol. 1, p. 117.

31 '*Bachellors Hall*': Still stands in Helpston in Heath Road.

32 *John and James Billings*: See pp. 41–3. They shared Clare's fondness for chapbooks. Clare began some of his prose writings to raise money for the brothers. See Tibble, *Prose of John Clare*, p. 5.

33 *gentlemen*: Edward Drury and Richard Newcomb, publisher of the *Stamford Mercury*. See p. 101.

34 *John Taylor*: (1781–1864) Publisher and bookseller, he had served with James Lackington and with Vernor and Hood. He had previously assisted in the publication of Robert Bloomfield. He founded the *London Magazine* and was also the publisher of Keats, Hazlitt, Reynolds, Cary, Lamb, De Quincey, and Landor. See E. Blunden, *Keats's Publisher* and T. Chilcote, *A Publisher and his Circle*.

35 *Patty*: Martha Turner, who became Clare's wife.

36 *Mary*: Mary Joyce, daughter of a farmer at Glinton, and Clare's first love.

37 *ranters*: Primitive Methodists. See Mark Minor, 'John Clare and the Methodists: A Reconstruction', *Studies in Romanticism*, 19, Spring 1980.

Autobiographical Fragments

1 *duck under water*: 'A game in which the players run, two and two, in rapid succession, under a handkerchief held up aloft by two persons standing apart with extended arms. Formerly, in the northern part of this county, even married

women on May Day played at this game, under the garland which was extended from chimney to chimney across the village street'. A. E. Baker, *Glossary of Northamptonshire Words and Phrases* (1854), 2 vols.

2 *eastwell spring*: A natural spring near Helpston which became a local meeting-place.

3 *Emmonsales*: Emmonsales, or Ailsworth, Heath – now a nature reserve.

4 *Langley Bush*: A favourite meeting-point for gypsies near Helpston and originally the site of the open courts. A gibbet once stood at the spot. Clare tells us that it was destroyed by vandalism.

5 *poor cade foal*: This story of the cade, or pet, foal is so near to Robert Bloomfield's poem, 'The Fakenham Ghost', that one wonders once again whether fact and fiction may not have become intertwined in Clare's mind.

6 'Rotten Moor', 'Dead Moor', *Eastwell moor, Banton green, Lolham Briggs, Rine dyke*: Many of these spots are identified in Daniel Crowson's pamphlet, *Rambles with John Clare*, 1798.

7 *Northborough*: This legend is clearly connected with the chapbook, *History of Gotham*.

8 *a young lady being killd . . . by a shield ball*: This may be connected with the unidentified book, *The Female Shipwright*. Stories of girls going to sea in search of their lovers were common.

9 *the old man and his ass*: A chapbook. Several editions in the Harding Collection, Bodleian Library, Oxford.

10 *Culpeppers Herbal*: Nicholas Culpepper, probably the edition by John Hill (London, 1792).

11 *the king and the cobler*: A chapbook. Several editions in the Johnson and the Harding Collections, Bodleian Library, Oxford e.g. *The Comical History of the King and Cobler, the Two Parts in One*, Liverpool, Printed for W. Armstrong, Banaster-Street. See also Briggs, op. cit., Part A, vol. 2, p. 437.

Seven Sleepers: A chapbook. Several editions in the Harding Collection, Bodleian Library, Oxford. See also R. Johnson, *The Most Famous History of the Seven Champions of Christendom*.

12 *the Pleasant art of money catching*: An anonymous publication, 1816–51. See *The Pleasant Art of Money-Catching and the Way to Thrive by Turning a Penny to Advantage* . . . Falkirk, Printed for the Booksellers, 1840, in the Harding Collection.

13 *Lord Radstock*: Admiral the Hon. William Waldegrave, second son of the third Earl Waldegrave, became the first Baron Radstock. Friend of Nelson and Naval Governor of Newfoundland, he quelled a mutiny on board HMS *Latona* at the mutiny of the Nore. He was an ardent evangelical and a very kindly man. See J. Marshall, *Royal Naval Biography* (1823–5), 8 vols, *The Annual Biography and Obituary* (1825), and D. W. Prouse, *A History of Newfoundland* (1896).

14 *Behnes*: Henry Burlow Behnes (d. 1837), the sculptor. Also made a bust of Clare now in Northampton Public Library. He tried to get S. C. Hall and others to pay Clare for his work.

15 *Lord Fitzwilliam*: Charles William Wentworth Fitzwilliam (1786–1857), third Earl Fitzwilliam, a man noted for his probity and independence of mind. See also pp. 116 and 118.

16 *Revd Holland*: Revd Isaiah Knowles Holland (d. 1873). Presbyterian minister at

Northborough and then St Ives, Huntingdon. Clare dedicated 'The Woodman' to him.

17 *Kirk White*: The poet, Henry Kirke White, author of *Remains*, 1824. Items nos. 396–7 in Clare's library. The book was also published as a chapbook.

18 *the Scotch Rogue*: A chapbook. Several editions in the Harding Collection, Bodleian Library, Oxford.

19 *Lord Milton*: Charles Fitzwilliam, usually so-called by Clare in his father's lifetime. See note 15 above.

20 *Milton*: The Fitzwilliam estate near Peterborough.

21 Identified titles are: *Dilworth Wingates Hodders Vyses and Cockers Arithmetic*: Thomas Dilworth, *The Schoolmaster's Assistant: being a compendium of arithmetic, both practical and theoretical* (London, 1744); Edmund Wingate, *Arithmetique made easie*, (London, 1652: 18th edn. by 1751); James Hodder, *Arithmetick* (London, 1702): item 242 in Clare's library; Charles Vyse, *The Tutor's Guide: being a complete system of Arithmetic* . . . (1770); Edward Cocker, *Cocker's Arithmetic*, (London, 1688): item 159 in Clare's library.

Horners Mensuration and Wards Mathematics Leybourns and Morgans Dialling: Horner: not identified. E. Ward, *The Elements of Arithmetic* (Liverpool, 1813); William Leybourne, *The Art of Dialling, by a Trigonal Instrument* (1699); Sylvanus Morgan, *Horologiographica: Dialling Universal and Particular* (London, 1652).

Female Shipwright: Unidentified chapbook. But see W. Clark Russell, *A Book for the Hammock*, 1887, pp. 91–114, for stories of women going to war in search of missing lovers or husbands.

Martindales Land Surveying and Cockers Land surveying: Alan Martindale, *The Country Survey-Book, or Land Meeter's Vade Mecum*, (London, 1682). Unidentified book by Edward Cocker, author of *Arithmetic*, 1678.

Hills Herbal: John Hill, *The British Herbal*, 1756. Clare requested the Revd Charles Mossop in a letter dated January 1832 to send back his copy of Hill's *Herbal*. Tibble, *Letters*, p. 260.

Balls Astrology: Richard Ball, *An Astrolo-Physical Compendium: or a brief introduction to astrology* (London, 1697).

Rays History of the Rebellion: James Ray, *A Compleat History of the Rebellion* . . . *in 1745*, 1749.

Sturms Reflections: Christopher Christian Sturm, *Reflections on the Works of God*, trans. from the German in 1788. Clare was presented with the same author's *Morning Communions with God*, 1825, by Herbert Marsh, Bishop of Peterborough, on 24 August 1827. Selections from Sturm were also published as a chapbook.

Harveys Meditations: James Hervey, *Meditations among the Tombs*, 1746 and many subsequent editions.

Thompsons Travels: Charles Thompson, *The Travels*, 1744.

Life of Barnfield: Probably *The Apprentices Tragedy or the History of George Barnwell*. A chapbook. See Harding Collection, Bodleian Library, Oxford.

more: Probably Thomas Moore, the Irish poet, unless he means Hannah More, whose *Spirit of Prayer*, 1825 was given to him by Lord Radstock (item 312 in Clare's library).

Duty of Man: Richard Allestree, *The Whole Duty of Man*, 1659. It was also published as a chapbook.

Lees Botany: James Lee, the elder, *An introduction to botany . . . extracts from the works of Linnaeus* (London, 1760).

Kings Tricks of London laid open: Richard King, *The new Cheats of London exposed; or, the frauds and tricks of the town laid open to both sexes* (Manchester, 1795).

The Fathers Legacy or seven stages of Life: A chapbook called 'The Seven Stages of Life' occurs in the Harding Collection, Bodleian Library.

22 *O. Gilchrist*: Octavius Graham Gilchrist (d. 1823). Grocer of Stamford, wrote on Clare in the *London Magazine*, January 1820. See also pp. 105, 117, and 129. He was editor of *Drakard's Stamford News*.

23 *Ray*: John Ray (1627–1705), author of the famous *Historia Plantarum* (1686–1704, 3 vols), also published a *Synopsis stirpium Britannicarum* (1690). It may be the shorter work to which Clare refers. Ray's interest in English words and proverbs would also have endeared him to Clare. See C. E. Raven, *John Ray Naturalist: His Life and Works* (Cambridge, 1950).

Parkinson: John Parkinson, *Theatrum Botanicum*, 1640.

Gerrard: John Gerard: *The Herball, or generall Historie of Plants . . .* (1630).

24 *my friend Artis*: Edmund Tyrell Artis. Butler to Lord Milton but famous as an archaeologist. Published the beautiful *Durobrivae of Antoninus* in 1828. Clare helped him with his digs. See also p. 126.

25 *Mrs Bellairs*: Owner of Woodcroft Farm. Clare was still enquiring after her as late as 15 June 1847. See Tibble, *Letters*, p. 297.

26 *'the milking pail'*: There are many songs of this name. This may be related to a chapbook entitled 'The Milk Pail' published by Aldermary Churchyard Press.

'Jack with his broom': To be found most easily as 'The Green Broom' in Lucy E. Broadwood, *English Country Songs*, pp. 88–9. It may also be found as 'The Jolly Broom-man: or, the Unhappy Boy turnd Thrifty' in Thomas d'Urfey, *Wit, and Mirth; or Pills to Purge Melancholy* (1719–20), 16 vols, vol. IV, p. 100.

27 *'Little red riding hood'* etc.: Most of these chapbook stories are familiar even to the modern reader, but see K. M. Briggs, *A Dictionary of British Folk Tales* and G. Deacon, *John Clare and the Folk Tradition*. R. Holmes, *The Legend of Sawney Bean*, 1975, p. 18 identifies four broadsheet versions in the National Library of Scotland. *The Seven Sleepers* appears in the W. W. H. Harding Collection, Bodleian Library. It is also printed in William Hone, *The Everyday Book*, vol. 1, pp. 1034–7, for 27 July 1838. *The History of Gotham* is discussed in J. E. Field, *The Myth of the Pent Cuckoo*, 1913. See Clare's passage about Northborough, p. 39 above. Clare made a note to purchase *Valentine and Orson* as a Christmas present for his daughter, Anna, and *Cock Robin* for Eliza (see D14, 7). 'Old mother Bunch' and 'Old Nixons Prophecys' are identified above, note to p. 2. Robin Hoods Garland was a 'special chapbook' published by the Aldermary Churchyard Press. It was a collection of songs and can be found as no. 29 in the John Johnson Collection at the Bodleian Library. *The History of Thomas Hickathrift*, Aldermary Churchyard Press, (London, 1790), is also to be found, with other editions, in the Harding Collection, Bodleian Library, Oxford.

28 *Rippingille*: Edward Villiers Rippingille (d. 1859). Painter of rural scenes. Worked in Bristol. See pp. 131, 140, and 143–4. These paintings have not yet been identified.

NOTES

29 *Tant Baker*: See *Drunken Barnaby's Four Journeys to the North of England*, 1822, edited by Gilchrist for an account of Baker's 'Hole in the Wall' or 'Hole of Sarah', the 'drunkard's cave'.

30 *Peter Pindar*: The pseudonym of John Wolcot (1738–1819), author of *The Lousiad*, 1785, in which he ridiculed the King, Pitt, and others.

31 *Tycho Wing*: (1696–1750). Astrologer and editor of *Olympia Domata*.

32 *Smiths*: Well-known gypsy name. In his *Journal*, Friday, 3 June 1825, Clare wrote: 'got the tune of Highland Mary from Wisdom Smith a gipsey and pricked another sweet tune without name as he fiddled it'. See note 4 to *Journey out of Essex*.

33 *Boswells*: Another well-known gypsy name. Tyso Boswell's daughter, Sophia, married John Grey, who taught Clare the fiddle. See Sylvester Boswell, *The Autobiography of a Gipsy*, ed. John Seymour, 1970.

34 *Mary –––––*: Mary Joyce.

35 *Elizabeth N[ewbon]*: Elizabeth, or Betty, Newbon. Wrongly identified as 'Newton' in F. Martin's *Life of John Clare*.

36 *Lord Napier Key*: John Napier, *A Plaine Discovery of the whole Revelation of Saint John*, 1593.

37 *Moors Almanack*: Old Moore's Almanack. An example is reproduced in L. James, *Print and the People, 1819–1851* (1976), p. 156.

38 *the lodge*: Walkherd Lodge, home of Patty (Martha Turner).

39 *Chatterton*: Thomas Chatterton (1752–70) who tried to pass off his poems as old MSS. He killed himself at the age of seventeen.

40 *'history of Joseph'*: *The History of Joseph and his Brethren*, a popular chapbook, was reprinted in J. Ashton, *Chapbooks of the Eighteenth Century*, 1882. There is an edition (no. 41) in the Johnson Collection at the Bodleian Library, Oxford, and several in the Harding Collection at the same library. Most editions are embellished with woodcuts.

41 *Revd Mr Mounsey*: Revd Thomas Mounsey, second master at Stamford Free Grammar School.

42 *Sir English Dobbin*: Sir John English Dobben of Finedon Place, Northamptonshire, ancestor of Robert Bridge's friend.

43 *Edwin and Emma*: David Mallet's 'Ballad of Edwin and Emma' was published as a chapbook. She also *Journal of the Folk Lore Society*, June 1909, no. 13 and no. 3.

The poems mentioned by Clare in this section, 'The Fate of Amy', 'The Lost Greyhound' or 'On a lost Greyhound lying on the Snow', and 'Crazy Nell' can be found in *Poems Descriptive of Rural Life and Scenery* (1820). These poems represent the genre of story-telling ballads describing pathetic rural events to which Clare was always strongly attracted. John Taylor, his publisher, while favouring them at first seems to have become increasingly critical of such poems.

44 *charlotte Smith*: Charlotte Smith (1749–1806). Her popular *Elegiac Sonnets* appeared in 1784.

45 *Dr Bell*: It was Dr J. G. Bell who secured a half yearly annuity from Earl Spencer for Clare. See Tibble, *Letters*, p. 86 and p. 122. He lived in Stamford and Clare met him at Edward Drury's.

46 *a young girl at Southorpe*: Betty Sell, daughter of a labourer at Southorp.

47 *Woods Historys*: This was the story of the king's chaplain, Dr Michael Hudson, who was trying to escape from Woodcroft Castle and had his hands cut off as he hung from the battlements. The story was told in Sir Walter Scott's *Woodstock* and in Clare's original version of 'The Village Minstrel'.

48 *Chauncy Hare Townsend*: The Revd Chauncy Hare Townshend (1798–1868), friend of Dickens. *Great Expectations* was dedicated to him. He published *Poems* in 1821 and *Sermons in Sonnets* in 1851. His letters to Clare are to be found in the Egerton MSS, The British Library.

49 *our parson*: Revd Charles Mossop, vicar of Helpston.

50 *Hon^{bl} Mr Pierpoint*: Henry Manvers Pierrepont, brother-in-law to the Marquis of Exeter.

51 *Blairs Sermons*: Hugh Blair, *Sermons*, 1819. Item 117 in Clare's library. See also Clare's *Journal* for 31 October 1824.

52 *Mrs Emmerson*: Eliza Louisa Emmerson (1782–1847). See below pp. 130–1. She was a poet and a keen admirer of Clare's work. Unfortunately much of her correspondence with Clare has disappeared. She was a friend of Lord Radstock and an evangelical.

53 *Captain Sherwell*: Captain Markham E. Sherwill, author of *Ascent to the Summit of Mount Blanc* (1825) and *Poems* (1832).

54 *Preston*: Edward Preston. F. Martin, *The Life of John Clare*, ed. E. Robinson and G. Summerfield (1964), p. 124 says of him: 'The first of the tribe [of writers of unpublished books visiting Clare] was an individual of the name of Preston, a native of Cambridge, and author of an immense quantity of poetic, artistic and scientific works, none of them printed . . .'

55 *Ireland the Shakespear Phantom*: William Henry Ireland (1777–1835) wrote verse imitations of early authors and then graduated to forging Shakespearian plays. When discredited he wandered almost penniless through Wales and Gloucestershire, visiting at Bristol in the autumn of 1796 the scenes connected with Chatterton's tragic death. He also wrote poems in imitation of Robert Bloomfield.

56 *Hilton*: William Hilton, painter, RA (1819) and Keeper of the Academy (1820). He painted portraits of both Clare and Keats.

57 *Ryde*: Henry Ryde, estate-agent at Burghley.

58 *Mr Hopkinson*: Hopkinson may have been the religious magistrate denounced by Clare for his unfeeling denunciation of gypsies. See p. 69. He lived at Morton in Lincolnshire. Clare once wrote to Taylor 'if I had an enemy I coud wish to torture I woud not wish him hung nor yet at the devil my worst wish shoud be a weeks confinment in some vicarage to hear an old parson and his wife lecture on the wants and wickedness of the poor . . .' (Northampton MS 30).

59 *Beatties Minstrel*: James Beattie, *The Minstrel*, 1819, presented by Chauncy Hare Townshend, 6 May 1820, is item 112 in Clare's library.

60 *never heard of him afterwards*: Clare was in fact to receive further letters from him.

61 *the Bishop of Peterboro*: Herbert Marsh.

62 *Miss Aikins Elizabeth*: Lucy Aikin, *Memoirs of the Court of Queen Elizabeth*, 1818.

63 *his Lady . . . Revd Mr Parsons*: Marsh's wife, Marianne . . . and presumably a chaplain to the Bishop of Peterborough.

64 *General Birch Reynardson*: Thomas Birch married Etheldred Ann Reynardson, eldest daughter of Jacob Reynardson of Holywell Hall in the county of Lincoln, and in 1801 assumed the additional surname of Reynardson.

65 *Henderson*: Head gardener at Milton Park.

66 *Madam Vestris*: John Clare's 'The Meeting', set to music by Haydn Corri, was sung by Madame Vestris and was published as a broadsheet. See Deacon, op. cit., pp. 64–5.

67 *Kean and Macready and Knight and Munden and Emmery*: Edmund Kean was playing at Drury Lane in *The Hebrew*, a drama based on *Ivanhoe*, Macready at Covent Garden in *Ivanhoe, or The Jewess*, a musical play. Munden and Emery were in a farce at the same theatre.

68 *fearful disclosures*: These stories suggest the chapbook, *Sweeney Todd*.

69 *Burkhardt*: J. C. Burkhardt, a London jeweller, and Gilchrist's brother-in-law.

70 *Beggars Opera*: Clare means Beggars Bush, a public house and vaudeville in Holborn.

71 *Allan Cunningham*: Writer and poet (1784–1842). His son was a patient at Dr Matthew Allen's asylum in Epping Forest at the same time that Clare was there.

72 *Wainwright*: Thomas Griffiths Wainewright. Friend of Charles Lamb, painter and forger. See J. Curling, *James Weathercock*. Did paintings from Walton's *Angler*.

73 *Reynolds*: John Hamilton Reynolds (1796–1832), friend of Keats and Byron, most famous for his 'Peter Bell', a very witty parody of Wordsworth. It is interesting to find him satirizing Wordsworth for mentioning the number of eggs in a nest since this would seem more appropriate as a criticism of Clare. ('Look! *five* blue eggs are gleaming there'). Reynolds published *The Naiad* and also a book of literary forgeries *The Fancy: A Selection from the Poetical Remains of Peter Corcoran* (1820). He contributed to the *London Magazine* under the name of Edward Herbert but eventually quarrelled with Taylor.

74 *Carey the translator of Dante*: The Revd H. F. Cary (1772–1844). The following description of the crane in Clare's *The Shepherd's Calendar* derives at least in part from Cary's *Dante* which Clare owned:

> the solitary crane
> Swings lonly to unfrozen dykes again
> Cranking a jarring melancholy cry
> Thro the wild journey of the cheerless sky.

See E. Robinson and G. Summerfield, *John Clare; The Shepherd's Calendar* (Oxford, 1964), p. 33.

75 *Gifford*: William Gifford, editor of the *Quarterly*. His translation of *The Satires of Aulus Persius Flaccus*, 1821, is item no. 221 in Clare's library.

76 *'Mohawks'*: A satirical poem by Sydney Owenson, later Lady Morgan.

77 *Murray*: John Murray, the publisher.

78 *Waithman*: Robert Waithman, Lord Mayor of London in 1823, was a political reformer. He was a linen-draper.

79 *Bullocks Mexico*: An exhibition of Mexican curiosities at the Egyptian Hall.

80 *D' Darling*: Dr George Darling (1782–1862), friend of John Taylor, physician to Keats, Wilkie, Haydon, Chantry and others.

81 *Devilles the Phrenologists*: Deville was one of the most respected 'professional' phrenologists in London, from the 1820s to the 1840s. See Clare's letter to Sir Charles Elton, Tibble, *Letters*, p. 164.

82 *Elton*: Sir Charles Abraham Elton (1778–1853), 6th baronet, was a scholar and author. His novel, *The Brothers*, 1820, is item 197 in Clare's library.

83 *Oliver*: Tom Oliver, famous pugilist.

84 *Jones the Sailor Boy*: A famous pugilist with whom Clare identified himself in his years of madness.

85 *Sir T.L.*: Sir Thomas Lawrence, painter. Clare always remained appreciative of his kindness.

86 *F freelings*: Sir Francis Freeling (1764–1836), Secretary to the General Post Office.

87 *the french Playhouse*: The Royal West London was known as the 'French Theatre'. See C. V. Fletcher 'The poetry of John Clare, with particular reference to poems written between 1837 and 1864', M.Phil. thesis, University of Nottingham, 1973.

88 *Astleys Theatre*: A low vaudeville in London.

89 *Van Dyk*: Harry Stoe Van Dyk helped Taylor to edit Clare's *Shepherd's Calendar*. He was the author of *English Romances and Songs of the Six Minstrels*. His poem, *The Gondola*, is item no. 382 in Clare's library.

90 *Etty the painter*: William Etty, RA (1787–1849), whom Clare classed alongside Hilton and Rippingille, as one of the neglected geniuses of the age.

Journey out of Essex

1 *my first wife*: Mary Joyce, Clare's childhood sweetheart. When Clare went mad he believed that he had married Mary and had had children by her, but that he had subsequently married Martha (Patty) Turner, his real wife, and had had a family also by her. His imprisonment at High Beach (actually a voluntary committal) he saw as punishment for his 'bigamy'.

2 *the 'Ram'*: See A. Tibble, *John Clare: The Journal, Essays, the Journey from Essex* (Manchester, 1980), p. 120 for a photograph and identification of this public house.

3 *Tollgate*: There was a turnpike gate at Temsford.

4 *highland Mary*: See Clare's *Journal*, Friday, 3 June 1825, where Clare says that he got the tune from a gypsy, Wisdom Smith. The words are by Burns but the air is much older and is called 'Katherine Ogie'. See broadside, John Johnson Collection, Box IV, no. 46, Bodleian Library. 'Highland Mary' was also published in several song-books, e.g. *The Garland of New Songs*, Harding, A31(9), A51(9) etc.

5 *Shefford Church*: See F. W. Martin's *The Life of John Clare*, ed. Eric Robinson and Geoffrey Summerfield (London, 1964), p. 310: Clare's narrative, understandably, is not entirely consistent. For example, when he met the young gypsy woman about a mile and a half West of St Neots it would have been impossible for her to have pointed to Shefford Church, if by Shefford is intended the town mid-way between Bedford and Hitchin. The confusion may have been due to the fact that Shefford was the home of Thomas Inskip, Clare's friend, and it is symptomatic of Clare's sense of urgency that he did not make the short detour to Shefford where Inskip could have been counted on for help and shelter. Some of

NOTES

Clare's landmarks, however, are tolerably clear and agree with those described in Cary's *New Itinerary*, 1815 edition. His route corresponded for the most part to the recognized Coach Road and Waggon Way.

6 *the Beehive*: There was a public house of this name at Stamford but none thus called that I have been able to trace at Werrington.

Appendix: Clare's Notes for his Autobiography

1 *Old B . . .* : Clare has written at the side of A33, 9 a note indicating that he is referring to Burbridge. I have not identified this work, entitled, according to Clare, *Old Burbridge's Journey to London wi 4ᵈ*.

2 *Sir M. B. Clare*: Sir Michael Benignus Clare, a rich West Indian, sent five guineas to Clare in September 1822, for the name's sake.

3 *Drury and Songs by Crouch*: At Edward Drury's suggestion, Clare's songs were set to music by Crouch who sold them on sheets embellished in a rather flamboyant manner. He never paid Clare for his work and Clare was reproved by John Taylor for entering into the arrangement with Drury. Crouch dedicated the songs to various notable people. F. Martin, *Life of John Clare* was the first to comment on this business. A single example of one of Crouch's settings of Clare survives in the British Library Music Collection. It is of 'Sweet the Merry Bells Ring Round'.

4 *French girl*: No account has survived in the autobiographical fragments of Clare's meeting with this girl who was probably connected with the French prisoners-of-war at Norman Cross. The following sonnet occurs, however, at A61, 40:

> I cannot know what country owns thee now
> With frances fairest lillies on thy brow
> When england knew thee thou wert passing fair
> I never knew a foreign face so rare
> The world of waters roll and rushes by
> Nor let me wander where thy vallies lie
> But surely france must be a pleasant place
> That greets the strange[r] with so fair a face
> The english maiden blushes down the dance
> But few can equal the fair maid of france
> I saw thee lovely and I wished thee mine
> And the last song I ever wrote is thine
> Thy countrys honour on thy face attends
> Man may be foes but beauty makes us friends

175

GLOSSARY

Abraham (to sham Abraham), to feign illness
ansel, *n.*, handsel, earnest of a bargain
apathisd, *a.*, apathetic
armorous, *a.*, amorous
Armours, *n.*, *amours*

bark men, *n.*, men who come to strip bark
bawks, *n.*, baulks
be, *prep.*, by
bee flye, *n.*, *Bombylius major*
blealy, *a.*, bleakly
bluebottles, bluecaps, blue corn bottles, *n.*, cornflowers (*Centaurea Cyanus*)
bogbean hiskhead, *n.*, bogbean huskhead, buckbean (*Meryanthes trifoliata*)
brancing, *a.*, prancing
brig, *n.*, bridge
buckbane, *n.*, buckbean (*Meryanthes trifoliata*)
Burvine, *n.*, probably burweed (*Xanthium Stramarium*)

cade, *a.*, pet
car, *n.*, care
childern, *n.*, children
chusd, *v.*, choosed
cite, *n.*, site
cloths, *n.*, clothes
clowns, *n.*, yokels
consieting, *part.*, conceiting, an obsolete form of conceiving
courtois, *a.*, courteous

cubbard, *n.*, cupboard
cuckoos, *n.*, cuckoo flowers. Red-flowered campion (*Lychnio dioica*)
cultured, *a.*, cultivated, ploughed
cumberground, *n.*, obstacle

descent, *a.*, decent
dilacet, *a.*, delicate
dinging, *part.*, struggling
dotterel, *n.*, a pollarded tree

edding, *n.*, heading
edling, *n.*, heading
eke, *v.*, increase

feelow, *n.*, fellow
feign, *a.*, fain
flower, *n.*, flour
forced, *a.*, obliged
fresh (to get fresh), to drink too much
frit, *a.*, frightened
frumity, *n.*, a dish of steeped wheat boiled in milk, with sugar and plums
furzebind, *n.*, tormentil (*Potentilla erecta*)

gighouse, *n.*, coach house
glegging, *part.*, peeping
grain, *n.*, branch
grip, *n.*, cart rut
gropes, *n.*, groups

head aches, *n.*, poppies
hernshaw, *n.*, heron (*Ardea cinerea*)

himny, *n.*, hymn
hip (to be in a), to be annoyed
hipt, *a.*, annoyed
horse bee, *n.*, horse-tick or gad-fly
hugd, *v.*, hugged
hurd, *n.*, hoard
huswife, *n.*, housewife

jeanty, *a.*, jaunty
jiant, *n.*, giant
joal, *n.*, gaol
jobbling, *part.*, moving unevenly
   like a choppy sea
jocolate, *a.*, chocolate
Joe Miller, joke
Jougler, Juggler

kidding, *part.*, cutting

lapt, *a.*, wrapped
learing, *part.*, learning
leiser, *n.*, leisure
listed, *v.*, enlisted
loath, *a.*, loth
long purples, *n.*, purple looestrife
   (*Lithrum salicaria*)
lordship, *n.*, the manor
lucifers, *n.*, matches

morts, *n.*, lots
mote, *n.*, moat
mystical, *a.*, mysterious

near, *adv.*, ne'er, never
nimble, *v.*, move quickly, dart
nimbling, *part.*, moving in a nimble
   fashion

orison, *n.*, horizon

pashd, *v.*, smashed
pawl, *n.*, pall
pested, *v.*, pestered

pill, *v.*, peel
pooty, *n.*, land snail, *Capaea*,
   particularly the shell of C.
   nemoralis

quick, *n.* (quick lines), quickset
   hedges

reddles, *n.*, riddles
rhyme, *n.*, rime

sat, *v.*, set
shanny, *a.*, shame-faced
shield ball, *n.*, cannon ball
sholl, *v.*, stroll, saunter
shony, *a.*, shame-faced
showing shony, appearing wary
shoy, *a.*, shy
siled, *v.*, slid
skreekers, *n.*, rattles
sock, *n.*, soak, damp of a ditch
sorcer, *n.*, saucer
spaws, *n.*, spas
stoven, *n.*, stump
stunt, *adv.*, abruptly
struttle, *n.*, minnow or stickleback
style, *n.*, stile
suds (in the), in the dumps
swarm, *v.*, climb
swarms, *n.*, throngs or crowds
sweeing, *part.*, swooping

tarbottles, *n.*, tar marks
tent, *v.*, attempt
threble fares, *n.*, three men in a bed:
   or an insect emitting a high
   (treble) note
tounge, *n.*, tongue
town, *n.*, sometimes a village
trays, *n.*, hurdles
two, *adv.*, too
tynes, *n.*, tines, prongs of a fork

waspweed, *n.*, water betony
(*Stachys palustris*)
water betony, *n.*, waspweed
(*Stachys palustris*)

wauk, *a.*, weak
waukly, *adv.*, weakly
water mouse ear, *n.*, blinks, water
chickweed (*Montia fontana*)

INDEX